HEINEMANN MATHEMATICS 9

Extension textbook

These are the different types of pages and symbols used in this book:

E6
Handling data 1: Interpretation of questionnaires

These pages develop mathematical skills, concepts and facts in a wide variety of realistic contexts.

E14
Detour: Rotational symmetry

Detours provide self-contained activities which often require an exploratory, investigative approach drawing on problem-solving skills.

This is a reminder of key information essential for the work of the page.

Challenges are more-demanding activities designed to stimulate further thought and discussion.

Investigations enhance the work of the page by providing additional opportunities to develop and use problem-solving skills.

Contents

. . . from little acorns

A prime number is a number which has only two factors.
11 is a prime number since 11 and 1 are its only factors.

$$30 = 5 \times 6 = 5 \times 3 \times 2$$

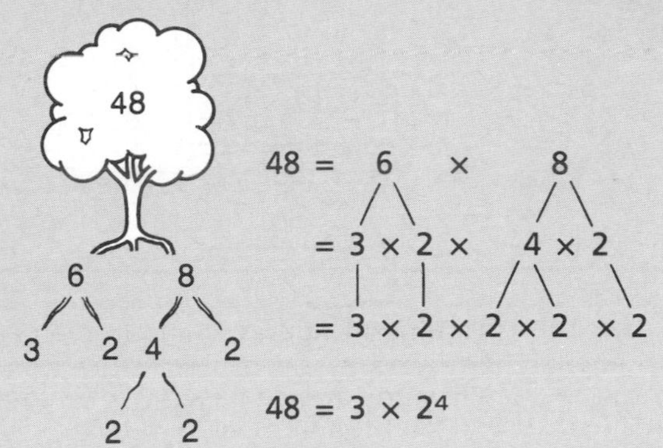

$$48 = 6 \times 8 = 3 \times 2 \times 4 \times 2 = 3 \times 2 \times 2 \times 2 \times 2$$

$$48 = 3 \times 2^4$$

5, 3 and 2 are the **prime factors of 30.**

3 and 2 are the **prime factors of 48.**

1 (a) Copy and complete.

$60 = 6 \times 10$
$= 2 \times 3 \times 2 \times \square$
$= 2^2 \times 3 \times \square$

$60 = 5 \times 12$
$= 5 \times \square \times \square$
$= \square$

$60 = 4 \times \square$
$= 2 \times \square \times \square \times \square$
$= \square$

(b) What do you notice?
(c) List the prime factors of 60.

2 Find the prime factors of each of these numbers.

(a) 45

(b)
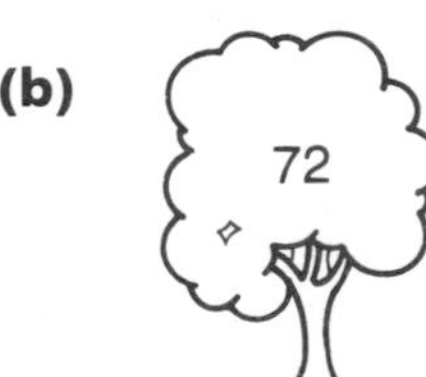

(c)
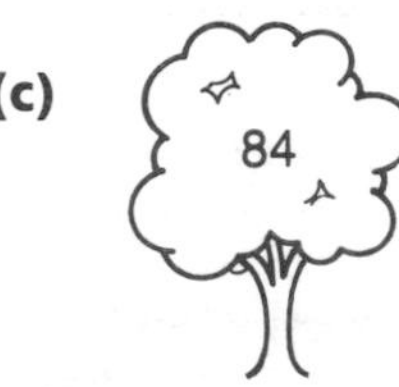

(d)
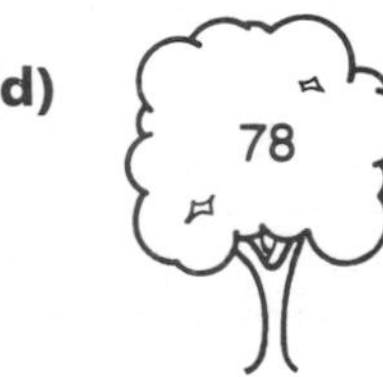

(e)

(f) 126

(g)
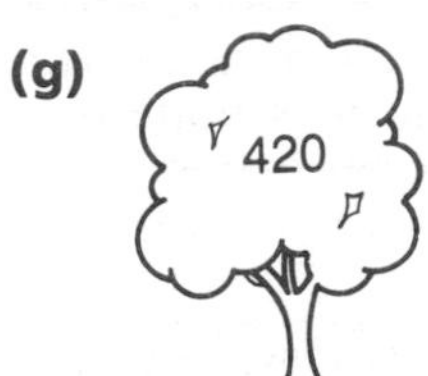

(h)

3 Find the prime factors of each of these numbers.

(a)	81	**(b)**	231	**(c)**	144
(d)	273	**(e)**	315	**(f)**	64
(g)	1080	**(h)**	1375	**(i)**	100 000

E2 Roll the dice

Whole numbers 1: Order of operations

Jim and Bill are playing a computer game. They put +, −, × or ÷ between the dice to make a number in the panel.

Their teacher, Mr Wright, settles the argument by explaining,

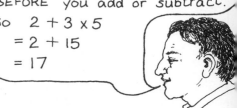

1 Use the rule to find

(a) $\boxed{5} + \boxed{3} \times \boxed{2}$ **(b)** $\boxed{4} + \boxed{6} \div \boxed{2}$ **(c)** $\boxed{6} - \boxed{2} \times \boxed{3}$

(d) $\boxed{4} - \boxed{2} \div \boxed{2}$ **(e)** $\boxed{2} \times \boxed{1} + \boxed{6}$ **(f)** $\boxed{4} \div \boxed{2} + \boxed{2}$

(g) $7 + 2 \times 5$ **(h)** $8 \div 2 - 1$ **(i)** $9 + 6 \div 3$

(j) $3 + 5^2$ **(k)** $2 + 2^3$ **(l)** $3 - 1^4$

2 Copy and complete by inserting signs.

(a) 7 3 2 = 1 **(b)** 6 6 2 = 3 **(c)** 2 3 6 = 0

Mr Wright tells them,

Always evaluate brackets first.

$$
\begin{aligned}
& (\boxed{2} + \boxed{3}) \times \boxed{5} \\
= \; & (2 + 3) \times 5 \\
= \; & 5 \times 5 \\
= \; & 25
\end{aligned}
$$

3 Use the bracket rule to find

(a) $(\boxed{2} + \boxed{3}) \times \boxed{4}$ **(b)** $\boxed{2} + (\boxed{3} \times \boxed{4})$ **(c)** $\boxed{6} \div (\boxed{2} + \boxed{1})$

(d) $(\boxed{6} \div \boxed{2}) + \boxed{1}$ **(e)** $\boxed{2} \times (\boxed{2} - \boxed{2})$ **(f)** $(\boxed{2} \times \boxed{2}) - \boxed{2}$

(g) $35 \div (2 + 3)$ **(h)** $(22 + 3) \div 5$ **(i)** $99 \div (3 + 6)$

(j) $2 \times (12 + 2)$ **(k)** $(2 + 9) \times (15 - 12)$ **(l)** $4\,(17 - 2) \div 20$

4 Copy and complete by inserting signs and brackets.

(a) 10 8 6 = 3 **(b)** 9 5 7 = 28 **(c)** 3 17 10 = 2

5 Calculate

(a) $(5 + 4)^2$ **(b)** $5 + 4^2$ **(c)** $(6 - 2)^2$ **(d)** $6 - 2^2$

(e) 3×3^3 **(f)** $(3 \times 3)^3$ **(g)** $(18 \div 3)^2$ **(h)** $18 \div 3^2$

6 **(a)** $17 - 5 \times 2$ **(b)** $(7 + 5) \div 4$ **(c)** $99 \div 3 + 6$

(d) $16 \div 2^3$ **(e)** $(3 + 3) \times (7 - 4)$ **(f)** $6 \div 1^2$

(g) $(6 \div 1)^2$ **(h)** $8 + 2 \times 3 - 5$ **(i)** $(8 + 2) \times 3 - 5$

(j) $48 \div (4 + 4) - 2$ **(k)** $48 \div 4 + 4 - 2$ **(l)** $48 \div (4 + 4 - 2)$

Top first

Bill evaluates expressions like these by first calculating the numerator and denominator.

$$\frac{43-3}{10}=\frac{40}{10}=40\div 10=4 \qquad \frac{5\times 5}{6+4}=\frac{25}{10}=25\div 10=2{\cdot}5 \qquad \frac{14-9}{40\div 5}=\frac{5}{8}=5\div 8=0{\cdot}625$$

$5 \div 8 \rightarrow 8\overline{)5{\cdot}000}$ = 0·625

1 Evaluate each expression.

(a) $\frac{8\times 5}{10}$ **(b)** $\frac{32}{4\times 2}$ **(c)** $\frac{11+7}{9}$ **(d)** $\frac{63}{8-1}$

(e) $\frac{52}{4\times 2}$ **(f)** $\frac{84}{2+4}$ **(g)** $\frac{48}{32\div 4}$ **(h)** $\frac{33}{103-98}$

(i) $\frac{9\times 4}{17-7}$ **(j)** $\frac{24+32}{36-29}$ **(k)** $\frac{123+24}{54\div 9}$ **(l)** $\frac{6^2}{5\times 2}$

(m) $\frac{5+3+7}{8-3}$ **(n)** $\frac{5\times 6\times 3}{25-19}$ **(o)** $\frac{3\times 5\times 7\div 2}{18+7-21}$ **(p)** $\frac{(5+4)^2}{6\div 3}$

(q) $\frac{7\times(18-9)}{12-16\div 4}$ **(r)** $\frac{16-2\times 5}{5\times 3-9}$ **(s)** $\frac{(12-4)\times 3^2}{(5+1)^2}$ **(t)** $\frac{10^2-8^2}{60\div(6-3)}$

Jim used his calculator to find $\frac{24}{3\times 4}$

If I enter 24 then press ÷3×4=
I think I'll be right.
Are you sure?

2 Was Jim correct? Explain.

3 Use your calculator to evaluate these expressions.

(a) $\frac{216}{9\times 5}$ **(b)** $\frac{138}{4\times 4}$ **(c)** $\frac{7\times 11}{5\times 4}$

(d) $\frac{8\times 9}{5\times 2}$ **(e)** $\frac{78}{3\times 4\times 5}$ **(f)** $\frac{108\times 72}{4^2\times 3\times 9}$

Ask your teacher what to do next.

E4 Walter's

Formulae 1: Symbolic formulae $y = ax - b$

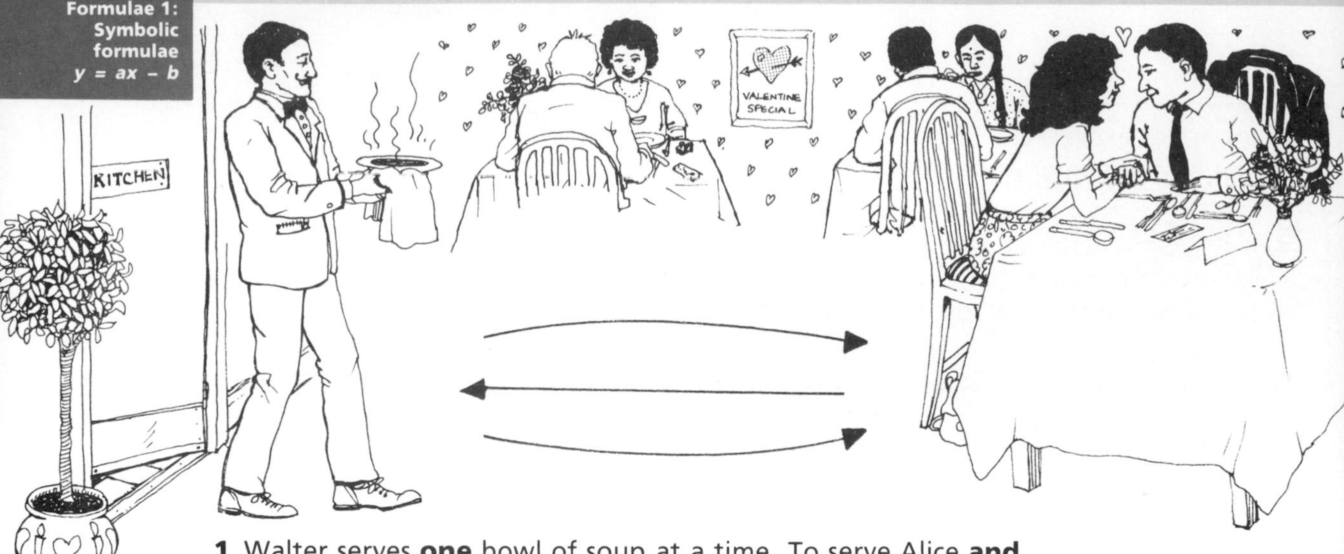

1 Walter serves **one** bowl of soup at a time. To serve Alice **and** Michael he crosses the restaurant floor 3 times.

(a) Copy and complete:

Number of soups (s)	2	3	4	5	6
Number of floor crossings (c)	3				

- The increase in the number of crossings each time is ☐.
  Number of crossings = ☐ × number of soups, **subtract** ☐.
  c = ☐ − ☐

(b) Use the formula to find how many times Walter crosses the dining room floor to serve • 10 soups • 20 soups.

SPECIAL SUPPER AT WALTER'S
— for —
ST. VALENTINE'S DAY
£7 per person
mints served with coffee.
WALTER'S
Bring this voucher and
SAVE £4
Only one voucher per table.
Minimum 2 persons per table.

2 (a) How much should Alice and Michael pay for their special supper when they use the voucher?

(b) Make a table to show the total cost in £ (t) of the special supper for different numbers of diners (d) sitting together.

(c) Write a formula for the total cost
- in words
- in letters.

(d) Use the formula to find the total cost when the number of diners at a table is • 8 • 12.

3 When Walter serves coffee he uses this table to find the number of mints to set out.

Number of diners	3	4	5	6	7
Number of mints	7	10	13	16	19

(a) Write a letter formula for the number of mints.

(b) Use your formula. Find the number of mints when the number of diners is • 9 • 15 • 20.

(c) Use your formula. Find the number of diners when Walter sets out • 28 • 37 • 52 mints.

The rules of the game

E5

Formulae 1: *n*th term

You need counters and squared paper. Work with a partner.

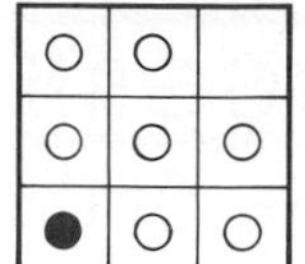

1 **(a)** Make a 3 by 3 square and place counters as shown.
Use these rules.

- A counter can move one square horizontally, vertically or diagonally.
- A counter can only move into an empty square.

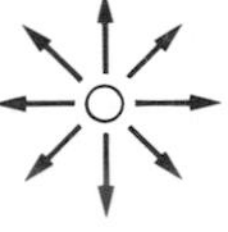

Find the least number of moves to position the black counter in the top right hand corner.

(b) Play the game using squares of different sizes.

(c) Copy and complete:

Size of square	2 by 2	3 by 3	4 by 4	5 by 5
Least number of moves		6		

2 Look at the numbers in the bottom row of the table. What do you think will be the least number of moves for a 6 by 6 square? Check by playing the game.

> The number of moves 1, 6, 11, 16, 21 . . . form a sequence.
> Each number in the sequence is called a **term**.
> The first term is 1, the second term is 6, the third term is 11, and so on.

3 **(a)** Copy and complete:

-

Term number (n)	1	2	3	4	5	6	7	8
Term	1	6	11	16				

- To find the term multiply the term number by ☐, subtract ☐.

(b) Find the • tenth term • twentieth term • *n*th term.

> If the term number is n then the term is given by $5n - 4$.
> $5n - 4$ is called the ***n*th term** of the sequence.

4 For each sequence make a table and find the *n*th term.

(a) 3, 5, 7, 9 . . . **(b)** 5, 8, 11, 14 . . . **(c)** 2, 6, 10, 14 . . .

5 For each sequence find the *n*th term.

(a) 1, 4, 7, 10 . . . **(b)** 4, 9, 14, 19 . . . **(c)** 6, 7, 8, 9 . . .

6 Write the first five terms of the sequence with *n*th term

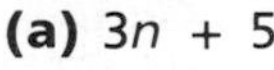

(a) $3n + 5$ **(b)** $2n - 1$ **(c)** $5n + 7$ **(d)** $4n - 3$

(e) n^3 **(f)** $\frac{1}{n}$ **(g)** $\frac{1}{n+1}$ **(h)** $\frac{n}{n+1}$ **(i)** $\frac{n}{2n+1}$

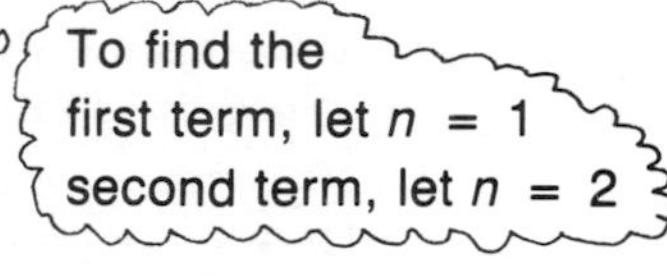

To find the
first term, let n = 1
second term, let n = 2

7 Find the *n*th term of each of these sequences.

(a) 1, 4, 9, 16 . . . **(b)** $\frac{1}{3}, \frac{1}{4}, \frac{1}{5}, \frac{1}{6}$ . . . **(c)** $1, \frac{2}{3}, \frac{3}{5}, \frac{4}{7}$, . . .

Challenge

Ask your teacher what to do next.

E6 Laggan Ski Club

Handling data 1: Interpretation of questionnaires

LAGGAN SKI CLUB

Connie Carr, Secretary
14 Glen Street, Laggan

Thank you for picking up this questionnaire from your local ski shop. We are trying to improve the facilities offered by Laggan Ski Club. Please help us by completing this questionnaire.

Connie Carr

Name.........................Address...

A Are you interested in skiing, or in learning to ski? yes/no

B Are you presently a member of Laggan Ski Club? yes/no

C If you are not a member, would you consider joining Laggan? yes/no

D How much would you be prepared to pay for membership? £25 £30 £35 £40

E At what level do you ski? Beginner Intermediate Advanced Expert

F Approximately how many days do you spend skiing each year? 5 10 15 20 More

G Do you have your own ski equipment? yes/no

H Give details of your measurements like this:
Height (185 cm), Weight (71 kg), Continental shoe size (41) 185, 71, 41

....

I What is your main summer sport? ....

Please place your completed questionnaire in the box provided or return it to the secretary.

1 Connie put questionnaires into the three local ski shops.
Why is question *A* unnecessary?

2 Why do you think Connie asked questions **(a)** *D* **(b)** *H* **(c)** *I* ?

Here is Connie's table for the first 10 replies.

Name	*A*	*B*	*C*	*D*	*E*	*F*	*G*	*H*	*I*
				Question					
P Taylor	Y	Y		£30	I	20	Y		Running
G Rodger	Y	N	Y	£25	B	5	Y		Golf
A Sneddon	Y	Y		£30	A	M	Y		Golf
A Hussain	Y	Y		£25	I	10	N	142,47,37	Walking
A Smythe	Y	N	Y	£25	I	15	N	151,51,39	Running
T Dalgleish	Y	Y	Y	£30	I	10	Y		Walking
R Clark	Y	N	Y	£35	B	5	N	172,68,41	Golf
V Thomas	Y	Y		£30	I	15	Y		Walking
J Queen	Y	Y		£40	E	M	Y		Sailing
C Howard	Y	Y		£25	I	10	N	178,65,42	Golf

3 **(a)** For the people who have replied so far, what is the mean membership fee they are prepared to pay?

(b) At what price do you think the membership fee should be set? Explain.

4 Who has answered question *C* incorrectly?

5 For R Clark, write his **(a)** height **(b)** shoe size.

6 List the members who do not have their own ski equipment.

7 List the intermediate skiers who spend approximately 15 days skiing each year.

8 Which non-member has his own skiing equipment?

9 List the members whose main summer sport is golf.

10 List the members who spend 12 or less days skiing each year.

Here are 5 more replies.

	Question								
Name	*A*	*B*	*C*	*D*	*E*	*F*	*G*	*H*	*I*
P Moore	Y	N	Y	£35	B	10	N	166,57,38	Tennis
C Thomson	Y	N	Y	£25	B	M	N	189,79,45	Fishing
F Terry	Y	Y		£30	A	M	Y		Golf
I Laing	Y	Y		£25	I	10	Y		Tennis
D Pritchard	Y	N	Y	£40	I	15	N	151,53,35	Running

11 For all the people who have replied so far, what is the mean membership fee they are prepared to pay?

12 From the fifteen replies list
(a) the members who ski for more than eight days each year and who play golf
(b) the beginners who do not have their own equipment and are over 170 cm tall
(c) the intermediate skiers who have their own equipment and ski 12 days or less per year.

13 The local council is considering building a new ski slope. There is some opposition from local residents. Here are some ways in which opinions can be sampled. Which of these sampling techniques are biased? Explain.

THE ADVERTISER
Ski slope developers barracked at village hall
The meeting in Laggan village hall to outline plans for the proposed new ski slope ended in uproar last night.

Telephone survey

Speak to skiers on the ski slopes

Interview people at the local sports centre

Street survey

Send a questionnaire to every hundredth person on the electoral register

E8 Giving it all away

Handling data 1: Mean, median and mode

Here are the contents of six collection cans. The average amount can be found in three different ways

Mean	Median	Mode
$\frac{2+9+3+8+5+3}{6}$ $= \frac{30}{6}$	Arrange the data in order. 2, 3, 3, 5, 8, 9 The median is the middle. There are the same number of values above and below it.	Arrange the data in order. 3, 2, 3, 5, 8, 9 The mode is the most frequent.
Mean = £5	**Median = £4**	**Mode = £3**

1 The table shows the charity donations of 25 people. Find

(a) the mean donation
(b) the median donation
(c) the modal donation.

Charity donations (£)				
2	1	5	1	2
1	1	10	1	1
5	20	400	20	5
1	1	10	1	1
2	1	5	1	2

2 One of these donors was selected at random and asked about her donation.

(a) Is her donation likely to be above or below the mean? Explain.
(b) How much is she most likely to have donated? Explain.

3 The graph shows the number and value of charity cheques donated on Tuesday.

(a) For these donations find
- the mean
- the median
- the mode.

(b) What would be the likely income from 800 cheques? Explain.

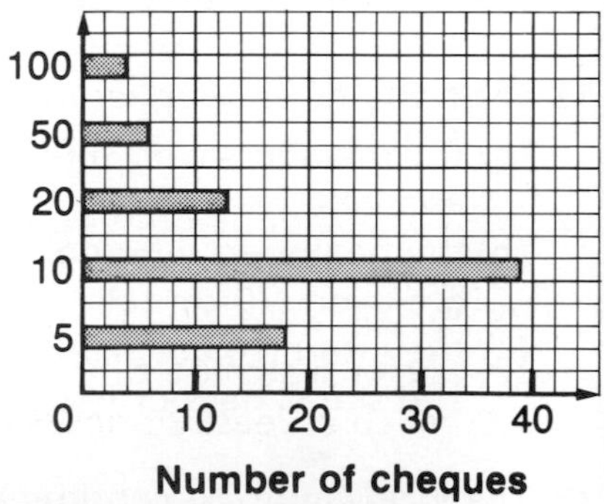

4 Find the mean, median and mode of the cheque donations for Thursday.

Thursday's cheque donations (£)				
50	5	50	10	20
10	50	10	5	50
20	100	20	50	10
50	10	50	100	5
10	50	20	5	50
5	20	5	50	10
50	5	50	10	5
5	50	10	20	50
20	5	100	50	5
5	10	50	5	20

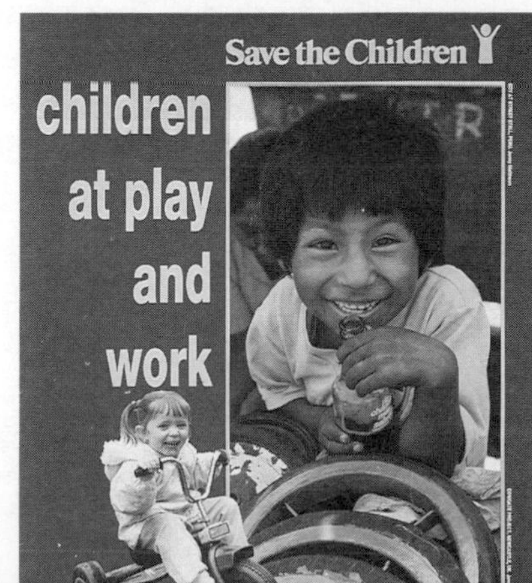

Save the Children
children
at play
and
work

RelaTiVity

E9

Handling data 1: Relative frequency

Rachel asked a sample of 53 students at Strangehill Secondary School about their TV viewing habits.

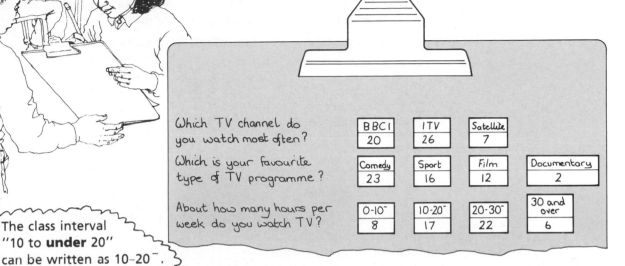

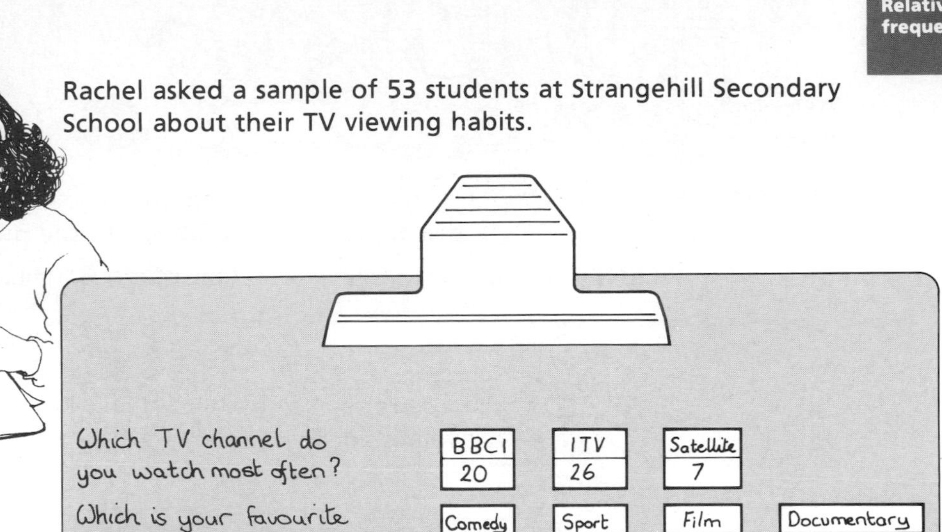

Which TV channel do you watch most often?
BBC1 20
ITV 26
Satellite 7
Which is your favourite type of TV programme?
Comedy 23
Sport 16
Film 12
Documentary 2
About how many hours per week do you watch TV?
0-10⁻ 8
10-20⁻ 17
20-30⁻ 22
30 and over 6

The class interval "10 to **under** 20" can be written as 10–20⁻.

2 of the 53 students in the sample preferred watching documentaries.

$\frac{2}{53}$ is the **relative frequency** of students preferring documentaries.

Relative frequency is an estimate of probability.

1 From the survey what are the relative frequencies of students who
- **(a)** prefer comedy programmes
- **(b)** watch ITV most often
- **(c)** watch 10–20⁻ hours of TV each week?

2 Estimate the probabilities that a student, chosen at random, will
- **(a)** prefer to watch BBC1
- **(b)** watch at least 30 hours of TV in a week
- **(c)** prefer watching films
- **(d)** watch at least 20 hours of TV each week.

3 When the average weekly viewing times were further analysed these results emerged.
Estimate the probabilities that
- **(a)** a girl watches 10–20⁻ hours each week
- **(b)** a girl watches at least 30 hours each week
- **(c)** a boy watches less than 10 hours each week
- **(d)** a boy watches 20–30⁻ hours each week
- **(e)** a student who watches 10–20⁻ hours each week is a boy
- **(f)** a student who watches less than 20 hours each week is a girl.

Hours	*Boys*	*Girls*	*Totals*
0–10⁻	2	6	8
10–20⁻	10	7	17
20–30⁻	12	10	22
30 and over	2	4	6
Totals	26	27	53

E10 Road safety

Handling data 1: Appropriate graphs

Strangehill Secondary School is conducting a road safety campaign. Sandie has to decide which **types** of graphs to use to best convey information to the public.

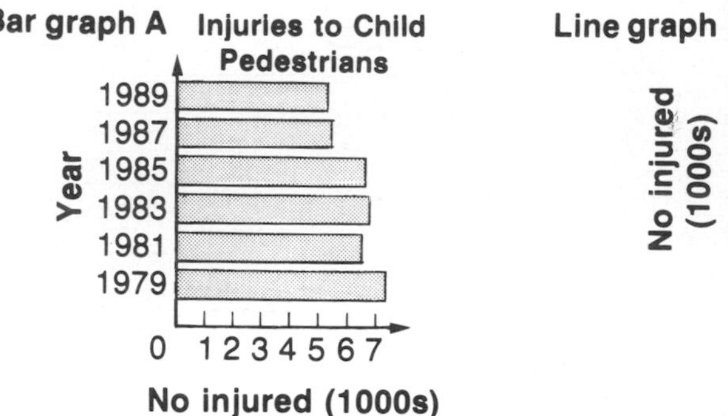

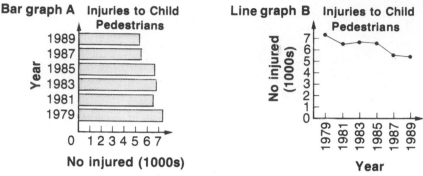

Line graph B **Injuries to Child Pedestrians**

No injured (1000s)

0 1 2 3 4 5 6 7

1979 1981 1983 1985 1987 1989

Year

1 These graphs show the number of child pedestrians who have been injured.

(a) In which year were most pedestrians injured? Which graph best shows this information?

(b) What is the trend in the number of injuries between 1979 and 1989? Which graph best shows this information?

(c) Which graph should Sandie use to highlight that

- a large number were injured in a year
- a decreasing number were injured each year?

2 Over the past few years 18 620 child cyclists have been injured.

(a) In which year did 25% of these injuries occur? Which display best shows this information?

(b) What is the trend in the number of cyclists injured between 1985 and 1989? Which display best shows this information?

(c) Which display should Sandie use to draw attention to

- the trend in cyclist injuries
- the proportion of injuries in each of the five years?

(d) Give a possible reason for the trend in child cyclist injuries.

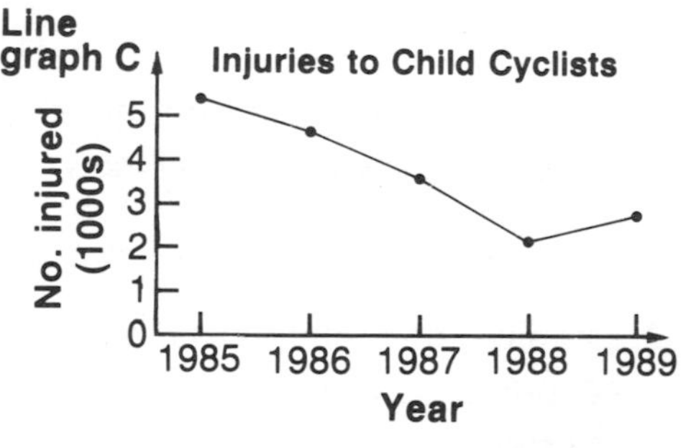

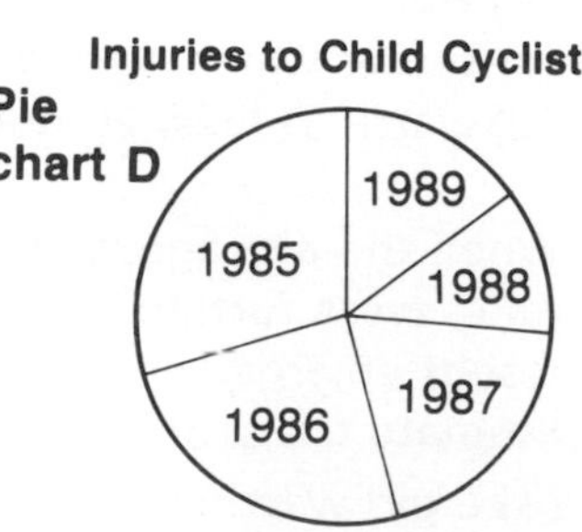

3 The numbers of children, of different ages, injured on the roads in one year are shown in the table.
Draw displays which will highlight

(a) the numbers of children injured

(b) the trend in the number of injuries with age

(c) the proportion of injuries for each age group.

Age	*Number of injuries*
0–4	1342
5–9	3094
10–14	3943
15–19	12 616

Ask your teacher what to do next.

Rivetting stuff

Laurie rivets steel plates together. The thickness of each plate is given in inches.

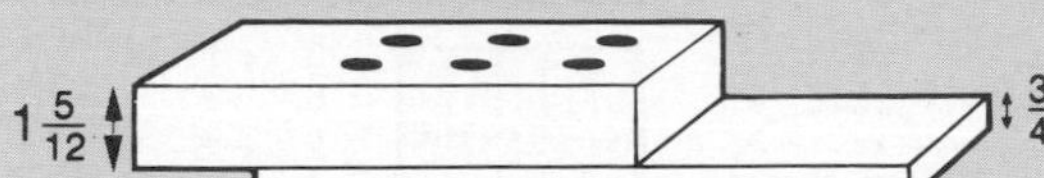

$2\frac{1}{2}$ $\frac{3}{4}$

To find the length of rivet needed for these two plates Laurie calculates the total thickness like this.

$1\frac{5}{12} + \frac{3}{4}$

$= 1\frac{5}{12} + \frac{9}{12}$

$= 1\frac{14}{12}$

$= 2\frac{1}{6}$

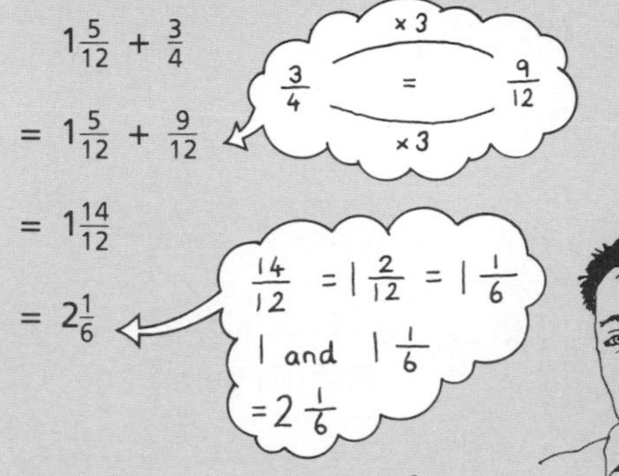

The total thickness is $\mathbf{2\frac{1}{6}}$ inches.

To find the thickness of plate needed to level this off Laurie calculates the difference in thickness like this.

$2\frac{1}{12} - \frac{3}{4}$

$= 2\frac{1}{12} - \frac{9}{12}$

$= 1\frac{13}{12} - \frac{9}{12}$

$= 1\frac{4}{12}$

$= 1\frac{1}{3}$

$2\frac{1}{12} = 1 + 1\frac{1}{12}$
$= 1 + \frac{13}{12}$
$= 1\frac{13}{12}$

The difference in thickness is $\mathbf{1\frac{1}{3}}$ inches.

To add or subtract fractions, the denominators must be the same.

1 For each pair of plates find • the total thickness • the difference in thickness.

(a) $\frac{1}{3}$ and $\frac{1}{6}$ **(b)** $1\frac{1}{2}$ and $1\frac{1}{12}$ **(c)** $2\frac{7}{8}$ and $1\frac{3}{4}$ **(d)** $2\frac{3}{5}$ and $1\frac{9}{10}$ **(e)** $1\frac{2}{3}$ and $1\frac{5}{6}$

For these plates Laurie did the calculations like this.

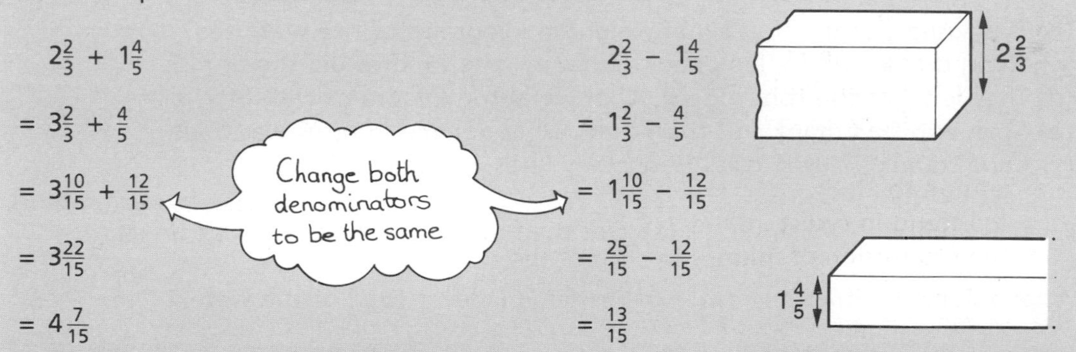

Change both denominators to be the same
$2\frac{2}{3}$
$1\frac{4}{5}$

$2\frac{2}{3} + 1\frac{4}{5}$

$= 3\frac{2}{3} + \frac{4}{5}$

$= 3\frac{10}{15} + \frac{12}{15}$

$= 3\frac{22}{15}$

$= 4\frac{7}{15}$

The total thickness is $\mathbf{4\frac{7}{15}}$ inches.

$2\frac{2}{3} - 1\frac{4}{5}$

$= 1\frac{2}{3} - \frac{4}{5}$

$= 1\frac{10}{15} - \frac{12}{15}$

$= \frac{25}{15} - \frac{12}{15}$

$= \frac{13}{15}$

The difference in thickness is $\mathbf{\frac{13}{15}}$ inches.

2 For each pair of plates find • the total thickness • the difference in thickness.

(a) $2\frac{1}{2}$ and $1\frac{1}{3}$ **(b)** $2\frac{1}{4}$ and $1\frac{2}{3}$ **(c)** $3\frac{2}{5}$ and $1\frac{1}{3}$ **(d)** $1\frac{3}{8}$ and $\frac{2}{3}$ **(e)** $2\frac{5}{6}$ and $1\frac{3}{8}$

3 Find **(a)** $1\frac{1}{3} + 2\frac{1}{5}$ **(b)** $5\frac{3}{5} - 4\frac{1}{4}$ **(c)** $2\frac{1}{7} + 7\frac{1}{2}$ **(d)** $2\frac{2}{3} - 1\frac{3}{4}$ **(e)** $4\frac{3}{5} + 3\frac{3}{8}$

(f) $6\frac{3}{7} - 2\frac{4}{5}$ **(g)** $6\frac{1}{2} + 2\frac{2}{5}$ **(h)** $4\frac{1}{8} - 2\frac{2}{3}$ **(i)** $3\frac{2}{5} + 1\frac{3}{4}$ **(j)** $5\frac{2}{7} - 1\frac{2}{3}$

E12 A sharing, caring family

Fractions: Fraction of a fraction

$\frac{1}{5}$	$\frac{1}{5}$	$\frac{1}{5}$	$\frac{1}{5}$	$\frac{1}{5}$

$\frac{1}{5}$ $\frac{1}{5}$ $\frac{1}{2}$ of $\frac{4}{5}$ $= \frac{2}{5}$

$\frac{1}{2} \times \frac{4}{5} = \frac{1 \times 4}{2 \times 5} = \frac{4}{10} = \frac{2}{5}$

$\frac{1}{3}$	$\frac{1}{3}$	$\frac{1}{3}$

$\frac{1}{6}$ $\frac{1}{6}$ $\frac{1}{2}$ of $\frac{1}{3}$ $= \frac{1}{2}$ of $\frac{2}{6}$

$\frac{1}{6}$ $= \frac{1}{6}$

$\frac{1}{2} \times \frac{1}{3} = \frac{1 \times 1}{2 \times 3} = \frac{1}{6}$

$\frac{1}{3}$	$\frac{1}{3}$	$\frac{1}{3}$

$\frac{1}{15}$ $\frac{1}{15}$ $\frac{1}{15}$ $\frac{1}{15}$ $\frac{1}{15}$ $\frac{2}{5}$ of $\frac{1}{3}$ $= \frac{2}{5}$ of $\frac{5}{15}$

$\frac{1}{15}$ $\frac{1}{15}$ $= \frac{2}{15}$

$\frac{2}{5} \times \frac{1}{3} = \frac{2 \times 1}{5 \times 3} = \frac{2}{15}$

1 Calculate **(a)** $\frac{1}{2}$ of $\frac{2}{3}$ **(b)** $\frac{1}{4}$ of $\frac{4}{5}$ **(c)** $\frac{1}{3}$ of $\frac{6}{7}$ **(d)** $\frac{2}{3} \times \frac{1}{4}$

(e) $\frac{3}{5} \times \frac{1}{8}$ **(f)** $\frac{1}{4}$ of $\frac{8}{9}$ **(g)** $\frac{3}{4} \times \frac{2}{7}$ **(h)** $\frac{2}{5}$ of $\frac{5}{7}$

The MacDonald family, Mum, Dad, Karim and Shirin buy these items.

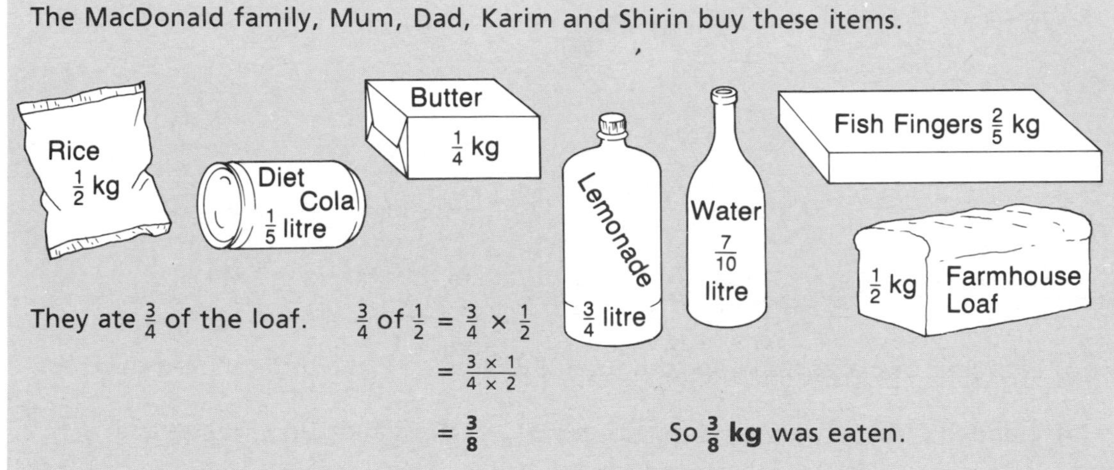

They ate $\frac{3}{4}$ of the loaf. $\frac{3}{4}$ of $\frac{1}{2} = \frac{3}{4} \times \frac{1}{2}$

$= \frac{3 \times 1}{4 \times 2}$

$= \mathbf{\frac{3}{8}}$ So $\frac{3}{8}$ **kg** was eaten.

2 **(a)** They used $\frac{1}{2}$ of the butter. What weight in kilograms was used?
(b) They used $\frac{1}{3}$ of the rice. What weight in kilograms of rice was used?
(c) Shirin drank $\frac{1}{3}$ of the lemonade. What volume in litres did she drink?
(d) They left $\frac{1}{6}$ of the fish fingers. What weight in kilograms was left?
(e) Mum and Dad drank $\frac{5}{7}$ of the water. What volume in litres was this?
(f) Karim drank $\frac{3}{4}$ of the cola. How many litres was this?

3 What weight in kilograms is **(a)** $\frac{2}{3}$ of the butter **(b)** $\frac{3}{4}$ of the fish fingers?

4 What volume in litres is **(a)** $\frac{5}{6}$ of the lemonade **(b)** $\frac{3}{4}$ of the water?

The MacDonald family shared $1\frac{1}{2}$ kg of grapes. They each had $\frac{1}{4}$ of $1\frac{1}{2}$ kg.

$= \frac{1}{4} \times 1\frac{1}{2}$

$= \frac{1}{4} \times \frac{3}{2}$

$= \frac{3}{8}$

They each had $\frac{3}{8}$ **kg** of grapes.

5 Calculate
(a) $\frac{1}{4} \times 1\frac{1}{3}$ **(b)** $\frac{1}{2} \times 2\frac{2}{3}$ **(c)** $\frac{5}{7} \times 5\frac{1}{4}$ **(d)** $1\frac{1}{3} \times \frac{1}{4}$ **(e)** $1\frac{1}{2} \times 2\frac{2}{5}$

E13

Fractions: Division by a fraction

Mrs MacDonald divides a cake into $\frac{1}{10}$ ths.

The whole cake has 10 slices.

$1 \div \frac{1}{10}$
$= 1 \times \frac{10}{1}$
$= \frac{10}{1}$
$= 10$

$\frac{1}{5}$ of the cake has 2 slices.

$\frac{1}{5} \div \frac{1}{10}$
$= \frac{1}{5} \times \frac{10}{1}$
$= \frac{10}{5}$
$= 2$

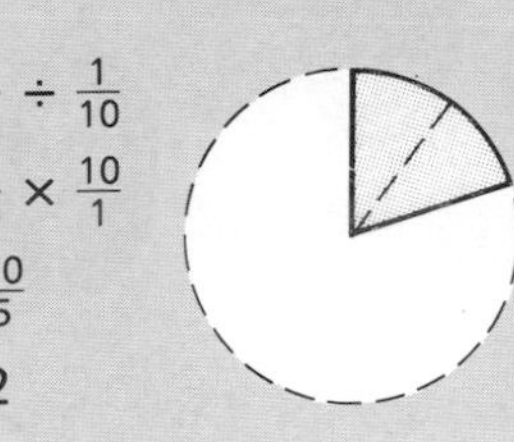

$\frac{3}{5}$ of the cake has 6 slices.

$\frac{3}{5} \div \frac{1}{10}$
$= \frac{3}{5} \times \frac{10}{1}$
$= \frac{30}{5}$
$= 6$

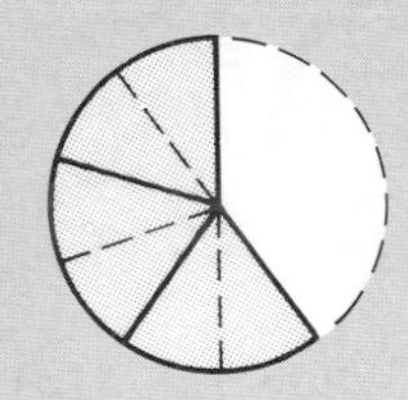

1 Karim divides a pie into $\frac{1}{12}$ ths. Copy and complete the calculations.

(a) How many pieces are in the pie?

$1 \div \frac{1}{12}$
$= 1 \times \frac{12}{1}$
$= \square$

(b) How many pieces are in $\frac{1}{3}$ of the pie?

$\frac{1}{3} \div \frac{1}{12}$
$= \frac{1}{3} \times \frac{12}{1}$
$= \square$

(c) How many pieces are in $\frac{3}{4}$ of the pie?

$\frac{3}{4} \div \frac{1}{12}$
$= \frac{3}{4} \times \frac{12}{1}$
$= \square$

Dividing by a fraction is the same as multiplying by the fraction "upside-down".

$\frac{5}{8} \div \frac{4}{5}$
$= \frac{5}{8} \times \frac{5}{4}$
$= \frac{25}{32}$

2 Calculate **(a)** $1 \div \frac{1}{4}$ **(b)** $3 \div \frac{1}{2}$ **(c)** $\frac{1}{4} \div \frac{1}{2}$ **(d)** $\frac{3}{4} \div \frac{1}{8}$

(e) $\frac{2}{5} \div \frac{2}{3}$ **(f)** $\frac{2}{7} \div \frac{2}{5}$ **(g)** $\frac{5}{6} \div \frac{1}{3}$ **(h)** $\frac{9}{10} \div \frac{3}{5}$

Later that evening friends visited the MacDonalds.
They shared sweets, nuts, drinks and ice cream.

3 Karim served the ice cream. How many scoops would she serve using **(a)** the $\frac{1}{6}$ litre scoop **(b)** the $\frac{1}{12}$ litre scoop?

4 Shirin set out the sweets in bowls each holding $\frac{1}{8}$ kg.
How many bowls did she fill?

5 Dad served the lemonade.

(a) How many $\frac{1}{6}$ litre glasses could he fill?

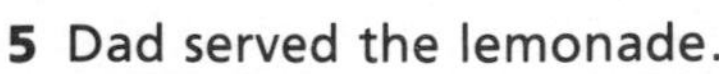

(b) How many $\frac{2}{9}$ litre tumblers could he fill?

6 **(a)** Mum divided the orange juice into $\frac{3}{10}$ litre tumblers.
How many full tumblers did she have?

(b) Shirin divided the peanuts into $\frac{2}{15}$ kg portions.
How many portions were there?

Ask your teacher what to do next.

E14 Wheelies

Detour: Rotational symmetry

1 Follow steps **(a)** to **(e)** to make a design for a wheel disc.

(a) Trace this starting shape and draw it on card.
Cut out the starting shape, make a hole in it and drawn an arrow as shown.

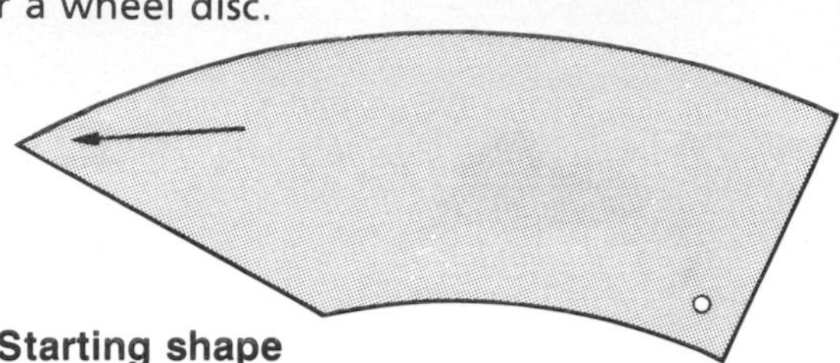

Starting shape

(b) Mark a point **P** near the centre of a sheet of paper.
Place the centre of a circular protractor at **P** and mark round its circumference every 60°.

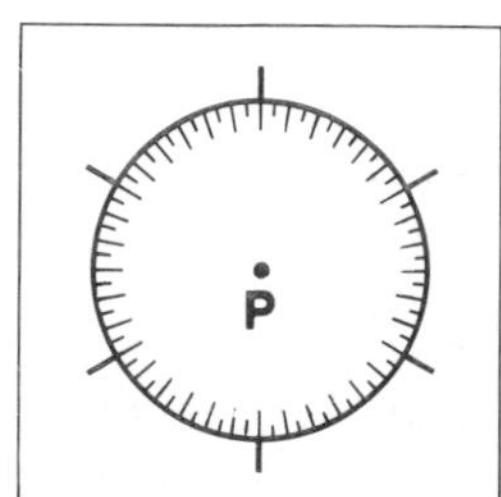

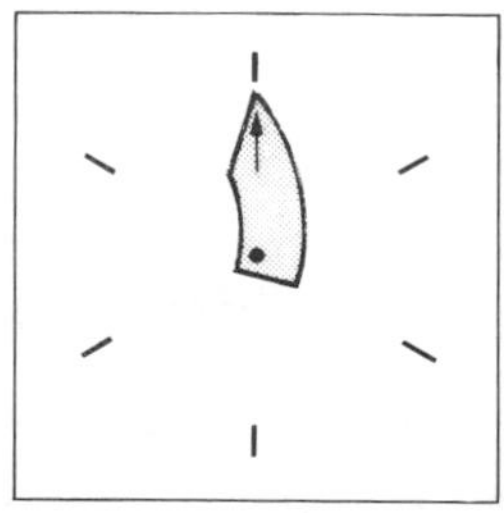

(c) Place the hole in the starting shape on top of point **P** with the arrow pointing to one of the marks. Draw round the starting shape.

(d) Repeat step **(c)** for each of the other marks.
(e) Draw a thick line round the perimeter.
Draw the circumference of the wheel disc.
Colour the design.

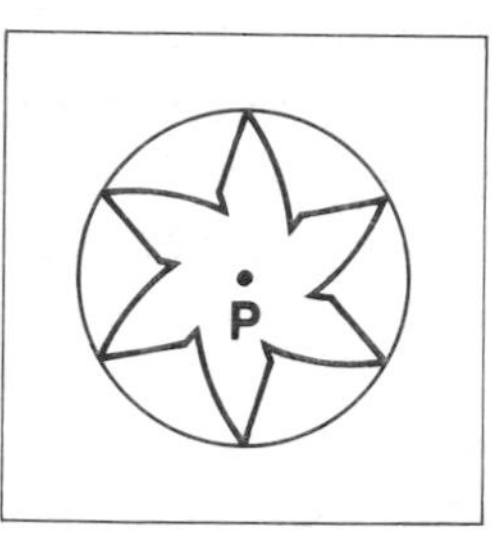

2 How many times does the finished design fit its own outline in one full turn?

This design has **rotational symmetry of order 6**.

Investigation

3 Draw your own wheel disc designs.
Investigate what happens if you change
- the starting shape
- the order of rotational symmetry to 3, 4, 5, 8 or 10.

Ask your teacher what to do next.

Numbers in space

Remember

For numbers > 1
- to round to **1** significant figure – round to the **highest place** value.
- to round to **2** significant figures – round to the **second highest** place value.

The space shuttle *Explorer* can carry a maximum load of 29 484 kg.
This weight is • **30 000** kg to **1 significant figure**
• **29 000** kg to **2 significant figures**.

The highest place value is tens of thousands, the second highest is thousands . . .

1 Round each piece of data about *Explorer* to
(a) 1 significant figure
(b) 2 significant figures
(c) 3 significant figures.

Space shuttle data – Explorer	
Weight of orbiter	77 320 kg
Total weight at lift off	2 081 168 kg
Thrust at lift off	30 740 000 Newtons
Fuel consumption	12 150 *l*/s

2 *Explorer* has a length of 37 metres and a wingspan of 24 metres. Round each dimension to 1 significant figure.

3 *Explorer* has a landing speed of 364 km/h. Give this speed correct to 2 significant figures.

Significant figures can be shortened to sig figs

The time taken for a radio signal to travel from Earth to the planet Neptune is 4·02778 hours.
This time is • **4** hours to **1 sig fig**
• **4·0** hours to **2 sig figs**
• **4·03** hours to **3 sig figs**.

The highest place value is units, the second highest is tenths . . .

4 These are the times for radio signals to travel from Earth to other planets. Round each time to
(a) 1 sig fig
(b) 2 sig figs
(c) 3 sig figs.

Radio Signals from Earth	
Planet	*Time*
Mars	4·3333 min
Jupiter	34·91667 min
Saturn	69·892 min
Uranus	2·52028 h
Pluto	5·32694 h

5 The length of a year on the planet Mars is 1·8808 Earth years. Round this time to
(a) 1 sig fig **(b)** 2 sig figs **(c)** 3 sig figs.

6 Repeat question **5** for each of these planets.
- Jupiter – 11·8617 Earth years
- Saturn – 29·473 Earth years
- Pluto – 248·552 Earth years
- Uranus – 84·019 Earth years.

E16 Beetling about

Decimals: Significant figures, numbers < 1

Dr Cheung is an entomologist. Today she is examining the lengths of her favourite insects – beetles. She uses a sophisticated measuring device which can record the length of a beetle in metres to four decimal places. Dr Cheung uses rounded lengths when she writes about her beetles in magazines.

For numbers <1
- to round to **1** sig fig – round to the **highest non-zero digit** place value.
- to round to **2** sig figs – round to the **next highest** place value.

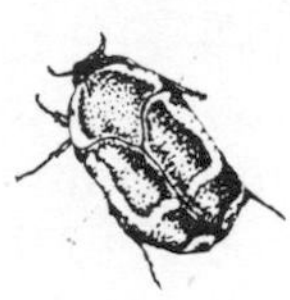

A Goliath beetle has a length of 0·1047 m.
This is • **0·1** m to **1 significant figure**
• **0·10** m to **2 significant figures.**

The highest non-zero digit place value is hundredths.

A Chafer beetle has a length of 0·0183 m.
This is • **0·02** m to **1 significant figure**
• **0·018** m to **2 significant figures.**

The highest non-zero digit place value is tenths.

1 Give the length of each of these beetles correct to
(a) 1 sig fig
(b) 2 sig figs.

Beetle lengths in metres	
Blister	0·0148
Colorado	0·0253
Golden	0·0267
Great Water	0·0314
Rhinoceros	0·0901
Rove	0·0239
Stag	0·0772

2 A Ladybird is 0·0066 m long. Write this length correct to 1 sig fig.

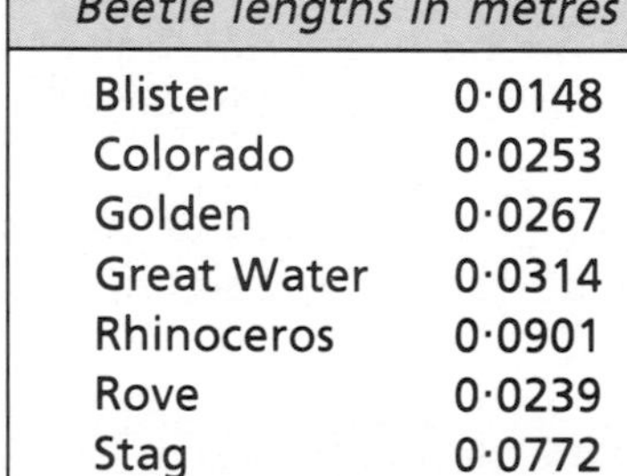

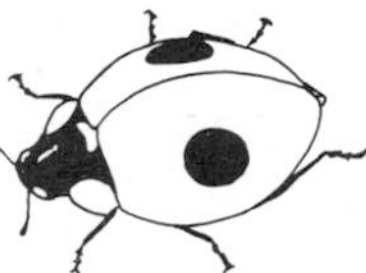

3 Round the length of each Weevil beetle to 1 sig fig.

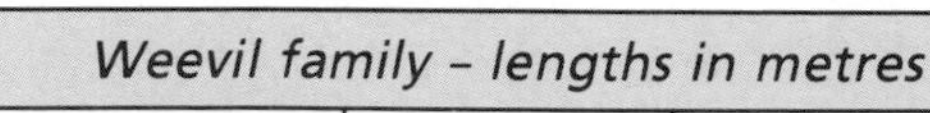

Weevil family – lengths in metres		
A 0·0032	B 0·0028	C 0·0057
D 0·0063	E 0·0044	F 0·0045

4 Round the length of each Hercules beetle to
(a) 1 sig fig
(b) 2 sig figs
(c) 3 sig figs.

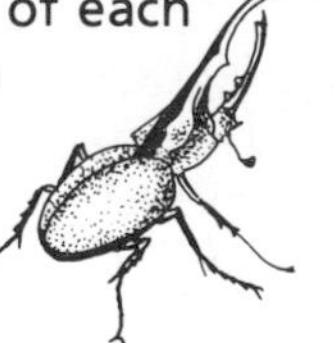

Hercules beetles – lengths in metres		
U 0·1528	V 0·1698	W 0·1467
X 0·1583	Y 0·1301	Z 0·1234

Challenge

5 How many Rhinoceros beetles placed end to end would fit the perimeter of your classroom?

Fuelling around

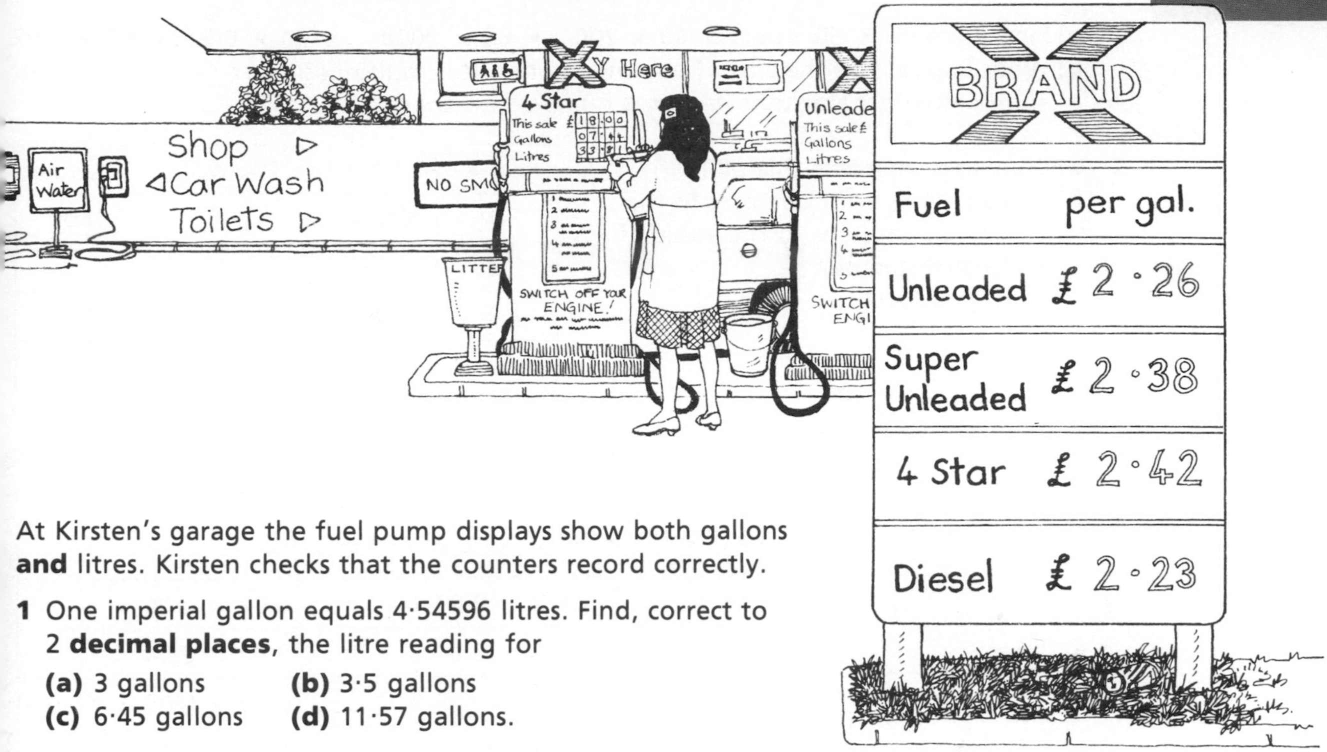

Fuel	per gal.
Unleaded	£2·26
Super Unleaded	£2·38
4 Star	£2·42
Diesel	£2·23

At Kirsten's garage the fuel pump displays show both gallons **and** litres. Kirsten checks that the counters record correctly.

1 One imperial gallon equals 4·54596 litres. Find, correct to 2 **decimal places**, the litre reading for

(a) 3 gallons **(b)** 3·5 gallons
(c) 6·45 gallons **(d)** 11·57 gallons.

2 Draw a display board to show the cost per **litre** of each type of fuel correct to 3 sig figs.

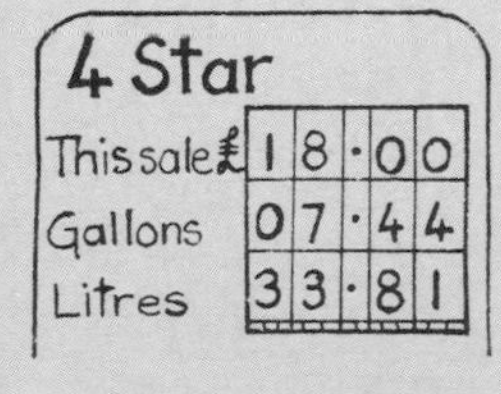

4 Star	
This sale £	18·00
Gallons	07·44
Litres	33·81

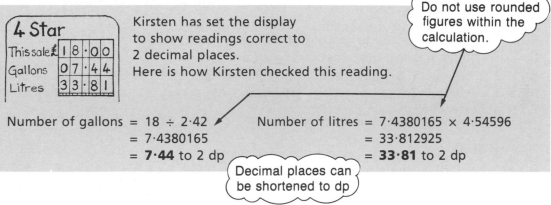

Kirsten has set the display to show readings correct to 2 decimal places.
Here is how Kirsten checked this reading.

Do not use rounded figures within the calculation.

Number of gallons = 18 ÷ 2·42
= 7·4380165
= **7·44** to 2 dp

Number of litres = 7·4380165 × 4·54596
= 33·812925
= **33·81** to 2 dp

Decimal places can be shortened to dp

3 Find the missing numbers in each of these displays.

(a)

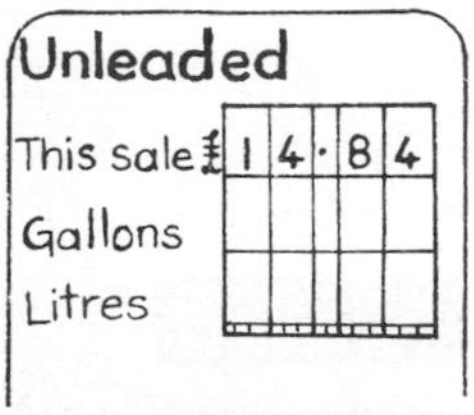

Unleaded	
This sale £	14·84
Gallons	
Litres	

(b)

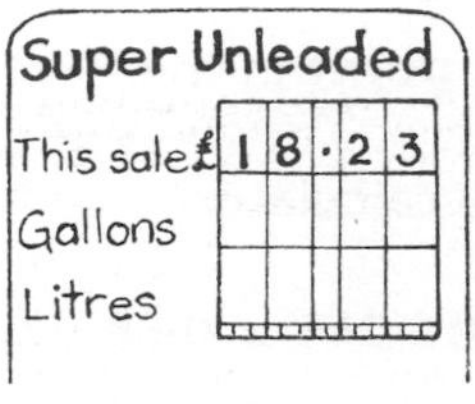

Super Unleaded	
This sale £	18·23
Gallons	
Litres	

(c)

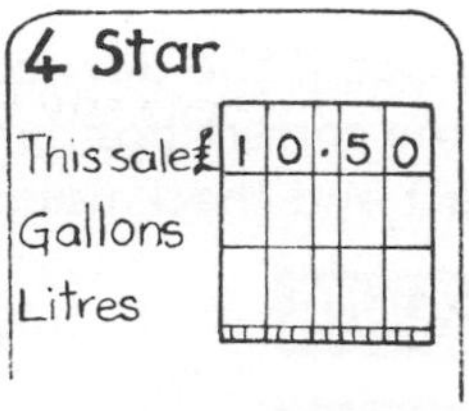

4 Star	
This sale £	10·50
Gallons	
Litres	

(d)

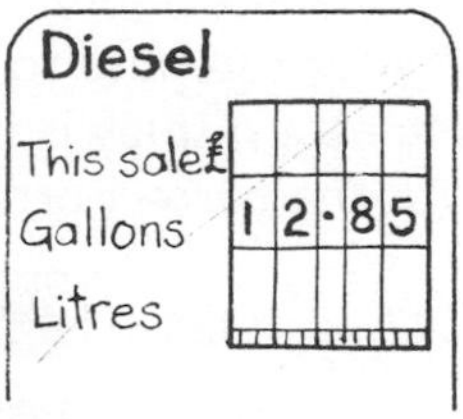

Diesel	
This sale £	
Gallons	12·85
Litres	

4 One US gallon equals 3·785306 litres.
A gallon of 4 star in the USA costs $2·68.

Which country has the better buy? Explain.

Country	Exchange rate per £
United States	1·74 dollars

The product of multiplying

1 **(a)** Find mentally • 60 × 2 • 60 × 200 • 60 × 2000 • 60 × 0·2 • 60 × 0·02
(b) What happens to the size of a number when it is multiplied by
- a number greater than 1
- a number less than 1?

2 **(a)** Copy and complete this table.
(b) As you move from one row to the next what happens to the value of
- the first number
- the product?

Row	*1st No.*		*2nd No.*		*Product*
1	8000	×	0·2	=	1600
2	800	×	0·2	=	
3	80	×	0·2	=	
4	8	×	0·2	=	

(c) Look at the number patterns in your table. Extend your table to rows 5 and 6. Check using your calculator.

3 **(a)** Use your calculator. Copy and complete.

2 × 0·6 =	0·2 × 0·6 =	0·2 × 0·06 =	0·02 × 0·06 =
3 × 0·4 =	0·3 × 0·4 =	0·3 × 0·04 =	0·03 × 0·04 =
0·3 × 5 =	0·3 × 0·5 =	0·03 × 0·5 =	0·03 × 0·05 =
1·4 × 7 =	1·4 × 0·7 =	0·14 × 0·7 =	0·14 × 0·07 =

(b) Write a rule for finding the number of decimal places in the product of two decimals.

4 How many decimal places do you **expect** in each product in the following multiplications? Check using a calculator.
(a) 1·2 × 3·4 **(b)** 1·23 × 4·5 **(c)** 0·06 × 6·66
(d) 9·8 × 0·076 **(e)** 5·3 × 1·924 **(f)** 9·8 × 7·65
Write about your answer in part **(f)**.

5 Find **mentally**
(a) • 0·3 × 0·8 • 0·3 × 0·08
(b) • 0·9 × 0·7 • 0·9 × 0·07
(c) • 0·4 × 0·6 • 0·04 × 0·6
(d) • 0·5 × 0·8 • 0·05 × 0·8

6 In each of the following
- estimate the product by first rounding each number to 1 significant figure
- use your estimate to decide if the **decimal point** in the calculator display is in the correct position
- write the correct product and check using a calculator.

(a) 0·047 × 0·328 = 15.416
(b) 0·246 × 0·68 = 1.6728
(c) 3·01 × 0·384 = 1.15584
(d) 72·352 × 0·065 = 47.0288
(e) 0·37 × 0·0061 = 2.257
(f) 0·0452 × 123·1 = 5.56412

Marina's Aquarium

E19

Decimals: Division by a decimal

1 Plants in a fish tank need light to help them stay healthy. When Marina makes a tank she uses 1 lamp for each 0·3 m of tank length.
Use a number line marked 0, 0·1, 0·2, . . . 2·4 to find how many lamps Marina should use for a tank of length
(a) 2·4 m **(b)** 1·8 m **(c)** 0·9 m

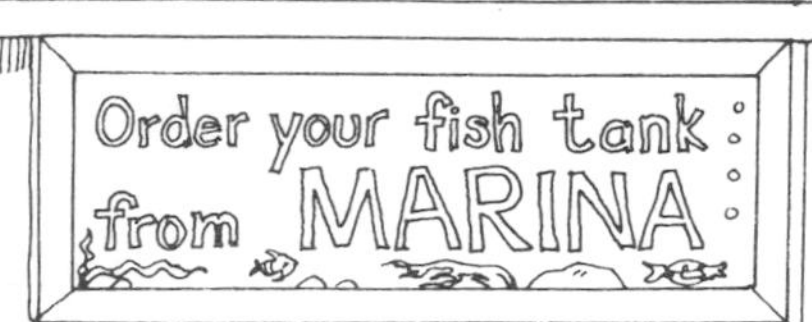

2 Marina works out the number of lamps in question **1(a)** like this:

$$2{\cdot}4 \div 0{\cdot}3 = \frac{2{\cdot}4}{0{\cdot}3} = \frac{2{\cdot}4 \times 10}{0{\cdot}3 \times 10} = \frac{24}{3} = 8$$

Use Marina's method to check your answers to questions **1(b)** and **(c)**.

To divide any number by a decimal, first make the divisor a **whole** number by multiplying **both** numbers by 10, or 100, or 1000 or . . .
For example:

$$0{\cdot}036 \div 0{\cdot}04 = \frac{0{\cdot}036}{0{\cdot}04} = \frac{0{\cdot}036 \times 100}{0{\cdot}04 \times 100} = \frac{3{\cdot}6}{4} = 0{\cdot}9$$

3 **(a)** Copy and complete. Work mentally if you can. Check using a calculator.

- 6·3 ÷ 0·7 = ☐
  6·3 ÷ 0·07 = ☐
- 0·81 ÷ 0·9 = ☐
  0·81 ÷ 0·09 = ☐
- 4 ÷ 0·8 = ☐
  4 ÷ 0·08 = ☐
- 0·054 ÷ 0·6 = ☐
  0·054 ÷ 0·06 = ☐

(b) What happens to the size of a number when it is divided by a number less than 1 ?

4 For each tank there is a fixed **total** length of fish that can be supported. Marina keeps one type of fish in each tank.
Estimate, by first rounding the lengths to 1 sig fig, the greatest number of each type of fish that can be supported by these tanks. Use your calculator to check your estimate.

Tank A *Total length of fish* $\leqslant$ *2·1 m*

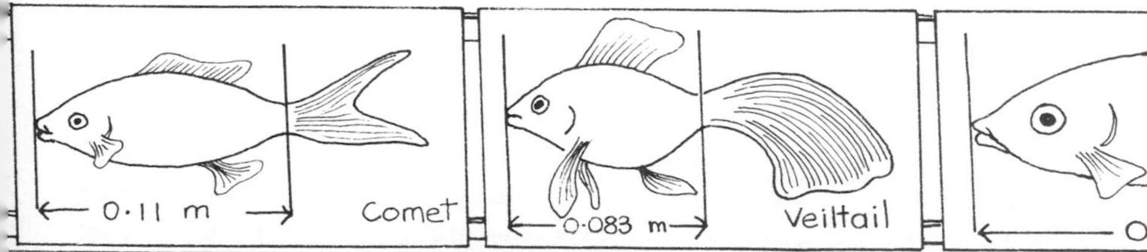

Tank B *Total length of fish* $\leqslant$ *0·88 m*

Ask your teacher what to do next.

E20 All at sea

Scale: Elevation and depression

Charlie is a coastguard based at Howard Point lighthouse.
He reports anyone in difficulty at sea to the rescue services.

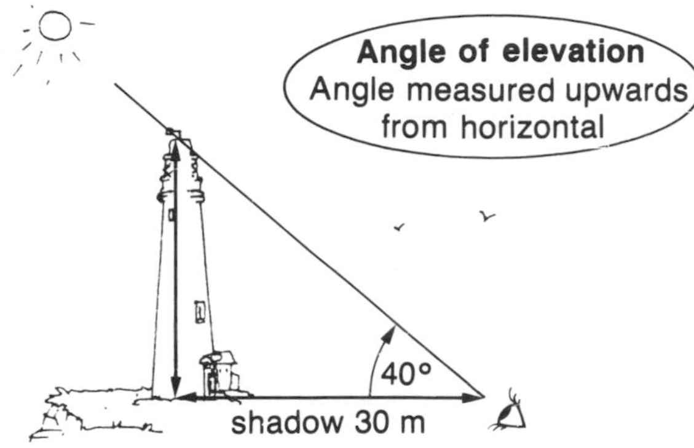

1 Charlie wants to find out the height of the lighthouse.
The angle of **elevation** of the sun is 40°.
The shadow of the lighthouse is 30 m long.

(a) Use a scale of 1:500 to make a scale drawing.

(b) What is the height of the lighthouse?

2 Charlie sees a windsurfer in difficulty. The angle of **depression** is 25°. The cliff is 70 m high. Choose a suitable scale and make a scale drawing.
How far is the windsurfer from the foot of the cliff?

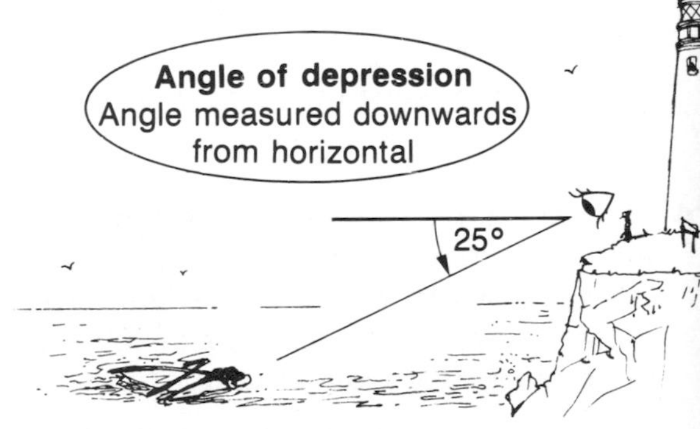

Angle of depression
Angle measured downwards from horizontal
25°

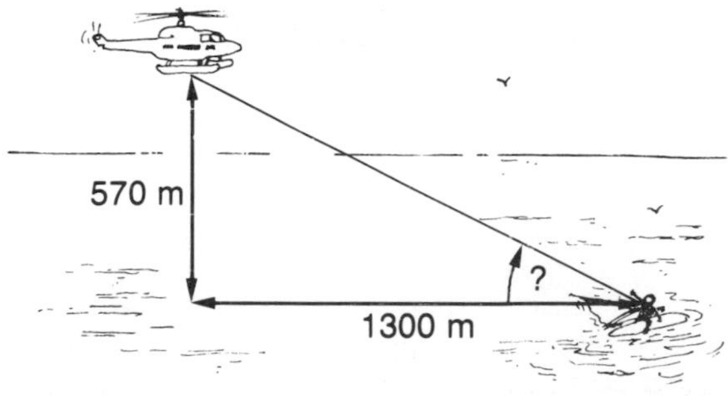

3 Charlie has alerted the rescue helicopter. It is flying at a height of 570 m and is 1300 m from the windsurfer.

(a) Find
- the angle of elevation of the helicopter from the windsurfer
- the angle of depression of the windsurfer from the helicopter.

(b) What do you notice about the two angles?

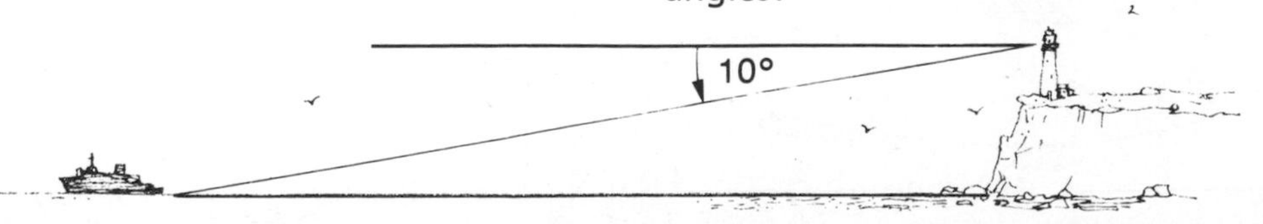

4 Looking out to sea from the top of the lighthouse, Charlie sees a ferry in the distance. The a of depression is 10°. How far is the ferry from the coast? Answer correct to the nearest 100 r

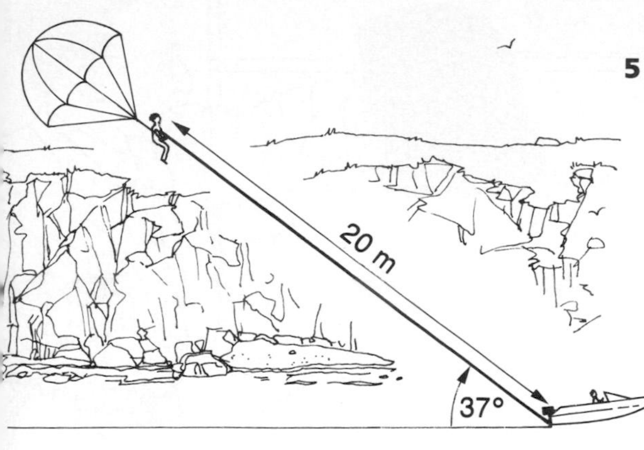

5 A paraglider is being towed at the end of a 20 m rope by a speedboat. The angle of elevation of the rope is 37°.

(a) What is the height of the paraglider above sea-level?

(b) The paraglider loses height. The rope is now inclined at an angle of 21° to the horizontal. How much height has the paraglider lost?

A **clinometer** is an instrument used by surveyors to measure angles of elevation and depression.

The clinometer shows a horizontal line of sight
Angle of elevation is 0°

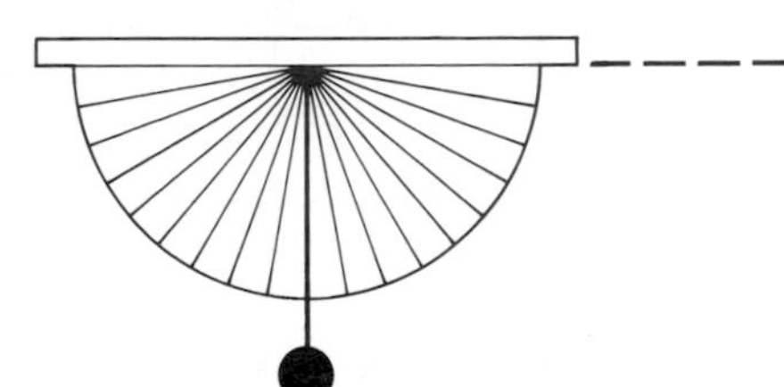

This clinometer shows an angle of elevation
Angle of elevation is 20°

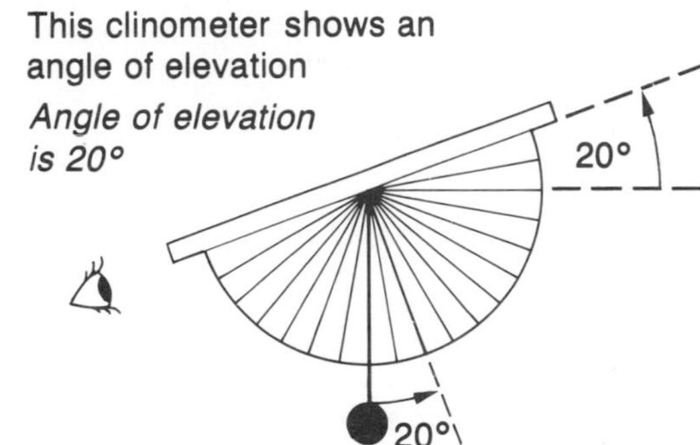

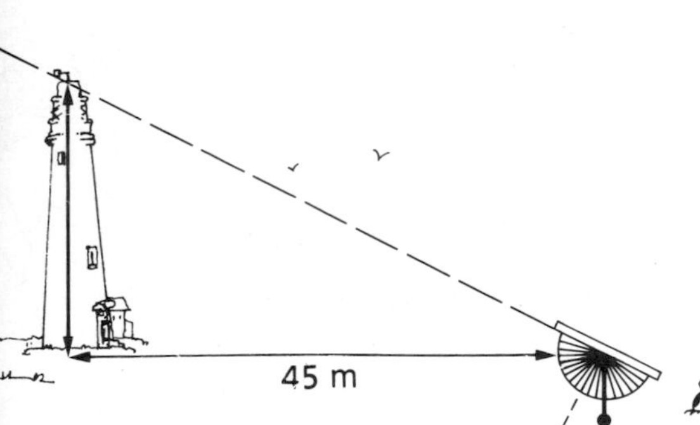

6 Tara, a surveyor, is measuring the height of Charlie's lighthouse.

(a) What is the reading of the angle of elevation on her clinometer?

(b) She is 45 m from the foot of the lighthouse. Does her calculation of the height of the lighthouse agree with Charlie's? Explain.

7 • Make a clinometer using a board protractor.
• Use your clinometer to find the height of your school building.

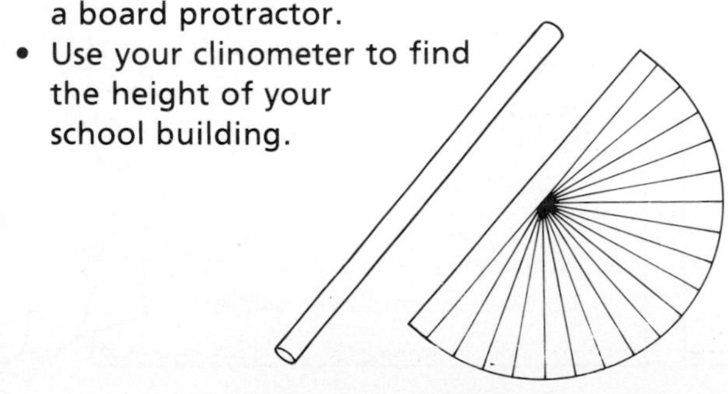

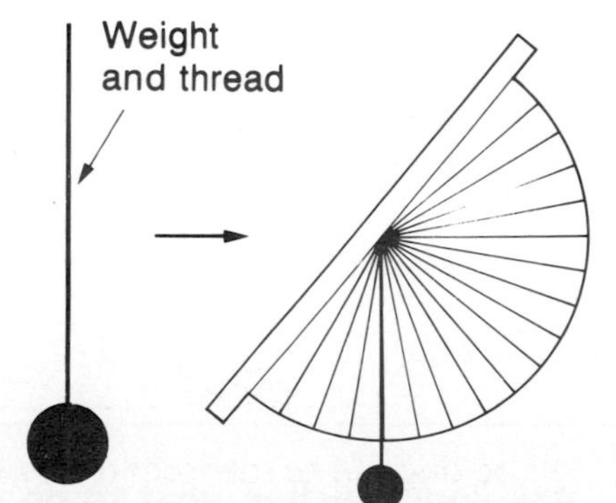

Designing Hall 2

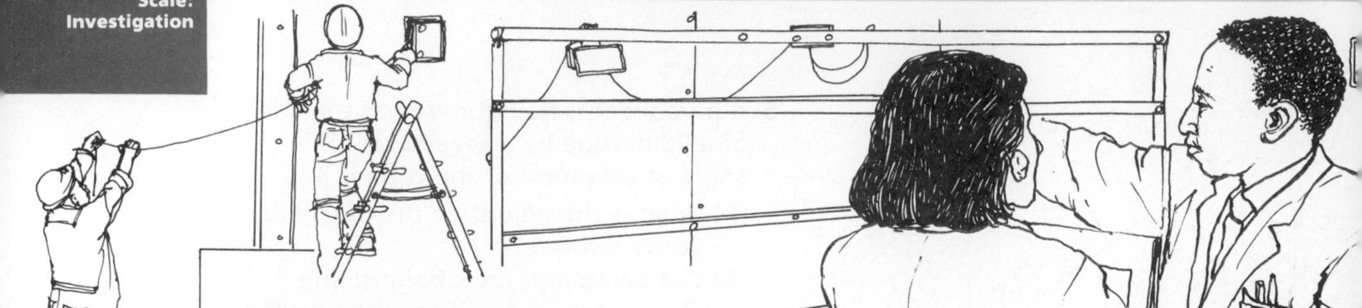

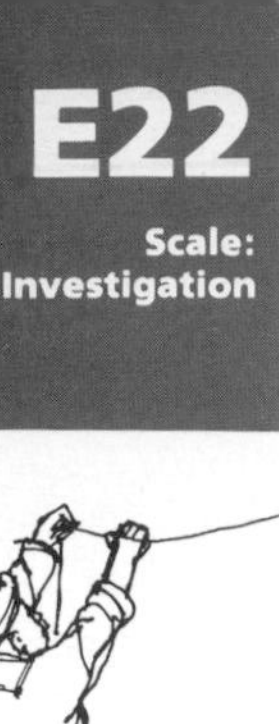

Alexis is organising Hall 2 of Lifescapes Exhibition Centre for the Modern House Exhibition. Her manager Peter gives her this note of the shapes and sizes of the display stands which will be used by the companies taking part.

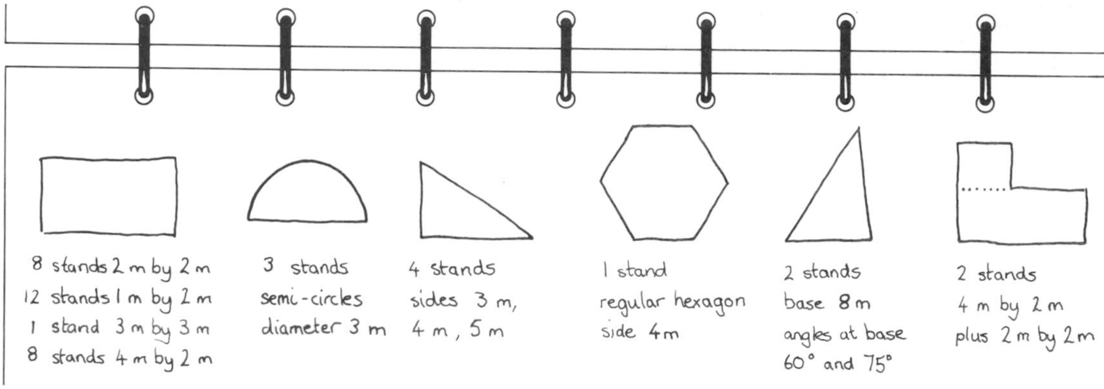

8 stands 2 m by 2 m
12 stands 1 m by 2 m
1 stand 3 m by 3 m
8 stands 4 m by 2 m
3 stands semi-circles diameter 3 m
4 stands sides 3 m, 4 m, 5 m
1 stand regular hexagon side 4m
2 stands base 8 m angles at base 60° and 75°
2 stands 4 m by 2 m plus 2 m by 2 m

Alexis checks the dimensions of the Hall and the rules which she has to follow when designing a layout for the stands. She tries various layouts on a scale diagram of the Hall before she makes her recommendations to Peter.

- Design a layout for the display stands.
- Write a report to Peter explaining your choice of design.

50 m
6 m
7 m
E Entrance
F Fire exit
F
E
8 m
6 m
10 m
F
18 m
F
18 m
≥2 m
≥2 m
≥2 m

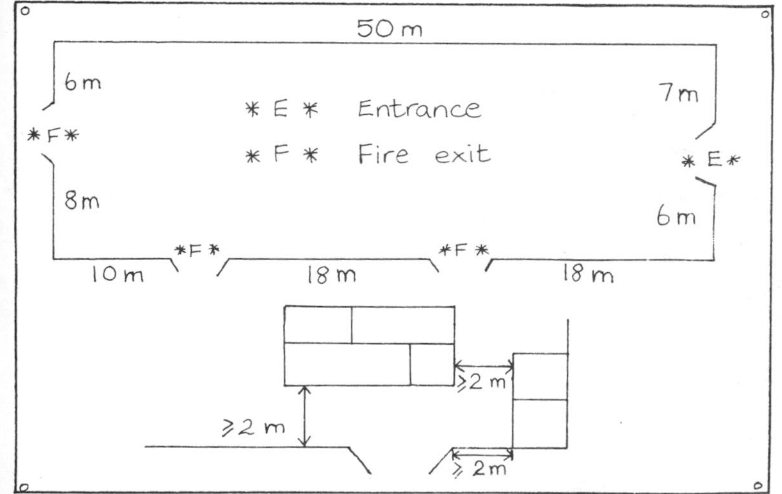

Hall 2

50 metres by 16 metres

The sketch shows the position of the entrance and fire doors.

Layout rules

- Each stand should be a minimum distance of 2 metres from any doorway.
- Stands may be arranged in groups but no more than four should be grouped together.
- Walkways should be at least 2 metres wide.

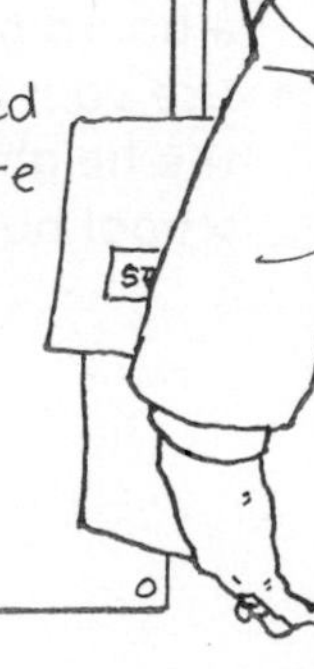

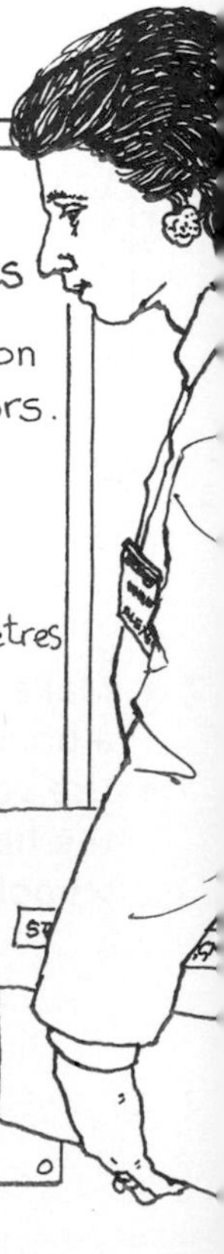

Ask your teacher what to do next.

Clock-wise

E23

Detour: Modular arithmetic

The pointer on this dial turns clockwise.
Check that 3 + 5 → 1.

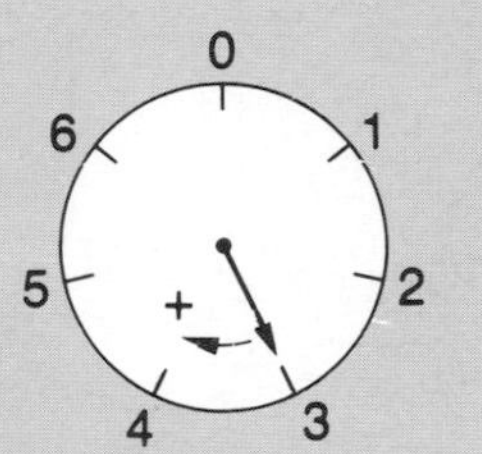

In this number system we use only the seven numbers 0, 1, 2, 3, 4, 5 and 6. This is called counting in **modulus 7**. We write **3 + 5 = 1 (mod 7)**.

1 Check that 4 + 5 = 2 (mod 7). In the same way find

(a) 4 + 4 **(b)** 6 + 3 **(c)** 1 + 5 **(d)** 6 + 6 **(e)** 3 + 4
(f) 5 + 5 **(g)** 4 + 5 + 3 **(h)** 6 + 1 + 2 **(i)** 3 + 2 + 2 **(j)** 6 + 6 + 6

2 Use the clock to solve these equations in modulus 7.

(a) $4 + y = 1$ **(b)** $p + 5 = 2$ **(c)** $t + 6 = 5$ **(d)** $3 + s = 6$
(e) $x + 3 = 1$ **(f)** $4 + q = 2$ **(g)** $x + 3 = 3$ **(h)** $5 + r = 0$

3 Draw the clock for the modulus 5 counting system. Use it to find

(a) 3 + 4 **(b)** 4 + 2 **(c)** 2 + 3 **(d)** 2 + 4 **(e)** 3 + 4 + 2

4 Draw the clock for the modulus 8 counting system. Use it to find

(a) 7 + 5 **(b)** 4 + 4 **(c)** 7 + 7 **(d)** 6 + 4 **(e)** 1 + 6 + 4

5 In which modulus has each calculation been done?

(a) 2 + 6 = 1 **(b)** 1 + 4 = 0 **(c)** 3 + 7 = 2 **(d)** 6 + 4 = 3
(e) 5 + 5 = 3 **(f)** 3 + 6 = 1 **(g)** 4 + 4 = 3 **(h)** 6 + 6 = 4

6 On this clock the pointer can turn in **either** direction.
Check that 4 − 6 = 9 (mod 11). Find

(a) 2 − 4 **(b)** 6 + 7 **(c)** 9 − 4
(d) 9 + 4 **(e)** 4 − 9 **(f)** 10 − 11
(g) 5 − 8 **(h)** 5 + 8 − 4 **(i)** 5 − 8 + 4

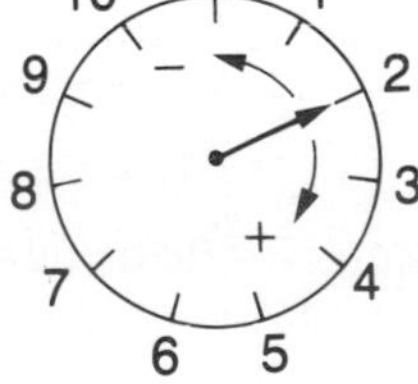

7 **(a)** Draw the clock for modulus 6.
(b) Copy and complete the table for $n \to n + 4$ (mod 6)

n	0	1	2	3	4	5
$n + 4$ (mod 6)	4			1		

(c) On your clock join each pair of numbers in the table.

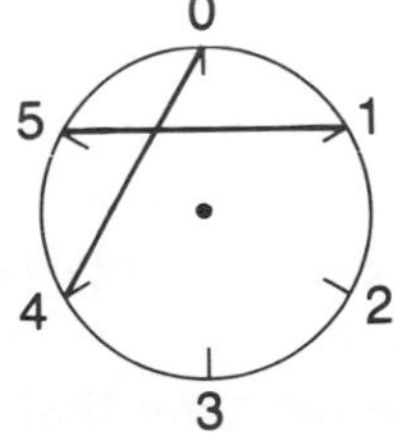

8 Draw the patterns for each of these clocks.

(a) modulus 8
$n \to n + 3$ (mod 8)

(b) modulus 9
$n \to n + 2$ (mod 9)

9 Find all possible patterns on a modulus 10 clock.

Ask your teacher what to do next.

E24 Concorde Couriers

Speed: Distance, speed, time formulae

Concorde Couriers operate a delivery service using motor cycles. John is the telephone receptionist. He tells customers when to expect delivery.

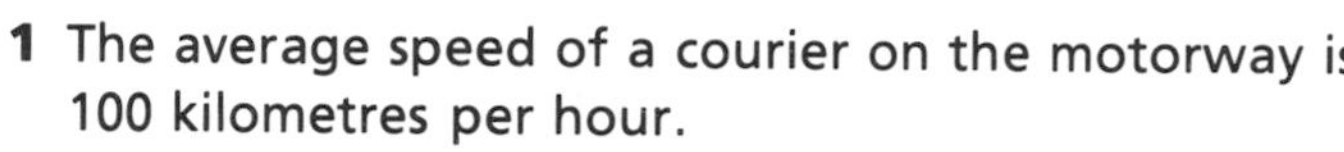

1 The average speed of a courier on the motorway is 100 kilometres per hour.

(a) How long should a delivery take when the distance is
- 200 km
- 300 km
- 450 km.

(b) Copy and complete:
- The time (T) equals the distance (D) ☐ by the average speed (S).
- The formula is $T = \frac{\square}{\square}$

For inter-city deliveries John uses an average speed of 90 km/h to calculate the expected time.
For a distance of 144 km:

$$T = \frac{D}{S} = \frac{144}{90} = 1{\cdot}6 \text{ hours.}$$

The time taken is 1 hour and 36 minutes.

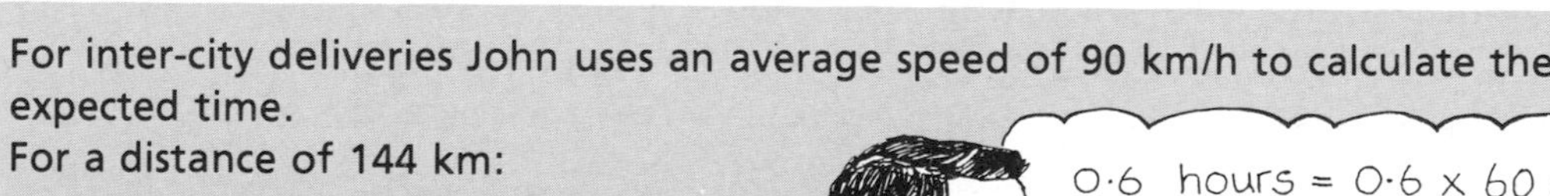

2 Change each of these times to hours **and** minutes.

(a) 1·25 hours **(b)** 1·7 hours **(c)** 2·4 hours **(d)** 3·35 hours

3 Use the formula to find the time in hours and minutes that John allows for an inter-city delivery of

(a) 117 km **(b)** 189 km **(c)** 243 km **(d)** 264 km.

4 Calculate the time that he allows for deliveries between

(a) Manchester and Newcastle
(b) Edinburgh and Leeds
(c) Sheffield and Manchester.

Inter-city Distance Chart (km)

	Edinburgh	Newcastle	Manchester	Sheffield
Newcastle	168			
Manchester	342	216		
Sheffield	376	208	63	
Leeds	315	147	64	54

5 It is 11.14 am. A customer in Edinburgh wants a delivery made to Manchester by 3 pm that day. Should John accept the job? Explain.

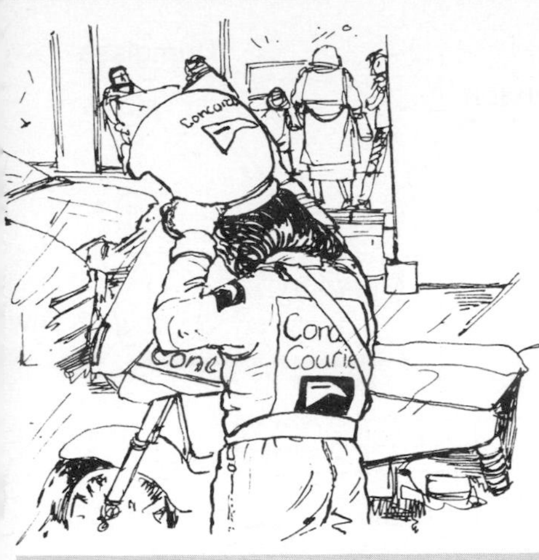

6 Maria can travel from

- Newcastle to Manchester in 2 hours
- Edinburgh to Leeds in 3 hours
- Sheffield to Edinburgh in 4 hours.

(a) Calculate her average speed for each journey.

(b) Copy and complete:

- The average speed (S) equals the distance (D) ☐ by the time (T).
- The formula is $S = \frac{\square}{\square}$

Maria delivered a package from Newcastle to Leeds in 1 hour 24 minutes.
You can calculate her average speed like this:

$$S = \frac{D}{T} = \frac{147}{84} = 1{\cdot}75 \text{ kilometres per } \textbf{minute}$$

$$= 1{\cdot}75 \times 60 \text{ kilometres per } \textbf{hour} = 105 \text{ km/h}$$

Maria's average speed was **105** km/h.

7 Find the average speed, in km/h, for each of these deliveries.

Distance	54 km	216 km	273 km	136 km
Time	36 min	2 h 15 min	2 h 48 min	1 h 20 min

8 Maria picked up a package in Leeds at 1.20 pm.
She delivered the package in Edinburgh at 4.50 pm.
Calculate her average speed.

9 Ron's average speed on the motorway is 100 km/h.

(a) What distance should he travel in

- 2 hours
- 3 hours
- 4 hours?

(b) Copy and complete:

- The distance (D) equals the average speed (S) ☐ by the time (T).
- The formula is $D = \square \times \square$

10 Using an average speed of 96 km/h find the distance travelled, to the nearest km, in

(a) 4 h **(b)** 3 h 15 min
(c) 2 h 18 min **(d)** 54 min

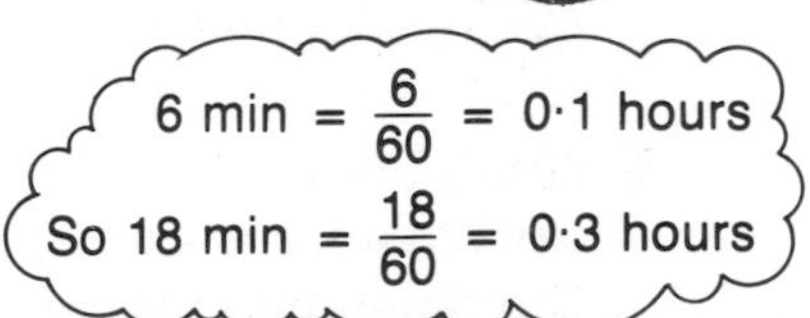

6 min = $\frac{6}{60}$ = 0·1 hours
So 18 min = $\frac{18}{60}$ = 0·3 hours

11 **(a)** How long should Sean take to travel from Belfast to Dublin at an average speed of 96 km/h?

(b) He took 1 hour 48 minutes to make a delivery between Dublin and Galway. Find his average speed.

(c) It took 2 hours 24 minutes at an average speed of 80 km/h to make a delivery between two of these towns. Name the towns.

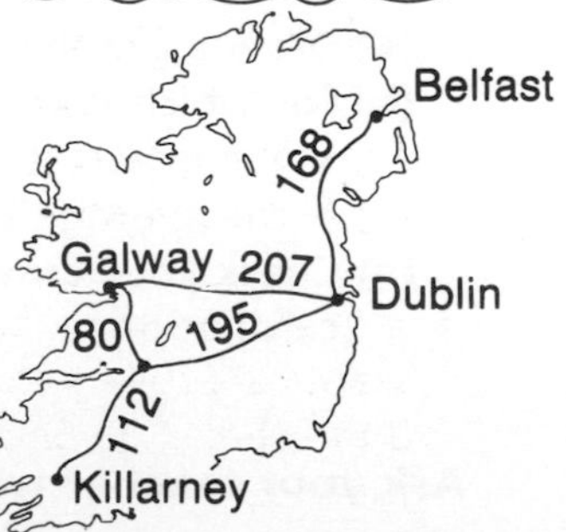

E26 Cora's coaches

Speed: Travel graphs

Each morning in summer Cora's coach company runs a tour from Dumglass to the coastal villages of Ferryton and Maryport.

The graph shows the coach's journey.

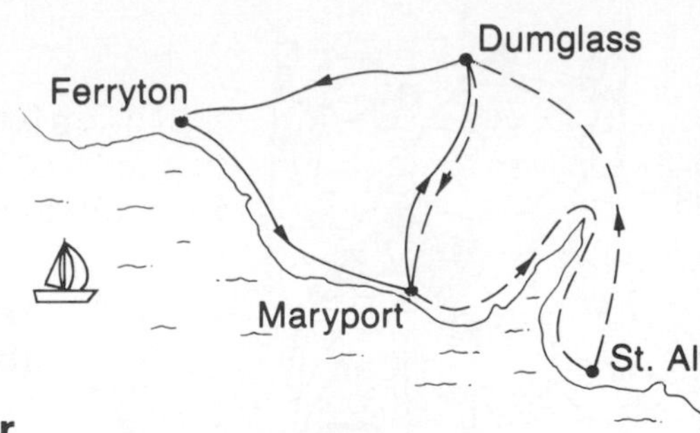

Cora's morning tour

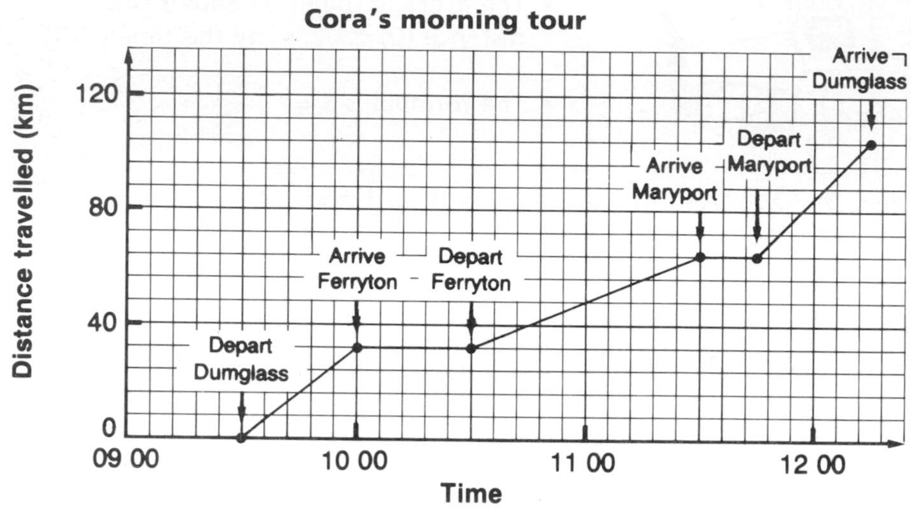

1 What does one small interval represent on
(a) the time axis **(b)** the distance axis?

2 Construct a timetable for Cora's morning tour.

3 How far does the coach travel during the tour?

4 For each of the three stages of the tour find
(a) the distance travelled
(b) the time taken
(c) the average speed in km/h.

5 For which stage of the tour is
(a) the average speed fastest
(b) the graph steepest?

6 Cora's afternoon tour from Dumglass visits Maryport and St. Alwin's. The timetable is shown.
(a) Draw a graph of the journey.
(b) For which stage of the tour is
- the graph steepest
- the average speed fastest?

(c) Check your answer to **(b)** by calculation.

Cora's afternoon tour

	Total distance travelled	*Arrive*	*Depart*
Dumglass	–	–	13 30
Maryport	40 km	14 00	14 30
St. Alwin's	96 km	15 54	16 12
Dumglass	144 km	17 00	–

Ask your teacher what to do next.

Rhodes to Crete

E27

Formulae 2: $y = ax - b$

1 There are four adults in the MacKay family. They have won a holiday discount voucher for £300. How much would the MacKay family pay for a holiday in

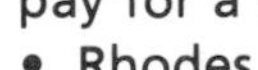

- Rhodes
- Malta
- Madrid?

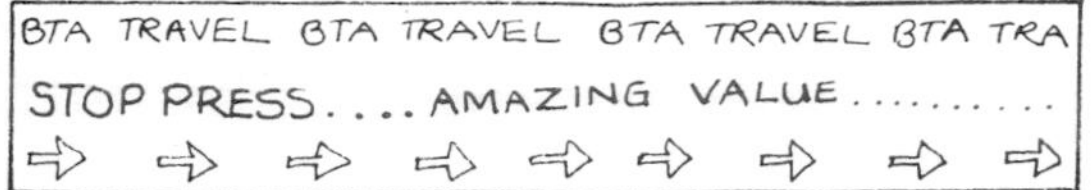

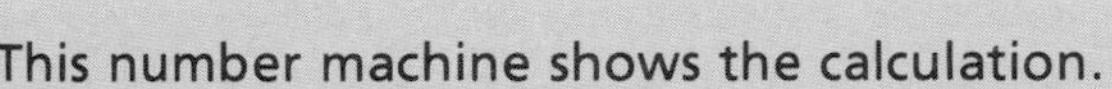

This number machine shows the calculation.

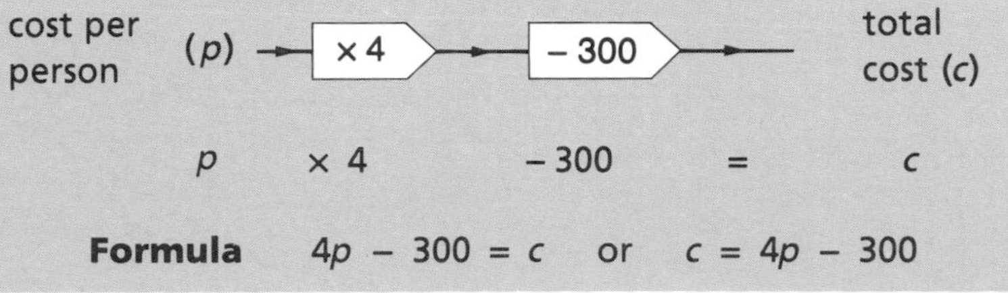

$p \quad \times 4 \quad - 300 \quad = \quad c$

Formula $4p - 300 = c$ or $c = 4p - 300$

2 Use the formula to find how much the MacKay family would pay for each of these holidays.

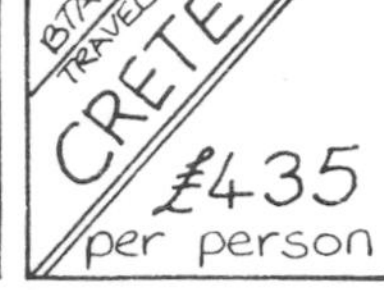

3 There are five people in the Hawkins family. They have a holiday discount voucher for £250.

(a) Write a formula to find the total cost of a holiday for this family.

(b) Use your formula to find the total cost of a holiday for the Hawkins family in • Rhodes • Rimini • Paris.

4 The MacKay family go to Paris. The exchange rate is £1 = 10 francs and the bank charges a fee of 25 francs for exchanging money.

(a) How many francs would they get for £50?

(b) Write a formula for the number of francs received for a number of pounds using
 p for the number of pounds
and f for the number of francs.

(c) Use your formula to find the number of francs the MacKay family would receive in exchange for
• £20 • £35 • £60 • £120 • £250.

5 The Hawkins family go to Crete. The exchange rate is £1 = 320 drachma and the bank charges a fee of 500 drachma for exchanging money.

(a) Write a formula for the number of drachma received for a number of pounds.

(b) Use your formula to find the number of drachma the Hawkins family would receive for
• £30 • £55 • £80 • £95 • £132.

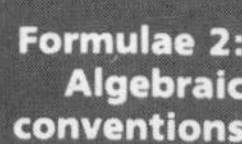

E28 Formula fun

Formulae 2: Algebraic conventions

1 Michael finds the perimeter of each drawing using the formula $P = 2(b + w)$, where b is the breadth and w is the width. Find the perimeter for each breadth and width.

(a) $b = 10$ cm, $w = 15$ cm **(b)** $b = 12$ cm, $w = 18$ cm
(c) $b = 20$ cm, $w = 24$ cm **(d)** $b = 32$ cm, $w = 44$ cm

2 Derek is investigating the areas of these shapes. He uses three formulae:

$P = d^2 \qquad Q = 3d^2 \qquad R = (3d)^2$

(a) Copy and complete his working, when d is 4 cm.

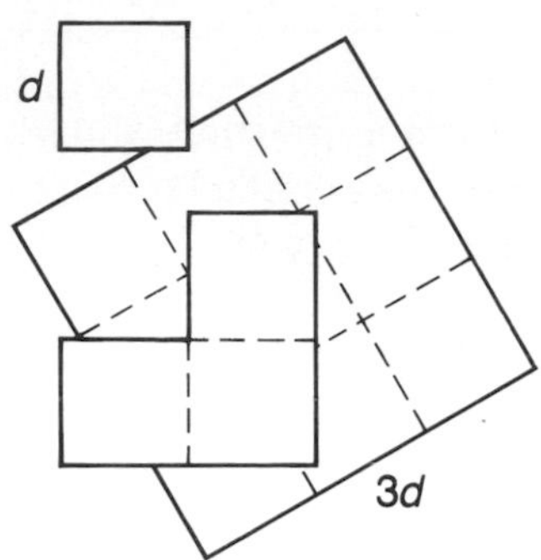

$P = d^2$
$= 4^2$
$= \square \text{ cm}^2$

$Q = 3d^2$
$= 3 \times 4^2$
$= 3 \times \square$
$= \square \text{ cm}^2$

$R = (3d)^2$
$= (3 \times 4)^2$
$= (\square)^2$
$= \square \text{ cm}^2$

(b) Find the value of P, Q and R when d is

- 5 cm
- 7 cm
- 12 cm
- 6·2 cm.

(c) Which is the correct formula for the area of the larger square?

3 Evaluate each formula.

(a) $A = 2d^2$ when $d = 3$
(b) $A = (2d)^2$ when $d = 3$
(c) $A = (4n)^2$ when $n = 2$
(d) $A = 4n^2$ when $n = 2$
(e) $A = x^2 + 5$ when $x = 7$
(f) $A = (x + 5)^2$ when $x = 7$
(g) $A = 2(p + 7)$ when $p = 3$
(h) $A = 3(2m - 3)$ when $m = 4$
(i) $A = \dfrac{12}{t}$ when $t = 6$
(j) $A = \dfrac{m}{5}$ when $m = 25$
(k) $A = \dfrac{p + 4}{6}$ when $p = 20$
(l) $A = \dfrac{2d + 3}{5}$ when $d = 6$
(m) $A = \dfrac{12}{f + 2}$ when $f = 4$
(n) $A = \dfrac{2r + 1}{r - 2}$ when $r = 7$
(o) $A = 5r^2 + 10$ when $r = 4$
(p) $A = (5r)^2 + 10$ when $r = 4$
(q) $A = (5r + 10)^2$ when $r = 4$
(r) $A = 2q^2 - 9$ when $q = 5$
(s) $A = (2q)^2 - 9$ when $q = 5$
(t) $A = (2q - 9)^2$ when $q = 5$

4 For a particular medicine Doctor Adams calculates a child's dose in milligrams using the formula

$$C = \frac{20y}{y + 12}$$ where y is the age of the child.

Calculate the correct dose of this medicine for each child.

(a) Tom aged 3 **(b)** Ali aged 8
(c) Kaj aged 12 **(d)** Senga aged 4

Just plug in the numbers

E29

Formulae 2: Substitution

Aunt Jemima uses recipes which have oven temperatures given in degrees centigrade, C. Her own oven is marked in degrees Fahrenheit, F. She converts the temperatures using the formula $\mathbf{F = 1{\cdot}8C + 32}$.

For gingerbread $C = 150°$ so $F = 1{\cdot}8 \times 150 + 32$
$= 270 + 32$
$= 302$

The dial is marked in 10° intervals so Jemima sets her oven at **300°F**.

1 At what temperature should Jemima set her oven to bake these cakes?

(a) Chelsea bun at 220°C
(b) Simnel cake at 230°C
(c) Sandwich cake at 190°C
(d) Porter cake at 140°C

2 Here are formulae for finding the volumes of three solids.

triangular prism
$V = Ah$

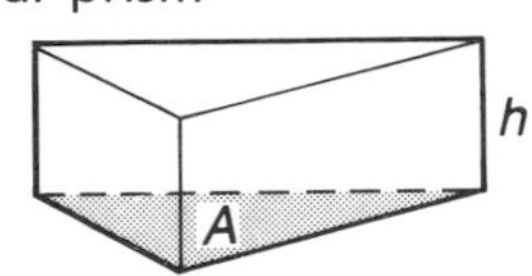

square-based cuboid
$V = b^2h$

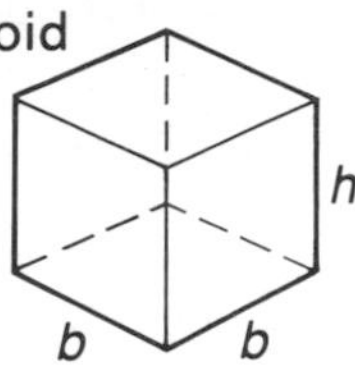

cone
$V = \frac{1}{3}Ah$

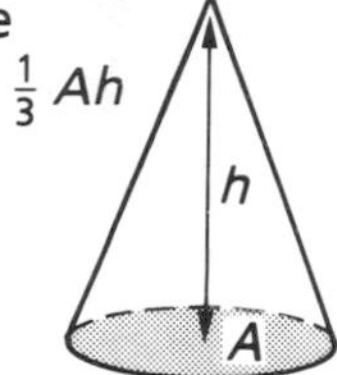

Find the volume (V) of each of these solids.

(a) A triangular prism with $A = 29$ mm² and $h = 5$ mm.
(b) A square-based cuboid with $b = 13$ cm and $h = 7$ cm.
(c) A cone with $A = 32$ m² and $h = 12$ m.
(d) A triangular prism with $A = 2{\cdot}3$ cm² and $h = 3{\cdot}2$ cm.
(e) A square-based cuboid with $b = 2{\cdot}5$ m and $h = 1{\cdot}2$ m.
(f) A cone with $A = 7{\cdot}6$ mm² and $h = 6{\cdot}6$ mm.

3 Here is a mixed bag of formulae.

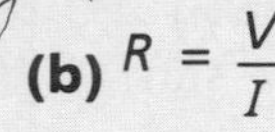

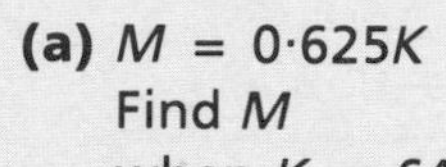

(a) $M = 0{\cdot}625K$
Find M
when $K = 64$

(b) $R = \frac{V}{I}$
Find R
when $V = 240$ and $I = 15$

(c) $w = \frac{1}{2}P - b$
Find w
when $P = 17{\cdot}5$
and $b = 3{\cdot}25$

(d) $v = u - 10t$
Find v
when $u = 75$
and $t = 2{\cdot}5$

(e) $A = 3{\cdot}14rs$
Find A
when $r = 9$
and $s = 15$

(f) $V = 4{\cdot}19r^3$
Find V
when $r = 3$

(g) $A = 2b^2 + 4bh$
Find A
when $b = 15$
and $h = 23$

(h) $D = v + \frac{v^2}{20}$
Find D
when $v = 75$

Ask your teacher what to do next.

E30 The planets

Whole numbers 2: Standard form

Neptune has a diameter of 49 600 km.
This can be written as $4{\cdot}96 \times 10\,000$ km
$= 4{\cdot}96 \times 10^4$ km

This number must lie between 1 and 10.

The diameter is now written in **standard form** or **scientific notation**.

1 Write the diameter of each of these planets in standard form.

(a) *Venus* diameter 12 000 km
(b) *Jupiter* diameter 139 000 km
(c) *Pluto* diameter 2280 km

2 Write each of these numbers in standard form.

(a) 65 000	**(b)** 3500	**(c)** 980	**(d)** 7560
(e) 315 000	**(f)** 20 500	**(g)** 235	**(h)** 4000
(i) 78 300	**(j)** 403 200	**(k)** 2 000 000	**(l)** 7 090 000

Mars has a diameter of $6{\cdot}79 \times 10^2$
$= 6{\cdot}79 \times 1000$
$=$ **6790 km**

3 Write each of these diameters as an ordinary number.

(a) *Earth* diameter $1{\cdot}3 \times 10^4$ km
(b) *Saturn* diameter $1{\cdot}2 \times 10^5$ km
(c) *Uranus* diameter $5{\cdot}11 \times 10^4$ km
(d) *Mercury* diameter $4{\cdot}9 \times 10^3$ km

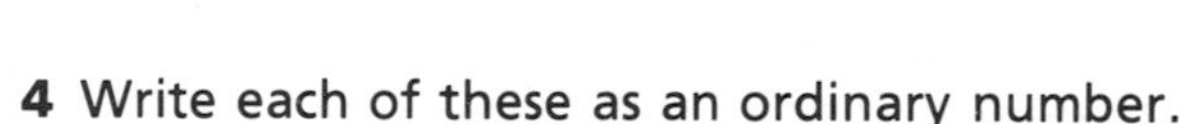

4 Write each of these as an ordinary number.

(a) $2{\cdot}3 \times 10^3$	**(b)** $5{\cdot}87 \times 10^6$	**(c)** $3{\cdot}1 \times 10^2$	**(d)** $7{\cdot}2 \times 10^7$	**(e)** $5{\cdot}0 \times 10^4$
(f) $8{\cdot}33 \times 10^4$	**(g)** $1{\cdot}35 \times 10^1$	**(h)** $9{\cdot}5 \times 10^5$	**(i)** $2{\cdot}07 \times 10^2$	**(j)** $5{\cdot}72 \times 10^9$

5 This table shows the mean distance in kilometres of each planet from the sun. Copy and complete the table.

Planet	*Mean distance in kilometres*	
	ordinary number	*standard form*
Mercury	58 000 000	
Venus		$1{\cdot}1 \times 10^8$
Earth	150 000 000	
Mars		$2{\cdot}28 \times 10^8$
Jupiter	778 000 000	
Saturn		$1{\cdot}4 \times 10^9$
Uranus	2 880 000 000	
Neptune		$4{\cdot}5 \times 10^9$
Pluto	5 910 000 000	

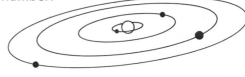

Ask your teacher what to do next.

Pick's Formula

E31

Detour: Investigation

This shape has
- 8 dots on its boundary
- 2 dots inside the boundary
- an area of 5 square units.

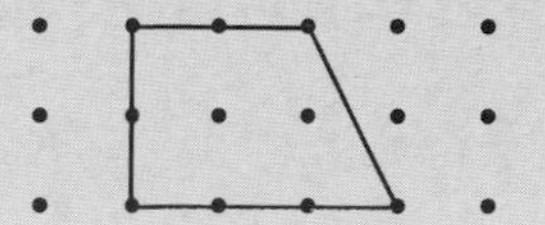

1 **(a)** Copy and complete the table for each of these shapes.

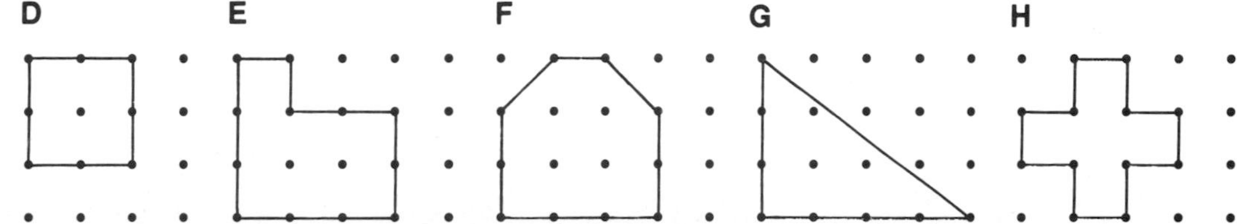

Shape	*Number of dots on boundary (b)*	*Number of dots inside boundary (i)*	$\frac{1}{2}b + i$	*Area (A) in square units*
D	8	1		
E				
F				

(b) Draw some shapes of your own and add the information to your table.
(c) Look at the last two columns in your table. What do you notice?
(d) Copy and complete the formula $A = \frac{1}{2}b + i - \square$.

This is called Pick's Formula.

2 Use the formula to find the area of each of these shapes.

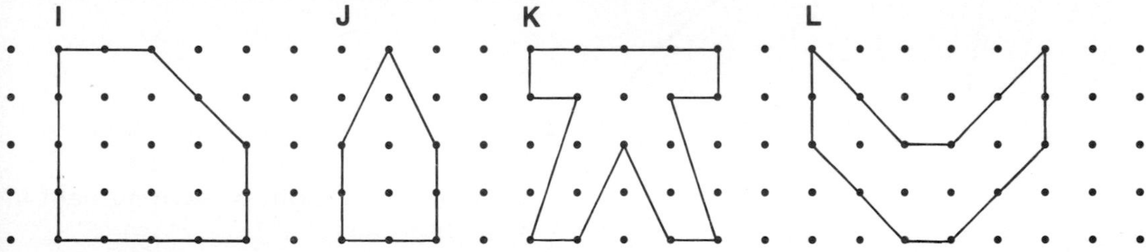

3 Use Pick's formula to find the shaded area in each of these shapes.

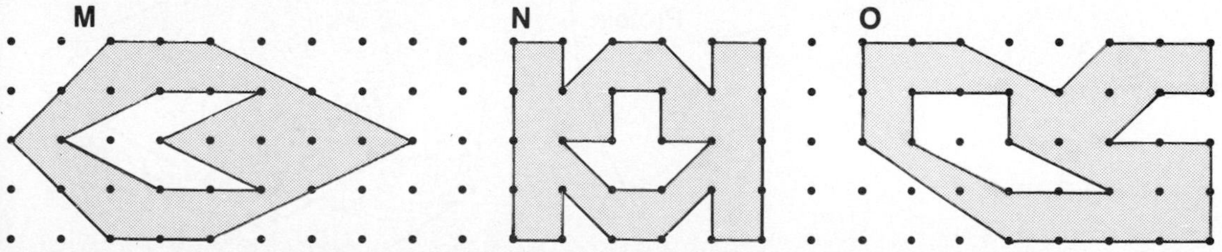

Ask your teacher what to do next.

E32 Chocolate pie

Handling data 2: Pie charts

You need a protractor.

Wild Bar

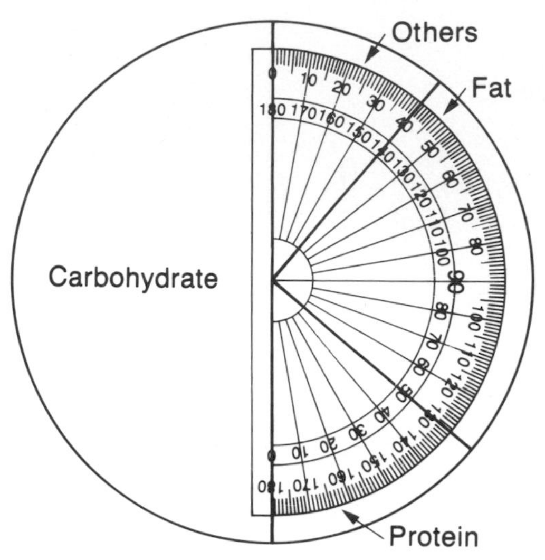

The pie chart shows the main nutritional contents of Wild Bar. A bar weighs 64g.
What is the weight of protein?
The sector representing protein has an angle of 50°.

This represents $\frac{50}{360}$ of a whole bar.

Weight of protein $= \frac{50}{360}$ of 64 g

$= \mathbf{8{\cdot}9g}$ to 1 dp.

$\frac{50}{360} \times 64$
$= 8{\cdot}8888888$

1 (a) Copy and complete the table for the weight of
- carbohydrate
- fat
- others.

(b) Complete the totals as a check.

Nutrient	*Angle*	*Calculation*	*Weig*
Protein	50°	$\frac{50}{360}$ of 64 g	8·9
Carbohydrate			
Fat			
Others			
Totals			

Coconut Ball

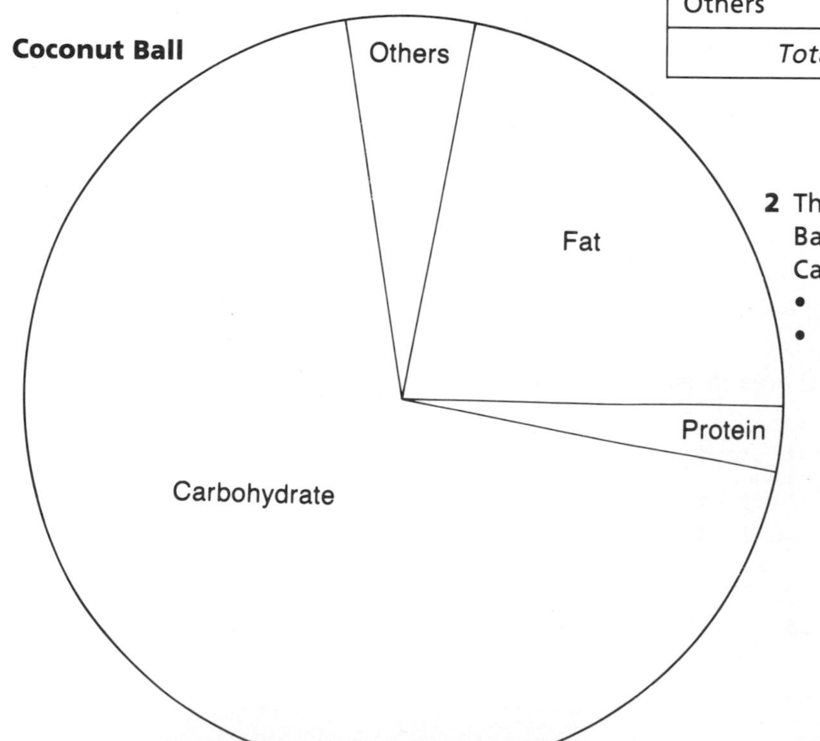

2 The nutritional contents of a Coconut Ball are shown in the pie chart.
Calculate the weight of each nutrient in
- an 18 g Ball
- a 500 g box of Coconut Balls.

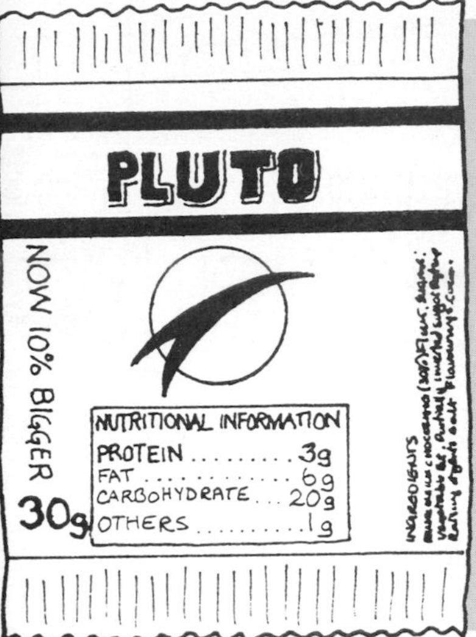

Carl wanted to display the information for a Pluto bar in a pie chart. He calculated the angle of the pie chart for protein like this.
The fraction of the bar which is protein is $\frac{3}{30}$.

Angle $= \frac{3}{30}$ of 360°

$= 36°$.

He drew a circle and a radius.
He then measured an angle of 36°.

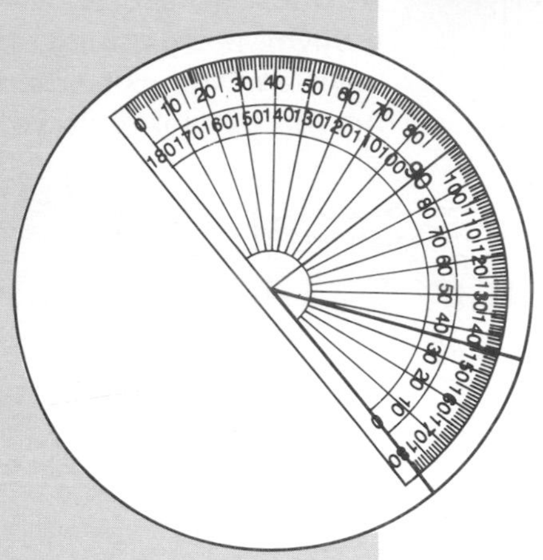

3 **(a)** For a Pluto bar draw a pie chart to show the weight of
- protein
- carbohydrate
- fat.

(b) Measure the angle of the *Others* sectors. Check it by calculation.

4 Draw pie charts to represent the nutritional information shown on each of these wrappers.

(a)

(b)

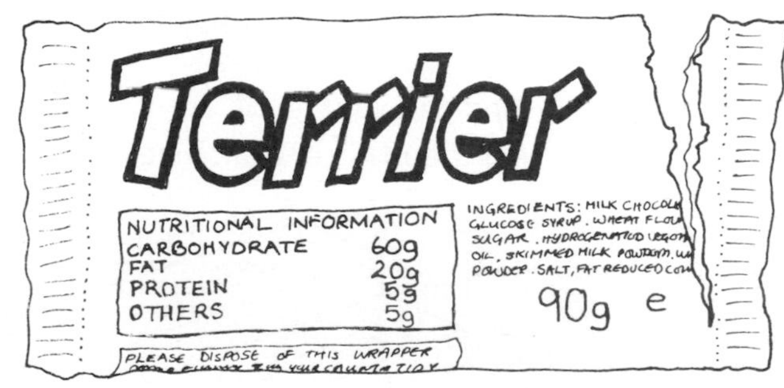

(c)

(d)

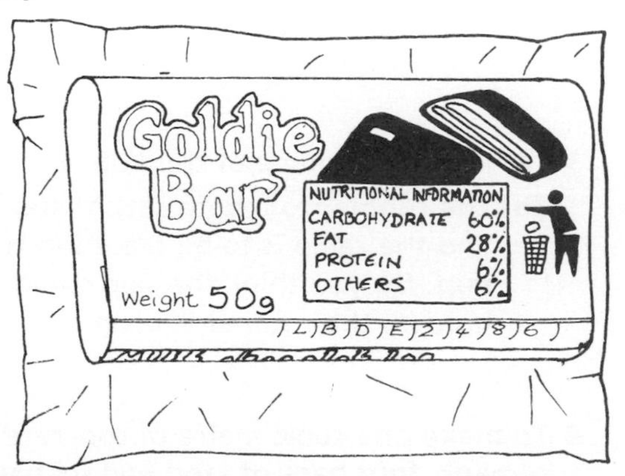

Ask your teacher what to do next.

E34 Step by step

Volume: Composite shapes, prisms

At the Astro Sports Centre, the manager, Gwilym, is organising repairs. Both sets of steps and the wheelchair ramp are to be broken up and replaced by new concrete ones.

1 Use each of the following methods to find the volume of the staff entrance steps.

Method A

- calculate the volume of step **P**
- calculate the volume of step **Q**
- find the total volume of the steps.

Method B

- find the area of the shaded cross section.
- multiply this area by the width of the steps.

1 m
1 m
2 m
0·3 m
0·6 m
Staff
Entrance
P
Q

2 Find the volume of

(a) the main entrance steps

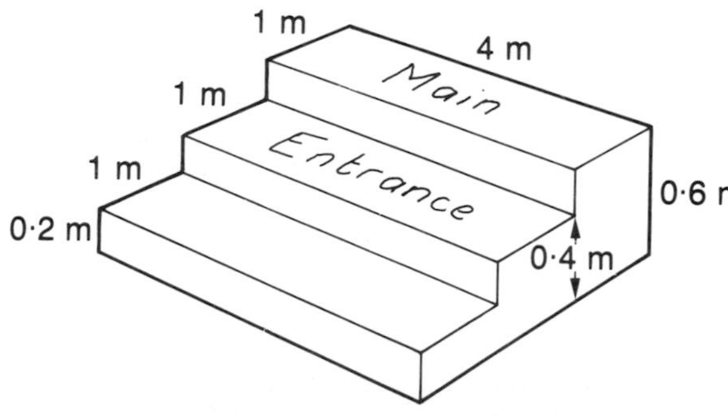

(b) the wheelchair ramp.

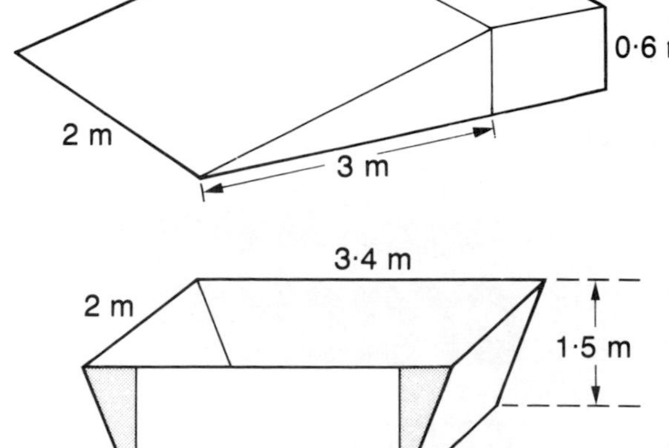

3 **(a)** Find the volume of the skip.

(b) The rubble from both sets of steps and the ramp is to be placed in the skip. Do you think the skip could hold all the rubble? Explain.

4 To make one cubic metre of concrete Bill uses two bags of cement, four bags of sand and six bags of chippings. How many bags of each does he need to replace both sets of steps and the ramp?

What's in a can?

E35

Volume: Cylinder, $V = Ah$

You need some containers which are cylinders, a measuring jar, 1 cm squared paper and a ruler.

I can find the volume of these prisms using the formula V = Ah

This cylinder is a prism with a circular base. Can I use V = Ah to find its volume ?
P

1 Copy this table.

Cylinder	*Area of base* *A*	*height* *h*	*Ah*	*Measured volume*
P	cm^2	cm	cm^3	ml

Write the answers to each part of question 2 in your table.

2 **(a)** Choose a cylinder. Draw round its base on 1 cm squared paper. By counting squares and part squares find the approximate area of the base, *A*.

(b) Measure the height, *h*, of the cylinder in centimetres.

(c) Calculate *Ah*.

(d) Fill the cylinder with water. Find the volume of the cylinder by measuring the volume of the water.

3 Repeat question **2** for each of your other cylinders.

4 Look at the last two columns in your table. Do you think you can use the formula $V = Ah$ to find the volume of a cylinder? Explain.

E36 Cecil's trays

Volume: Maximum volume investigation

Cecil makes trays at the Cardboard Container Company. He makes the nets by cutting small congruent squares from each corner of large 10 cm by 10 cm cardboard squares.

1 Cecil's small squares have an edge length which is a **whole number of centimetres.**

(a) Make all the different trays Cecil could produce.
(b) What is the volume of each tray?
(c) What is the edge length of the small squares which give the tray with the greatest volume?

Can I make a tray which holds even more?
I wonder what would happen if the edges of the small squares could be any length?

2 Cecil had a brainwave! He measured the edges of the small squares to **the nearest $\frac{1}{4}$ centimetre**. Answer **without** making trays:

(a) What is the volume of a tray made by cutting off small squares with edge length $2\frac{1}{2}$ cm?
(b) Using Cecil's brainwave, what is the edge length of the small squares which gives the tray with the greatest volume?

3 What did Cecil find?

Ask your teacher what to do next.

Sarah's garden

E37

Detour: Ellipses

Colin is a landscape artist. He designs flower beds and layouts for plants. Sarah has asked Colin to redesign her circular flower bed which has a diameter of 20 metres.

1 **(a)** Follow these instructions to make Colin's design:
- Draw a circle with diameter 20 **centimetres**.
- Draw lines at right angles to the diameter.
- Mark the mid-points, between the diameter and the circumference, of each of these lines as shown.
- Join the mid-points to form a smooth curve.

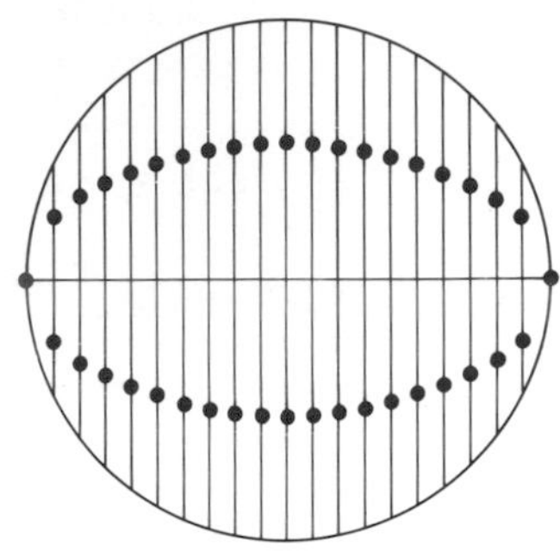

This curve is an **ellipse**.

(b) Investigate what would happen if you marked the **three-quarter** points instead of the mid-points . . . or the **one-quarter** points . . . or . . .

2 Colin advises Sarah to make her new flower bed like this:
- Loop 32 m of rope round two pegs in the ground, X and Y, 12 m apart.
- Pull the rope taut to form a triangle. **Keeping the rope taut** walk round marking out the perimeter of the flower bed.

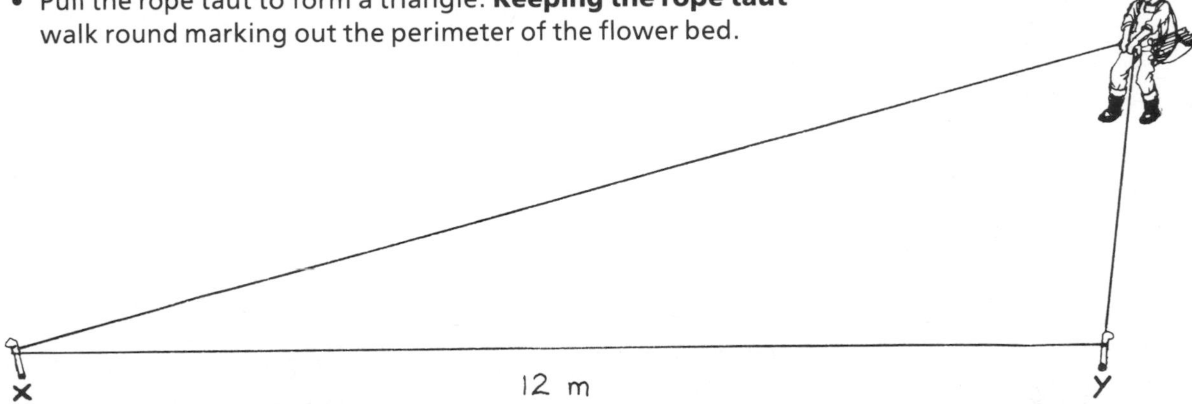

(a) **You need a 32 cm loop of string, two drawing pins and a pin board**. Use a scale of 1 cm to 1 m to make a scale drawing of Sarah's new flower bed.

(b) Compare this drawing and your drawing of Colin's design in question **1(a)**. What do you notice?

3 Sarah decides to place pegs X and Y 8 m apart. She still wants her new flower bed to fit **inside** the old circular flower bed. What is the greatest length she can make her loop of rope? Explain.

4 Colin designs a layout for the flowers using two sets of **concentric** circles. The shading shows where the flowers are to be planted.

(a) What do you notice about the shape of the layout?

(b) Draw a layout like Colin's.

Ask your teacher what to do next.

E38 The Lunchbox Café

Algebraic expressions: Like terms

Elma makes up packed lunches at the Lunchbox Café.
A sandwich costs s pence

Debbie's sandwiches cost $6 \times s = 6s$ Mike's sandwiches cost $4 \times s = 4s$

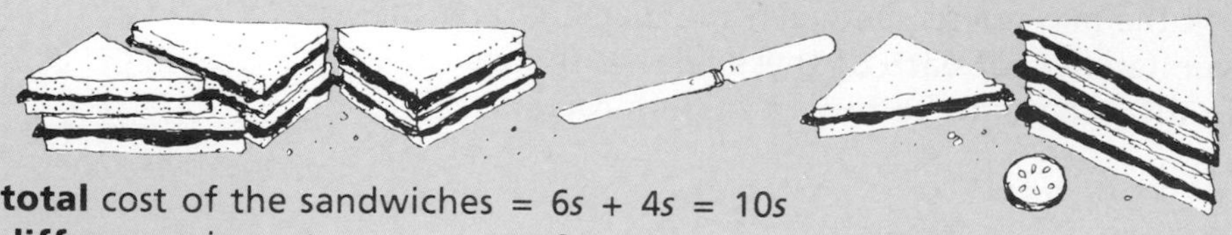

The **total** cost of the sandwiches $= 6s + 4s = 10s$
The **difference** in cost $= 6s - 4s = 2s$

1 Find each total

(a) $4s + 2s$ **(b)** $7s + s$ **(c)** $15s + 5s$ **(d)** $3s + 6s + 5s$

2 Find each difference

(a) $7s - 4s$ **(b)** $12s - 3s$ **(c)** $4s - s$ **(d)** $55s - 15s$

3 A carton of juice costs, c pence. Find

(a) $6c + 3c$ **(b)** $5c + 9c$ **(c)** $7c + 3c + c$
(d) $10c - 5c$ **(e)** $20c + 15c - 3c$ **(f)** $24c + 5c - 7c$

David orders these 2 lunches.

The total cost of these lunches is

$4s + 2c + 3s + c$
$= 4s + 3s + 2c + c$
$= 7s + 3c$

$4s$ and $3s$ are like terms.
$2c$ and c are like terms.
You can add and subtract like terms.
This is called simplifying.

The difference in cost of these lunches is

$4s + 2c - 3s - c$
$= 4s - 3s + 2c - c$
$= s + c$

(a) $3s + 2c + 5s + c$ **(b)** $2s + 2c + 4s + 3c$ **(c)** $8s + 5c + 7s + 4c$
(d) $5p + 3q - 2p - 2q$ **(e)** $6p + 3q - 2p - q$ **(f)** $4p + 3q - 3p - q$

We can also simplify expressions with a mixture of letter terms and number terms.

$3c + 7 + 6c + 2$
$= 3c + 6c + 7 + 2$
$= 9c + 9$

$7f + 6 - 3f - 5$
$= 7f - 3f + 6 - 5$
$= 4f + 1$

$8 - 3p - 3 + 4p + 7$
$= 8 - 3 + 7 + 4p - 3p$
$= 12 + p$

5 Simplify

(a) $5k + 8 + 2k + 3$ **(b)** $4g + 9 - 3g + 5$ **(c)** $7t + 3 - 2t - 2$
(d) $6 + 8x + 9 + 3x$ **(e)** $5 + 4y - 2 + 9y$ **(f)** $5s + 7 - 3s - 3$
(g) $4y + 8 - 3y - 6$ **(h)** $4 - 3a + 7 + 8a$ **(i)** $3 - d + 7 + 5d - 6$
(j) $30x + 5 + 20 - 15x$ **(k)** $20r + 25 + 30r + 12$ **(l)** $5v + 4v - 9 + 2v + 15$

The Lunchbox Café

E39

Algebraic expressions: Distributive law

Gordon buys three identical packed lunches.

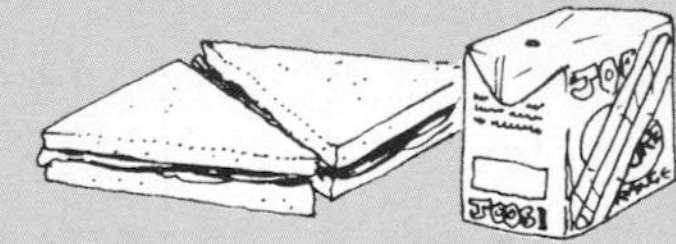
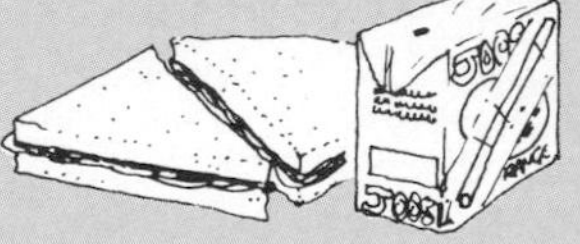

The total cost of the lunches is

$2s + c \quad + \quad 2s + c \quad + \quad 2s + c$ or $3(2s + c)$

$= 2s + 2s + 2s + c + c + c$ $\qquad = 3 \times 2s + 3 \times c$

$= 6s + 3c$ $\qquad = 6s + 3c$

1 Copy and complete the expressions.

(a)

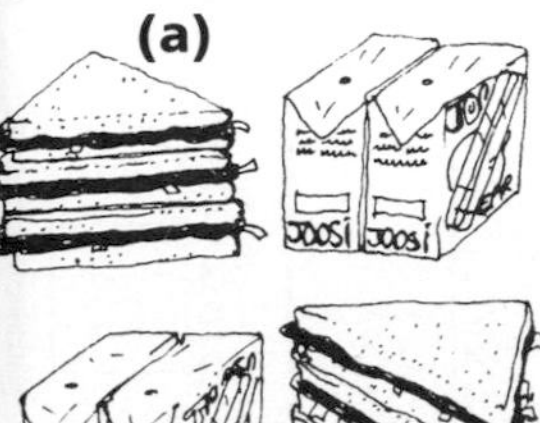
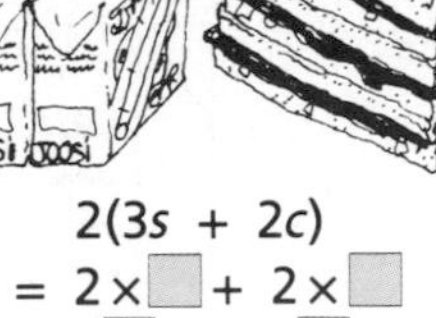

$2(3s + 2c)$
$= 2\times\square + 2\times\square$
$= \square + \square$

(b)

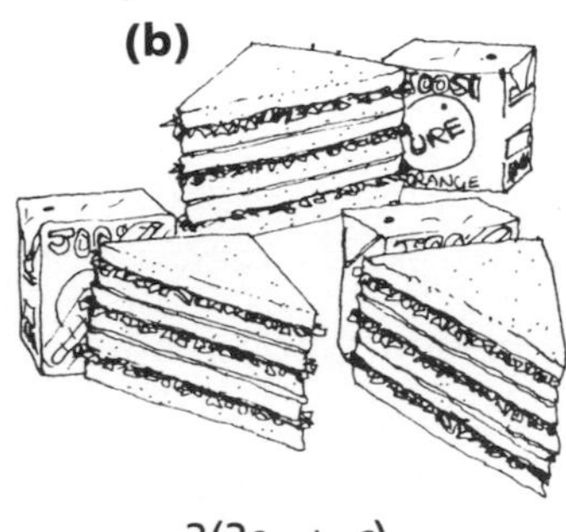

$3(3s + c)$
$= 3\times\square + 3\times\square$
$= \square + \square$

(c)

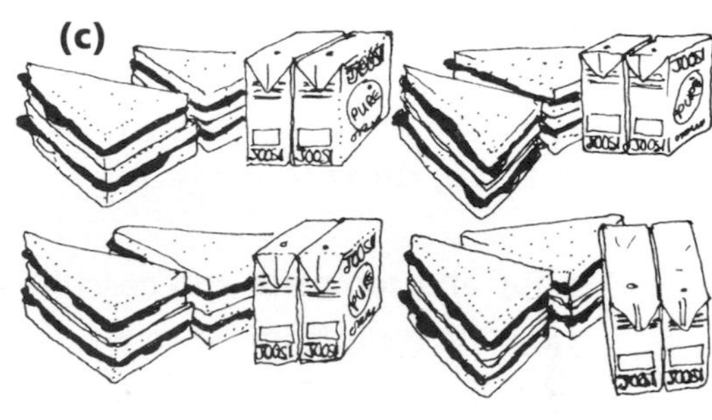

$4(4s + 2c)$
$= 4\times\square + \square\times\square$
$= \square + \square$

2 Multiply out these brackets.

(a) $5(2x + 4y)$ **(b)** $4(5t + 2u)$ **(c)** $2(3x + 9y)$ **(d)** $7(3s + 8t)$
(e) $8(g + 7h)$ **(f)** $3(5d + 10e)$ **(g)** $6(k + 6m)$ **(h)** $8(7g + 6h)$

The difference in cost between the sandwiches and the cartons is

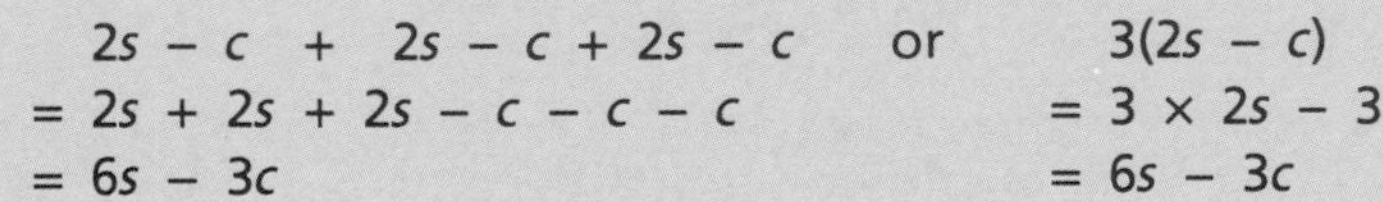

$2s - c \quad + \quad 2s - c + 2s - c$ or $3(2s - c)$

$= 2s + 2s + 2s - c - c - c$ $\qquad = 3 \times 2s - 3 \times c$

$= 6s - 3c$ $\qquad = 6s - 3c$

3 Multiply out these brackets.

(a) $5(3s - c)$ **(b)** $4(5s - 2c)$ **(c)** $7(3s - 4c)$ **(d)** $8(s - 2c)$
(e) $4(p - 8q)$ **(f)** $10(6d - 10e)$ **(g)** $4(3a - 11b)$ **(h)** $5(v - 15w)$

We can also multiply out brackets with a mixture of letter terms and number terms.

$5(3c + 8)$
$= 5 \times 3c + 5 \times 8$
$= 15c + 40$

$6(7c - 5)$
$= 6 \times 7c - 6 \times 5$
$= 42c - 30$

$7(2c + 5 - 3d)$
$= 7 \times 2c + 7 \times 5 - 7 \times 3d$
$= 14c + 35 - 21d$

4 Multiply out these brackets.

(a) $5(7t + 9)$ **(b)** $9(5 + 3r)$ **(c)** $5(2s - 6)$ **(d)** $3(9 - 5t)$
(e) $8(3s + 2t - 3)$ **(f)** $7(a + 2b - 4)$ **(g)** $2(4f - 3g + 7)$ **(h)** $5(3p - 6 - 8q)$

Ask your teacher what to do next.

E40 The Jupiter rocket

Negative numbers: Subtraction of a negative integer

On the ladders outside the Jupiter rocket:
Jill starts at 3 and goes to 8. We can write this as

$3 + ? = 8$ **or** $8 - 3 = ?$
$? = 5$

Jill goes **up 5** rungs.

Jim starts at $^-4$ and goes to 3. We can write this as

$^-4 + ? = 3$ **or** $3 - {}^-4 = ?$ **or** $3 + 4 = ?$
$? = 7$ so $3 - {}^-4 = 3 + 4$

Jim goes **up 7** rungs.

Zoë starts at $^-3$ and goes to $^-7$. We can write this as

$^-3 + ? = {}^-7$ **or** $^-7 - {}^-3 = ?$ **or** $^-7 + 3 = ?$
$? = {}^-4$ so $^-7 - {}^-3 = {}^-7 + 3$

Zoë goes **down 4** rungs.

1 Copy and complete and describe each person's movements.

(a) John goes from $^-2$ to 6.
$^-2 + \square = 6$ or $6 - {}^-2 = \square$ or $6 + 2 = \square$.
John goes $\square\,\square$ rungs.

(b) Jo goes from $^-7$ to $^-3$.
$^-7 + \square = {}^-3$ or $^-3 - {}^-7 = \square$ or $^-3 + 7 = \square$.
Jo goes $\square\,\square$ rungs.

(c) Lisa goes from $^-3$ to $^-8$.
$^-3 + \square = {}^-8$ or $^-8 - {}^-3 = \square$ or $^-8 + 3 = \square$.
Lisa goes $\square\,\square$ rungs.

2 Write additions and subtractions and describe Jill's movements when she goes from
(a) $^-4$ to 3 **(b)** $^-3$ to 1 **(c)** $^-3$ to $^-5$ **(d)** $^-4$ to $^-8$

Subtracting a negative number is the same as adding the positive number.

3 Copy and complete:

(a) $5 - {}^-2$
$= 5 + 2$
$= \square$

(b) $3 - {}^-6$
$= 3 + 6$
$= \square$

(c) $^-2 - {}^-5$
$= {}^-2 + 5$
$= \square$

(d) $^-6 - {}^-3$
$= {}^-6 + 3$
$= \square$

(e) $^-9 - {}^-7$
$= {}^-9 \ \square$
$= \square$

(f) $^-8 - {}^-4$
$= {}^-8 \ \square$
$= \square$

(g) $5 - {}^-3$
$= \square$
$= \square$

(h) $^-7 - {}^-1$
$= \square$
$= \square$

4 Find
(a) $5 - {}^-3$ **(b)** $3 - {}^-5$ **(c)** $^-7 - {}^-2$ **(d)** $^-2 - {}^-7$ **(e)** $^-5 - {}^-5$
(f) $^-2 - {}^-8$ **(g)** $8 - {}^-2$ **(h)** $^-9 - {}^-1$ **(i)** $^-1 - {}^-9$ **(j)** $^-3 - {}^-3$

5 Find
(a) $5 + 6 - 9$ **(b)** $4 + 1 - 7$ **(c)** $3 - 2 - 4$ **(d)** $3 - 8 + 7$
(e) $5 - 7 + {}^-4$ **(f)** $8 + {}^-2 + {}^-5$ **(g)** $4 + {}^-6 + 8$ **(h)** $3 - {}^-2 + 4$
(i) $7 - {}^-1 - 8$ **(j)** $5 - {}^-3 - 4$ **(k)** $3 - {}^-7 + 3$ **(l)** $8 - {}^-2 + {}^-9$
(m) $^-2 - {}^-7 + 3$ **(n)** $^-5 - {}^-2 + 8$ **(o)** $^-2 - {}^-5 + {}^-9$ **(p)** $^-9 - {}^-5 - {}^-8$

Number patterns

1 Copy and complete each of these number patterns.

(a)	(b)	(c)	(d)
$2 \times 3 =$	$4 \times {}^{-}3 =$	${}^{-}5 \times 2 =$	$3 \times {}^{-}7 =$
$2 \times 2 =$	$3 \times {}^{-}3 =$	${}^{-}5 \times 1 =$	$2 \times {}^{-}7 =$
$2 \times 1 =$	$2 \times {}^{-}3 =$	${}^{-}5 \times 0 =$	$1 \times {}^{-}7 =$
$2 \times 0 =$	$1 \times {}^{-}3 =$	${}^{-}5 \times {}^{-}1 =$	$0 \times {}^{-}7 =$
$2 \times {}^{-}1 =$	$0 \times {}^{-}3 =$	${}^{-}5 \times {}^{-}2 =$	${}^{-}1 \times {}^{-}7 =$
$2 \times {}^{-}2 =$	${}^{-}1 \times {}^{-}3 =$	${}^{-}5 \times {}^{-}3 =$	${}^{-}2 \times {}^{-}7 =$
$2 \times {}^{-}3 =$	${}^{-}2 \times {}^{-}3 =$	${}^{-}5 \times {}^{-}4 =$	${}^{-}3 \times {}^{-}7 =$

Look at your number patterns. Check that when you multiply two numbers
- the answer is **positive** when their **signs are the same**.
- the answer is **negative** when their **signs are different**.

2 Find **(a)** $3 \times {}^{-}4$ **(b)** ${}^{-}7 \times 6$ **(c)** ${}^{-}6 \times {}^{-}4$ **(d)** $8 \times {}^{-}2$ **(e)** ${}^{-}5 \times {}^{-}9$
(f) ${}^{-}6 \times {}^{-}6$ **(g)** ${}^{-}4 \times 7$ **(h)** $7 \times {}^{-}5$ **(i)** ${}^{-}3 \times {}^{-}3$ **(j)** $({}^{-}9)^2$

3 Copy and complete.

(a) ${}^{-}2 \times 3 \times 4$
$= {}^{-}6 \times 4$
$= \square$

(b) $5 \times {}^{-}4 \times {}^{-}7$
$= {}^{-}20 \times \square$
$= \square$

(c) $3 \times {}^{-}2 \times {}^{-}1$
$= \square$
$= \square$

4 Find **(a)** $3 \times {}^{-}4 \times 2$ **(b)** $5 \times {}^{-}2 \times {}^{-}1$ **(c)** ${}^{-}5 \times {}^{-}1 \times {}^{-}6$ **(d)** $({}^{-}4)^3$
(e) $0 \times {}^{-}8 \times {}^{-}9$ **(f)** $2 \times {}^{-}5 \times {}^{-}1 \times {}^{-}4$ **(g)** $3 \times {}^{-}2 \times 4 \times {}^{-}5$ **(h)** $({}^{-}5)^3$

Since	$5 \times 3 = 15$	then	$15 \div 3 = 5$	and $15 \div 5 = 3$
Since	$5 \times {}^{-}3 = {}^{-}15$	then	${}^{-}15 \div {}^{-}3 = 5$	and ${}^{-}15 \div 5 = {}^{-}3$
Since	${}^{-}5 \times 3 = {}^{-}15$	then	${}^{-}15 \div 3 = {}^{-}5$	and ${}^{-}15 \div {}^{-}5 = 3$
Since	${}^{-}5 \times {}^{-}3 = 15$	then	$15 \div {}^{-}3 = {}^{-}5$	and $15 \div {}^{-}5 = {}^{-}3$

Look at these examples. When you divide two numbers
- the answer is **positive** when their **signs are the same**
- the answer is **negative** when their **signs are different**.

5 Find **(a)** ${}^{-}8 \div 2$ **(b)** $20 \div {}^{-}5$ **(c)** ${}^{-}35 \div {}^{-}7$ **(d)** ${}^{-}24 \div 3$ **(e)** ${}^{-}36 \div {}^{-}6$
(f) $5 \div {}^{-}1$ **(g)** ${}^{-}21 \div {}^{-}3$ **(h)** ${}^{-}63 \div {}^{-}3$ **(i)** $56 \div {}^{-}8$ **(j)** ${}^{-}80 \div {}^{-}8$

6 Copy and complete:

(a) $\dfrac{5 \times {}^{-}6}{{}^{-}2} = \dfrac{{}^{-}30}{{}^{-}2} = \square$

(b) $\dfrac{5 \times {}^{-}8}{2 \times {}^{-}4} = \dfrac{{}^{-}40}{{}^{-}8} = \square$

(c) $\dfrac{{}^{-}8 \times {}^{-}3}{4 \times {}^{-}2} = \dfrac{24}{{}^{-}8} = \square$

(d) $\dfrac{{}^{-}36}{({}^{-}3)^2} = \dfrac{{}^{-}36}{9} = \square$

7 Find **(a)** $\dfrac{4 \times {}^{-}6}{3}$ **(b)** $\dfrac{8 \times {}^{-}6}{2 \times {}^{-}4}$ **(c)** $\dfrac{{}^{-}9 \times 5}{{}^{-}3 \times {}^{-}3}$ **(d)** $\dfrac{7 \times {}^{-}4}{({}^{-}2)^2}$

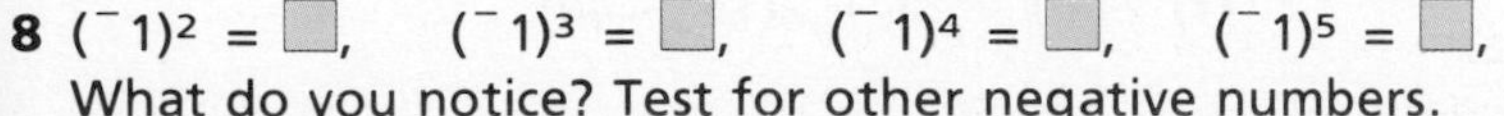

8 $({}^{-}1)^2 = \square$, $({}^{-}1)^3 = \square$, $({}^{-}1)^4 = \square$, $({}^{-}1)^5 = \square$, . . .
What do you notice? Test for other negative numbers.

E42 What an expression!

Negative numbers: Distributive law

1 Multiply out the brackets.

(a) $5(a + 3)$ **(b)** $3(2b + 1)$
(c) $4(c - 7)$ **(d)** $2(5d - 3p)$

$2(3a + 1)$
$= 6a + 2$

$5(2b - 3)$
$= 10b - 15$

2 Copy and complete.

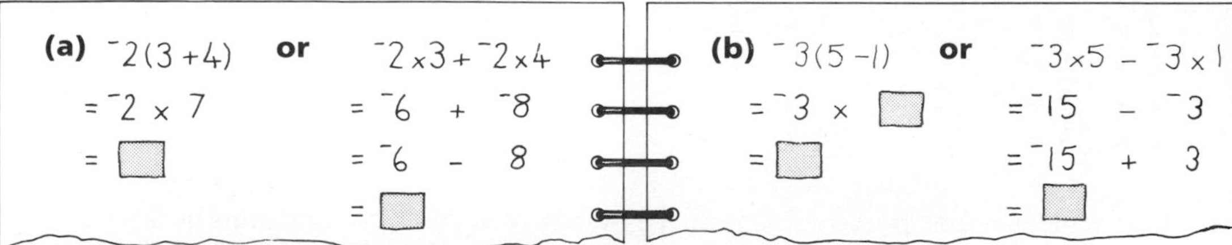

You can multiply brackets like this.

$$
\begin{aligned}
&{}^-3(a + 4) \\
&= {}^-3 \times a + {}^-3 \times 4 \\
&= {}^-3a + {}^-12 \\
&= {}^-3a - 12
\end{aligned}
\qquad
\begin{aligned}
&{}^-3(a - 4) \\
&= {}^-3 \times a - {}^-3 \times 4 \\
&= {}^-3a - {}^-12 \\
&= {}^-3a + 12
\end{aligned}
$$

3 Copy and complete:

(a) $^-3(a+5)$
$= {}^-3a + {}^-15$
$=$ □ − □

(b) $^-2(5b+7)$
$= {}^-10b +$ □
$=$ □

(c) $^-5(c-2)$
$=$ □ $- {}^-10$
$=$ □

(d) $^-4(3f-8)$
$=$ □
$=$ □

4 Multiply out the brackets.

(a) $^-4(p + 3)$ **(b)** $^-3(2q + 7)$ **(c)** $^-5(3r + 7s)$ **(d)** $^-7(x - 3)$
(e) $^-1(3w - 2z)$ **(f)** $^-7(4 - 5j)$ **(g)** $^-2(t + 2u + 3)$ **(h)** $^-4(3n - 7m + 5)$

You can simplify expressions like this.

$$
\begin{aligned}
&6 - (a + 4) \\
&= 6 + {}^-1(a + 4) \\
&= 6 - a - 4 \\
&= 2 - a
\end{aligned}
\qquad
\begin{aligned}
&2a - (a - 4) \\
&= 2a + {}^-1(a - 4) \\
&= 2a - a + 4 \\
&= a + 4
\end{aligned}
$$

5 Copy and complete.

(a) $5 - (a+2)$
$= 5 + {}^-1(a+4)$
$= 5 -$ □ − □
$=$ □ − □

(b) $7b - (2b+1)$
$= 7b + {}^-1($□ + □$)$
$= 7b -$ □ − □
$=$ □

(c) $^-2d - (7-3d)$
$= {}^-2d + {}^-1($□ − □$)$
$= {}^-2d -$ □ + □
$=$ □

6 Simplify

(a) $4a - (a + 5)$ **(b)** $8f - (f - 8)$ **(c)** $4 - (3c + 7)$ **(d)** $^-5h - (7 - 3h)$

Challenge

7 Multiply out the brackets and then simplify.

(a) $3(a + 1) - 2(a + 2)$ **(b)** $4(3b + 1) - 5(2b - 1)$
(c) $5(2 - 3c) - (c - 2)$ **(d)** $9(2d - 6) - (10 + 3d)$
(e) $7(1 - 2e) + (e - 1)$ **(f)** $6(2h - 3) + 2(15 - 4h)$

Ask your teacher what to do next.

Very cross roads

E43

Detour: Investigation

Tom designs road systems. All the streets in this new town are to be straight lines. At each crossroads a control box will be needed to operate the traffice lights.

Three roads **could** cross in the following ways.

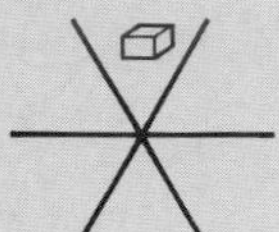

1 control box is needed.

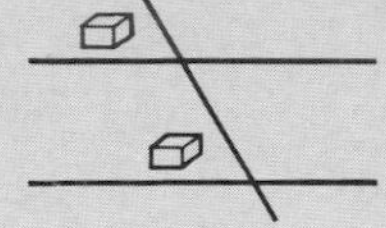

2 control boxes are needed.

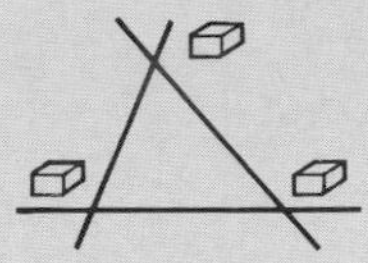

3 control boxes are needed.

The **maximum** number of control boxes needed for 3 roads is **3**.

1 Draw a diagram to show the maximum number of control boxes needed for a design with

(a) 2 roads **(b)** 4 roads.

2 Copy this table. Record the maximum number of control boxes needed for designs with 2, 3 and 4 roads.

Number of roads	1	2	3	4	5	6
Maximum number of control boxes	0					

3 **(a)** What do you think is the maximum number of control boxes needed for 5 roads? Check by drawing a diagram.

(b) Complete your table.

4 Tom's design has 8 roads in the centre of the new town. What is the greatest number of control boxes needed for the town centre?

5 **(a)** Look at the diagram for 3 roads.
There are 2 control boxes on each road.
How many control boxes are there altogether?

(b) Look at **your** diagram for 4 roads.
How many control boxes are there on **each** road?
How many control boxes are there altogether?

(c) Repeat **(b)** for 5 roads.

(d) Describe how Tom could find the maximum number of control boxes when he knows the number of roads.

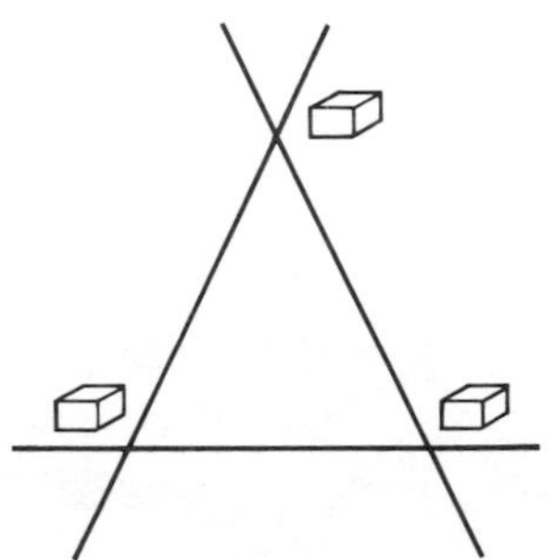

6 There are to be 20 roads in the new town. What is the greatest number of control boxes needed?

7 Write a formula to find the maximum number of control boxes needed for a design with n roads. Check your formula.

Ask your teacher what to do next.

E44 Motorway repairs

Proportion: Inverse

1 A new drainage pipe is to be laid along 120 metres of motorway. The pipe is available in sections of different lengths.

(a) Copy and complete the table.

Length of each section in metres	*Number of sections needed*
1	120
2	
4	
6	20
12	

(b) When the length of each section is doubled, what happens to the number of sections needed?

2 A crash barrier is to be fitted along a 200 metre stretch of motorway.

(a) How many sections of barrier will be needed when the length of each section is
- 2 metres
- 4 metres
- 8 metres?

(b) When the length of each section is **doubled**, what happens to the number of sections needed?

3 New kerb-stones are to be laid along one side of a 200 m stretch of motorway. The stones are available in three different lengths.

(a) Copy and complete the table.

(b) When the length of each stone is **halved**, what happens to the number of stones needed?

Length of each stone in metres	*Number of stones needed*
0·5	
1·0	200
2·0	

4 This crane can lift 2800 kg. How many kerb-stones can it lift when each stone weighs

(a) 20 kg

(b) 40 kg

(c) 80 kg?

These are examples of **inverse proportion**.

5 Copy and complete these statements about **inverse proportion**.

(a) When one quantity is **doubled**, the other is ______.

(b) When one quantity is **halved**, the other is ______.

6 One machine can tar a stretch of road in 3 hours. How long will 2 machines take to do the job?

7 Two road rollers can roll a stretch of road in 30 minutes. How long will the rolling take when
(a) one road roller is used
(b) four road rollers are used?

8 A car travelling at 30 mph takes 40 seconds to pass the roadworks. How long will it take for a car travelling at
(a) 60 mph **(b)** 15 mph?

9 White lines have to be painted along a stretch of road using a line painting machine. Copy and complete the table.

Speed of the machine in mph	*Time taken in minutes*
0·5	
1	24
2	
	6

10 A worker has to move 48 cones to another part of the roadworks. If he moves one cone at a time he will have to make 48 trips.
(a) Copy and complete the table.

Number of cones on each trip	*Number of trips needed*
1	48
2	
3	
	12
6	
8	
	4
	3

(b) When the number of cones per trip is **trebled** what happens to the number of trips needed?

11 Three dumper trucks will take 6 hours to remove a pile of rubble.
(a) How long will it take if only one truck is used?
(b) How many trucks would be needed to do the job in
- 3 hours
- 2 hours?

12 Copy and complete these statements about **inverse proportion**.
(a) When one quantity is **trebled**, the other is ____.
(b) When one quantity is **divided by 3**, the other is ____.

E46 Proportion: Inverse

Pump action

Three pumps will take 8 days to empty a pond.
With one pump it will take three times as long.

	Number of pumps	*Number of days*
3 pumps take 8 days	3	8
1 pump takes 8 × 3 = **24 days**.	1	8 × 3 = 24

1 How long will it take **one** pump to empty each of these ponds?

(a) 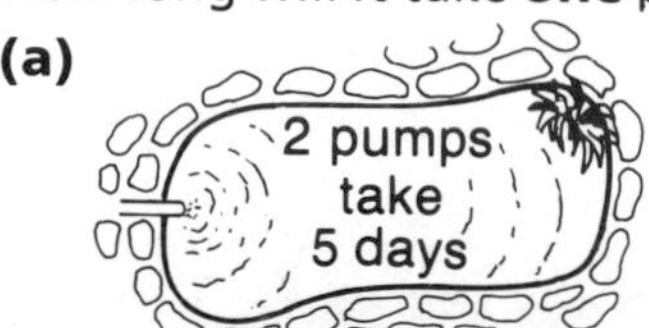

(b) 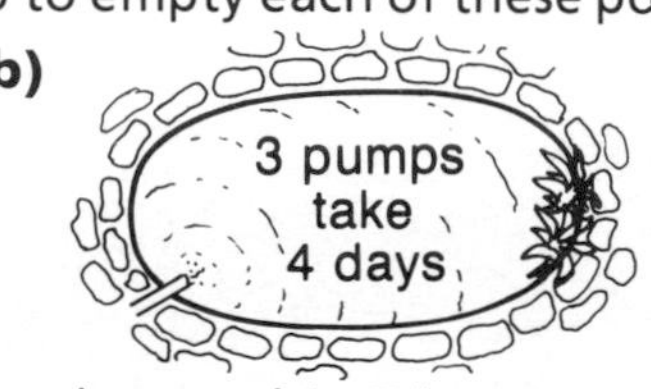

(c) 

2 Three pumps can empty a swimming pool in 5 hours.
How long will it take if one pump is used?

An engineer calculates that two pumps will take 30 hours to clear the water from a mine shaft. Another pump becomes available.

	Number of pumps	*Number of hours*
2 pumps take 30 hours	2	30
1 pump takes 30 × 2 = 60 hours	1	30 × 2 = 60
3 pumps take 60 ÷ 3 = **20 hours**.	3	60 ÷ 3 = 20

3 How long would it have taken to clear the mine shaft with
(a) 4 pumps **(b)** 5 pumps **(c)** 6 pumps **(d)** 8 pumps?

4 Three pumps can remove the water from a flooded basement in 12 hours. How long would it have taken
(a) 2 pumps **(b)** 4 pumps **(c)** 6 pumps **(d)** 8 pumps?

5 Two lorries can "in-fill" a pond in sixty hours.
(a) How long will it take three lorries?
(b) How many lorries will be needed to do the job in 20 hours?
(c) How many lorries will be needed to do the job in 25 hours?

Ask your teacher what to do next.

Patchworks

Detour: Making shapes from shapes

1 Alistair works for Patchworks. He designs decorative shapes foı patches on clothing.

(a) Copy these shapes on 1 cm isometric paper.

(b) Glue the paper onto card and cut out each shape.

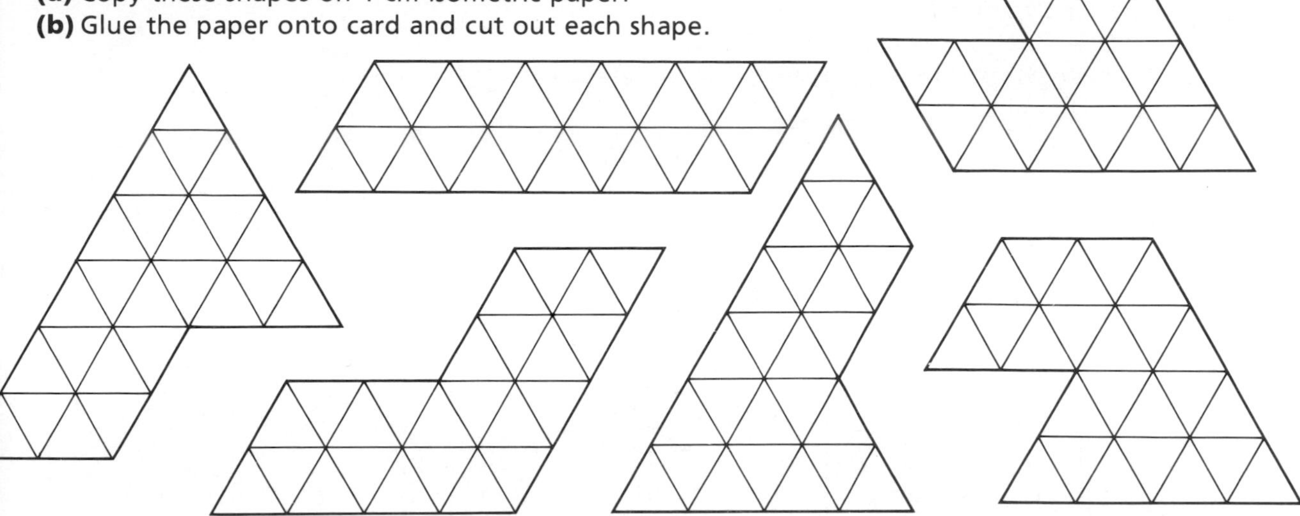

2 Susan buys these shapes and sews them together to make patches for her jeans.

(a) Show how Susan could make this parallelogram patch using four of the shapes.

(b) Show how she could make
- a different parallelogram patch using four of the shapes
- another parallelogram patch using five of the shapes.

3 Using some or all of the shapes each time show how she could make these patches.

(a) a rhombus **(b)** a regular hexagon

(c) an equilateral triangle.

4 Use the shapes to design some patches of your own.

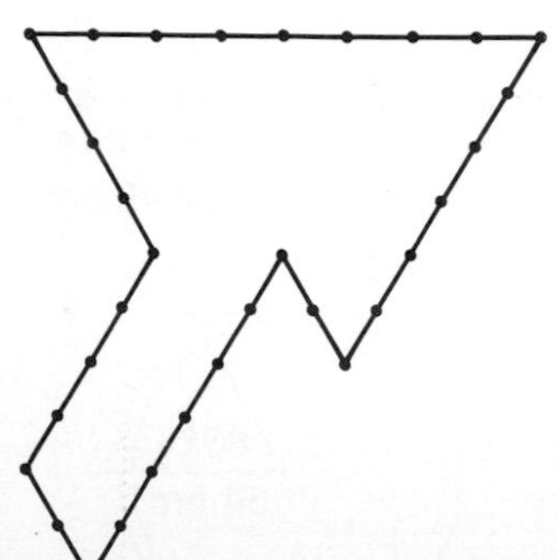

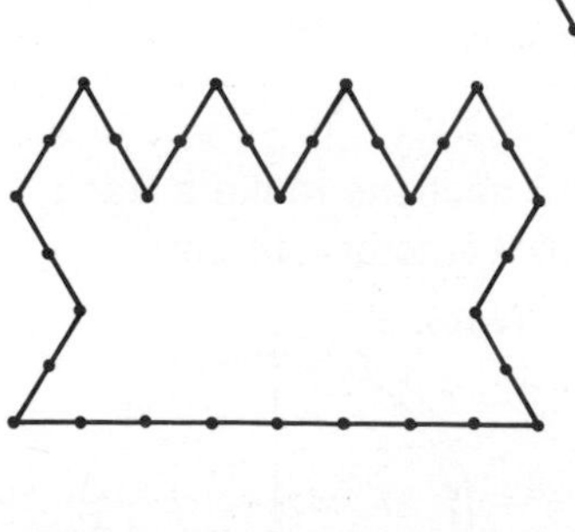

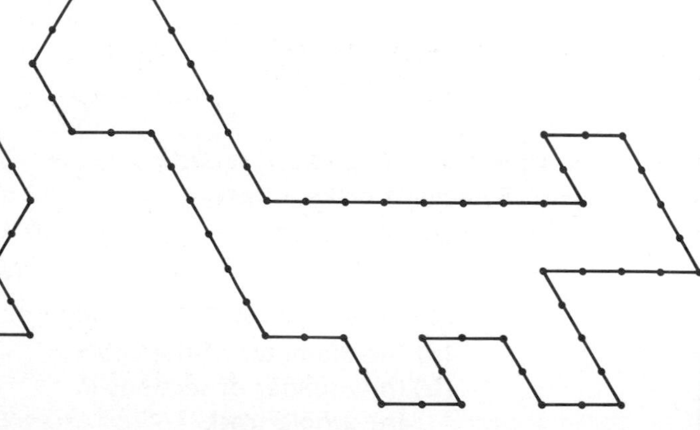

Ask your teacher what to do next.

E48 Holby Trains

Circle: Arc length

Holby makes train sets. The basic monorail track is made from four sections which fit together to make a circle of diameter 70 cm. Find the length of each section.

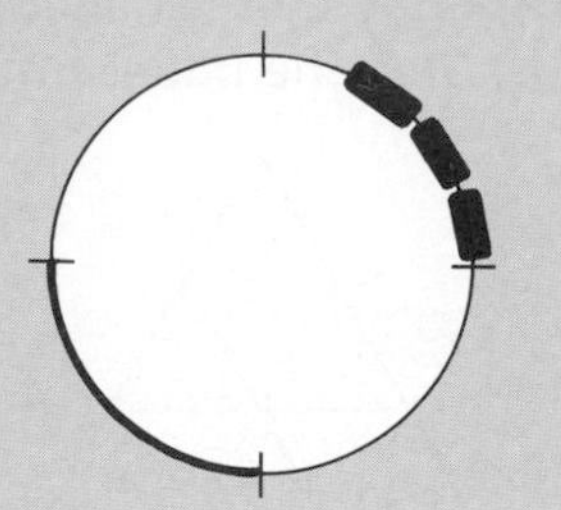

Length of one section $= \frac{1}{4}$ of circumference

$= \frac{1}{4} \times \pi d$

$= \frac{1}{4} \times 3{\cdot}14 \times 70$

$= 54{\cdot}95$

Length of each section is **55 cm**, to the nearest cm.

1 Find the length of one section, to the nearest cm, in each of these monorail sets.

(a)

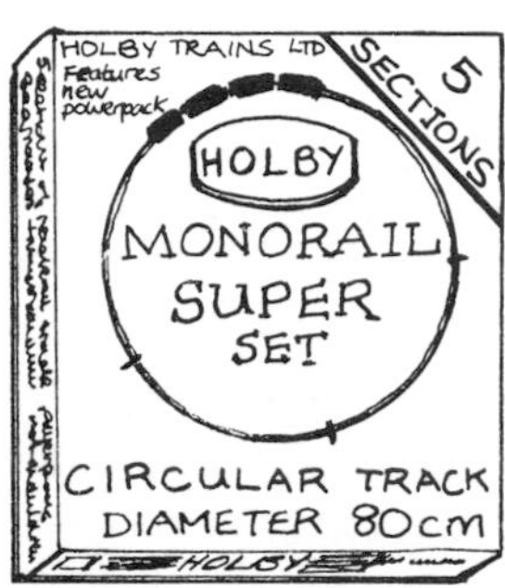

(b)

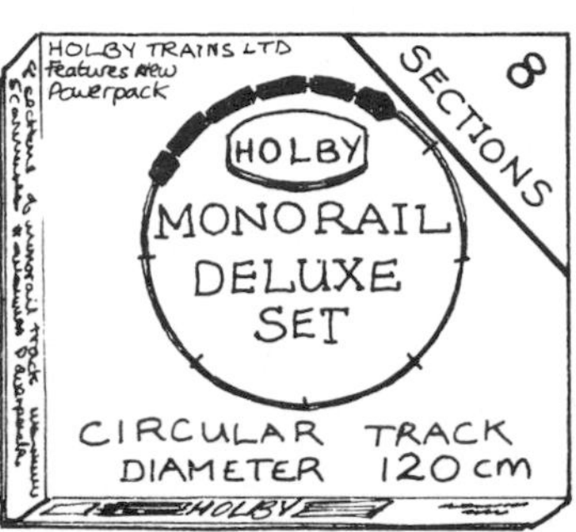

(c)

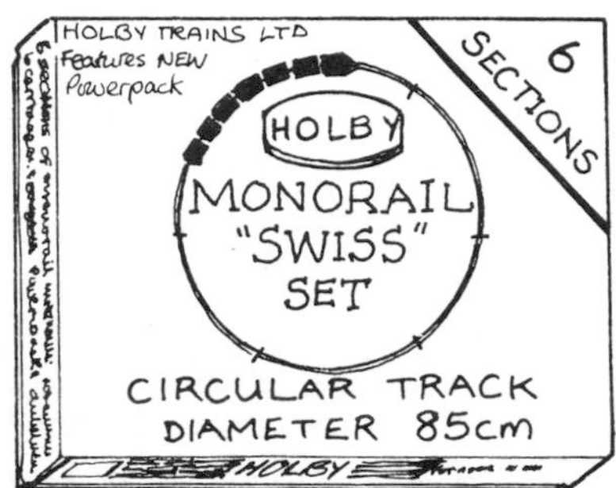

This railway track has eight sections which fit together to make a circle of diameter 76 cm. These three sections of track form an **arc**. Find its length.

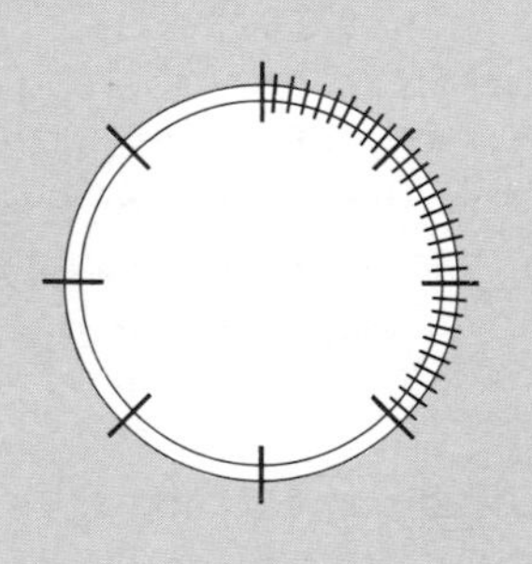

Length of one section $= \frac{1}{8} \times \pi d$

$= \frac{1}{8} \times 3{\cdot}14 \times 76$

$= 29{\cdot}83$

Length of three sections $= 3 \times 29{\cdot}83 = 89{\cdot}49$.

Length of arc is **89 cm**, to the nearest cm.

2 Find the length of each arc, to the nearest cm.

(a)

8 sections make a track of diameter 112 cm

(b)

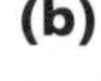

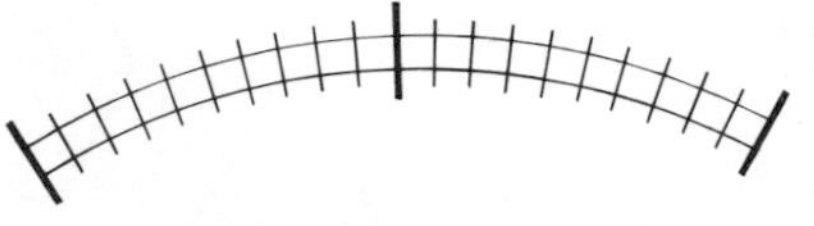

12 sections make a track of diameter 144 cm

(c)

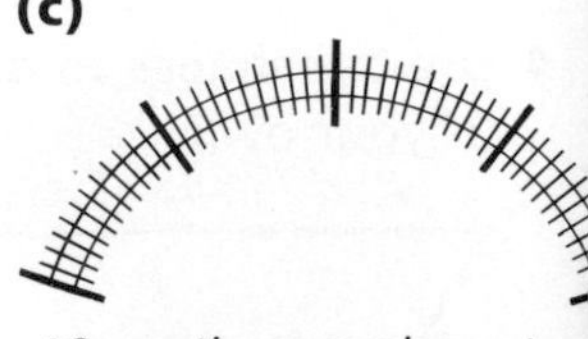

10 sections make a track of diameter 95 cm

3 For each of these tracks, find
(a) the diameter of the circle
(b) the number of sections in the whole track
(c) the length of each section, to the nearest cm.

Track 1

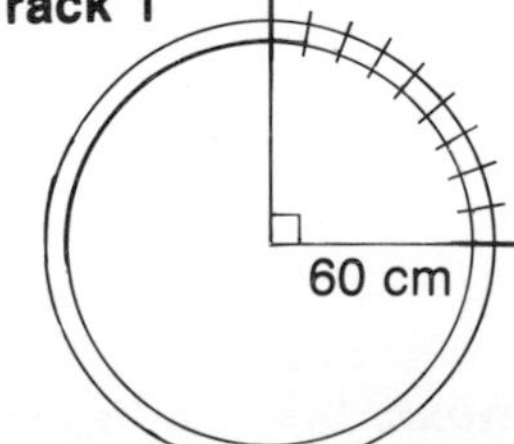

Track 2

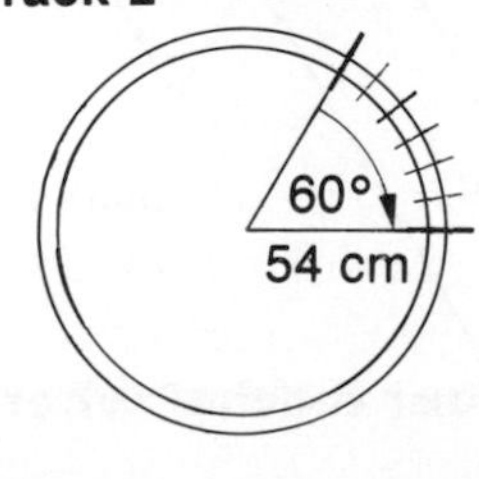

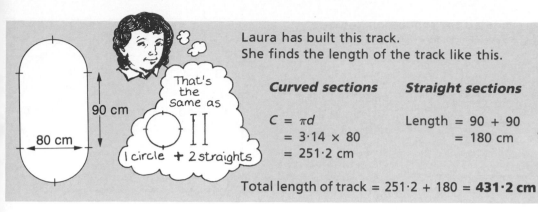

Holby Trains

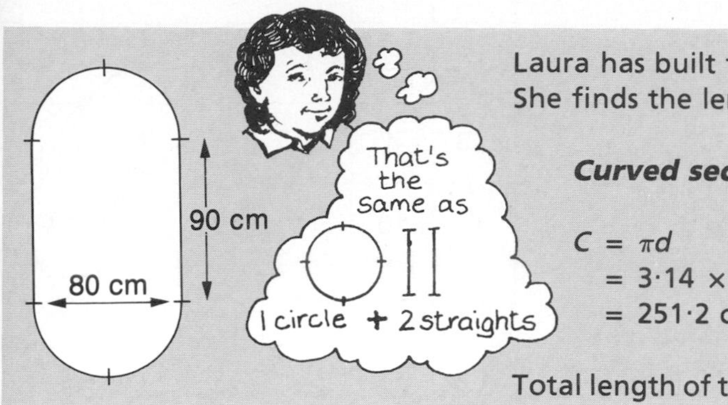

Laura has built this track.
She finds the length of the track like this.

Curved sections	***Straight sections***
$C = \pi d$	Length = 90 + 90
$= 3{\cdot}14 \times 80$	= 180 cm
$= 251{\cdot}2$ cm	

Total length of track = 251·2 + 180 = **431·2 cm**

1 Find the total length of each of these tracks.

(a)

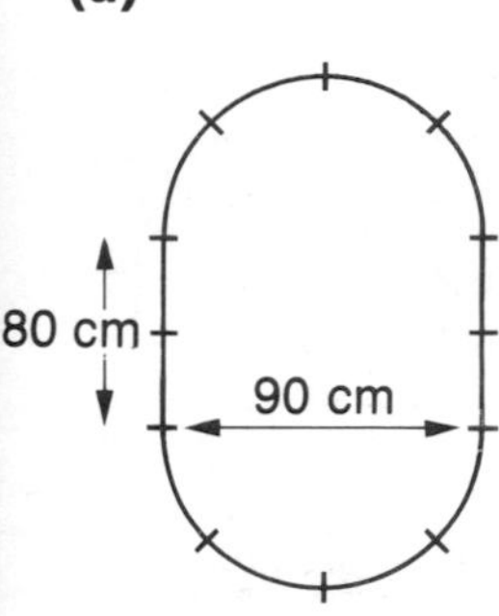

(b)

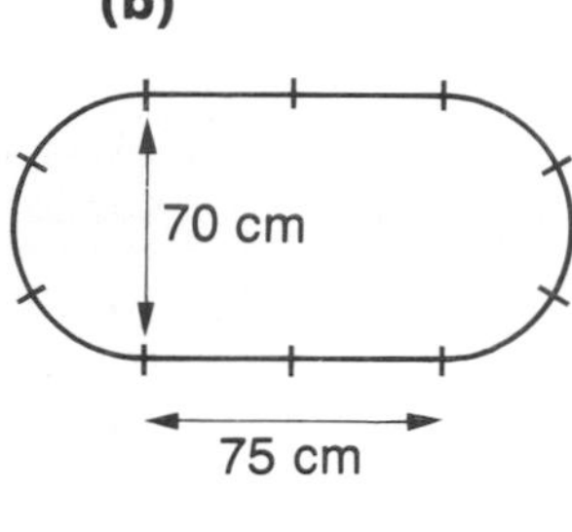

(c)

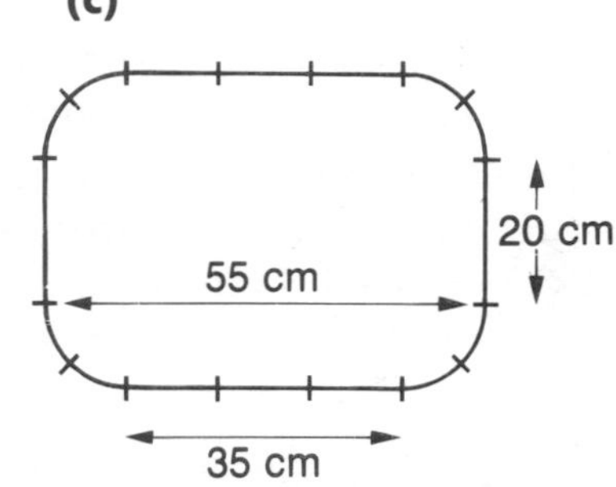

2 This is the technical data sheet for the track in the 'Trick Track' monorail racing set.

(a) Find the distance travelled in one lap of the inside lane.

(b) The two tracks are 7·5 cm apart.
Find the distance travelled in one lap of the outside lane.

(c) How much further would a train on the outside lane travel in a 10-lap race?

'TRICK TRACK' MONORAIL RACING SET

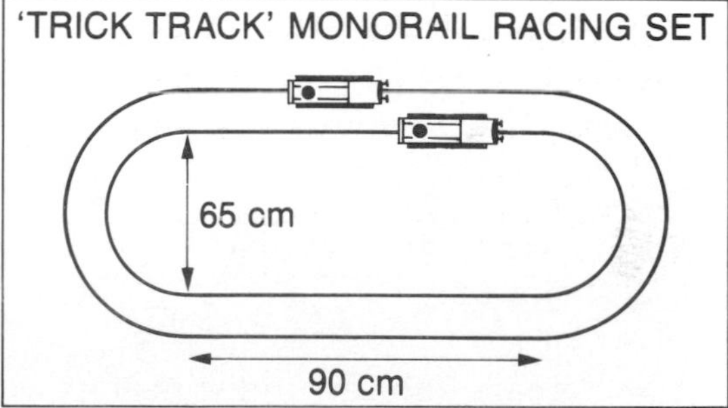

The Wild West railway set comes with a circular track of circumference 240 cm. Find its diameter.

$$C = \pi d$$
$$240 = 3{\cdot}14 \times d$$
$$\frac{240}{3{\cdot}14} = d$$
$$d = 76{\cdot}433121$$

$240 = 3{\cdot}14 \times ?$

so $? = \dfrac{240}{3{\cdot}14}$

$= 76{\cdot}433121$

The diameter is **76·4 cm**, to one decimal place.

3 Find the diameter, to one decimal place, of the circular track in each of these sets.

(a) Continental set – circumference 280 cm.

(b) Flying Scotsman – circumference 330 cm.

(c) Thomas the Tank Engine – circumference 255 cm.

E50 Squares from circles

Circle: Area, $A = \pi r^2$

Ian investigated the connection between the area and the radius of a circle.

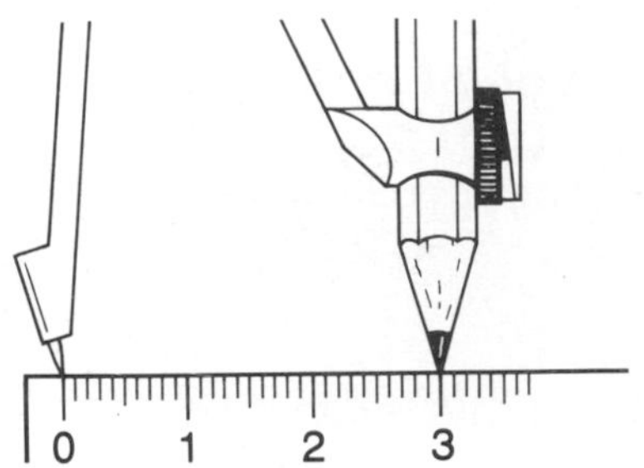

On 1 cm squared paper he drew a circle with radius 3 cm.

He estimated its area by counting squares.

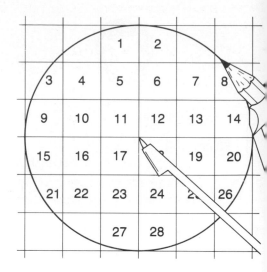

1 On 1 cm squared paper draw circles of radius 2 cm, 4 cm, 5 cm and 6 cm.

(a) Estimate their areas by counting squares.

(b) Copy and complete the table.

(c) Copy and complete:
The area of a circle is about ☐ × r^2.

radius, r	r^2	*Area, A*
2 cm	4 cm²	
3 cm	9 cm²	28 cm²
4 cm		

It is more accurate to say that the Area, $A = \pi r^2$ where $\pi = 3{\cdot}14$.

The radius of this circle is 9 cm.
Calculate its area.

$A = \pi r^2$
$A = 3{\cdot}14 \times 9^2$
$A = 3{\cdot}14 \times 81$
$A = 254{\cdot}34$

The area is **254 cm²** to the nearest whole number.

2 Calculate the area of each of these circles to the nearest whole number.

(a)

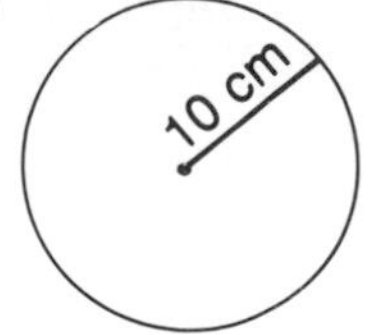

(b)

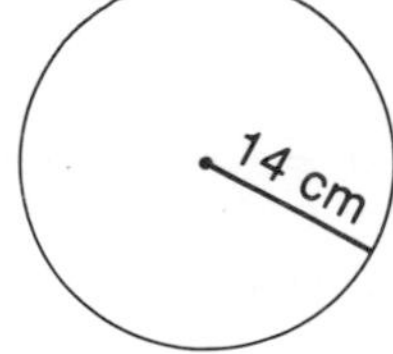
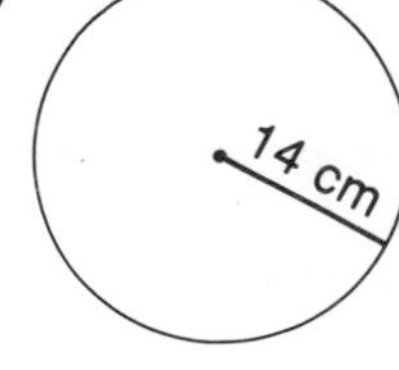

(c)

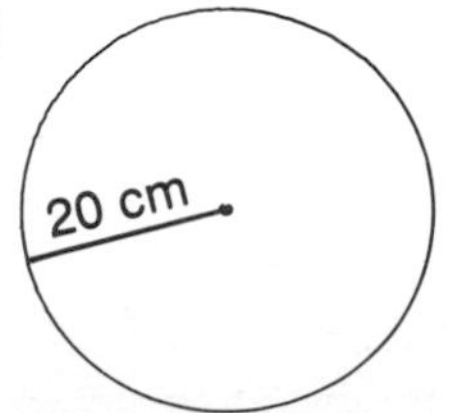

(d)

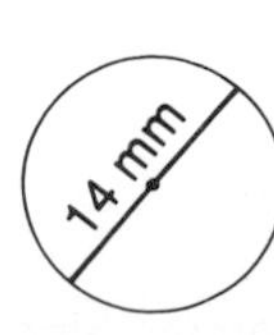

(e)

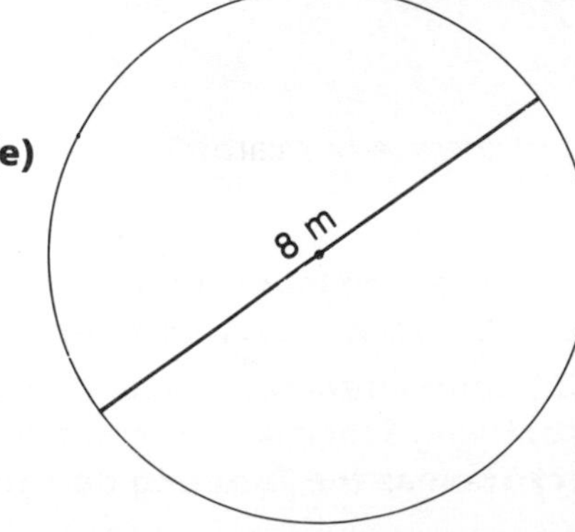

The Friday Fun Club

Patrick and Val present the Friday Fun Club television programme.

1 Last week Patrick demonstrated how to make lavender bags. Find the area of each circular piece of material, to the nearest cm^2.

(a)

(b)

(c)

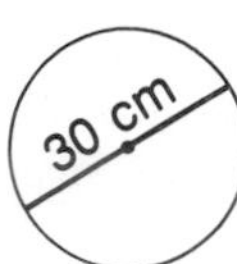

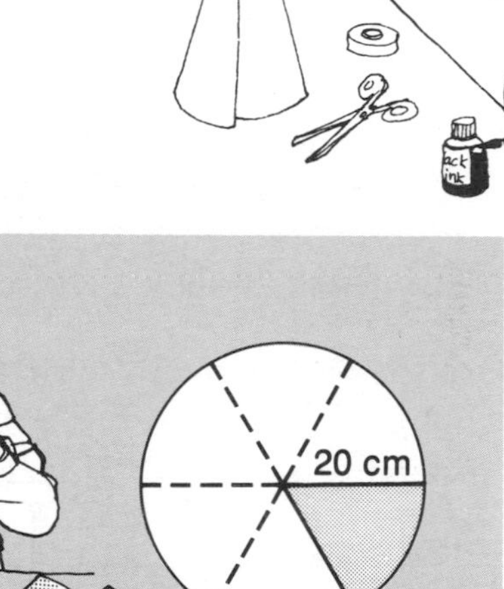

2 Val made magicians' hats from sheets of card. She used a semi-circle of card for each one. Find the area of card used for each hat.

(a)

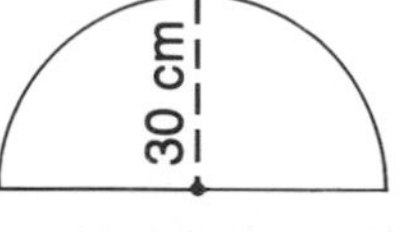

(b)

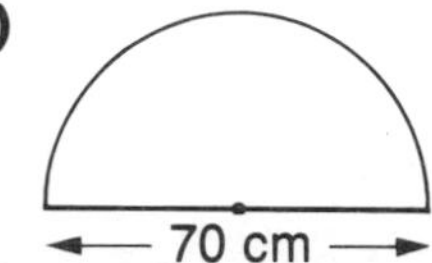

Patrick cuts patchwork pieces from circles.
Find the area of one patch.

$$A = \frac{1}{6}\pi r^2$$
$$= \frac{1}{6} \times 3{\cdot}14 \times 20^2$$
$$= \frac{1}{6} \times 3{\cdot}14 \times 400$$
$$= 209{\cdot}33333$$

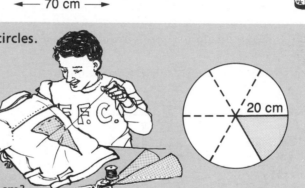

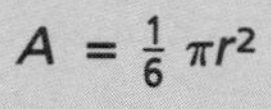

20 cm

The area is **209 cm²**, to the nearest cm^2.

3 Find the area of each of these shaded patches, to the nearest cm^2.

(a)

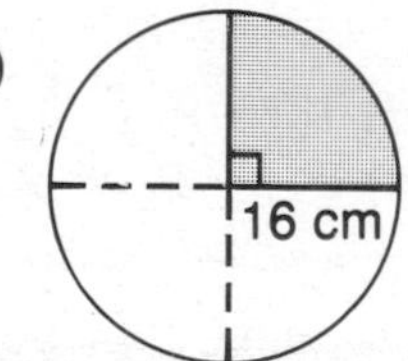

(b)

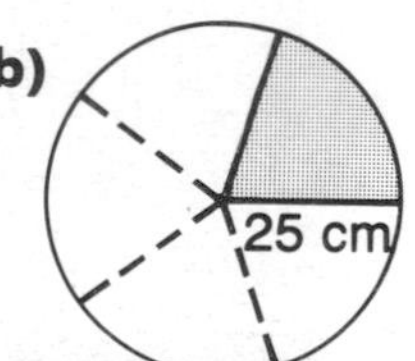

(c)

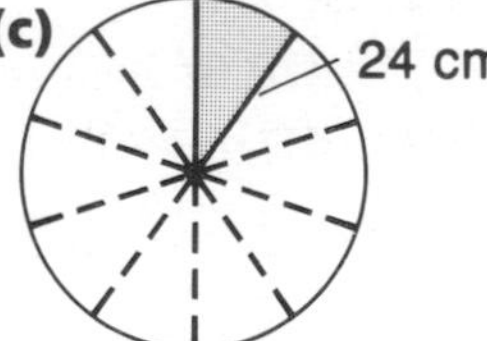

(d)

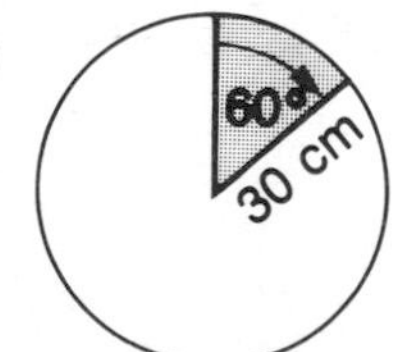

(e)

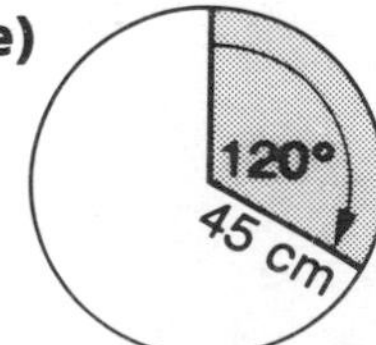

(f)

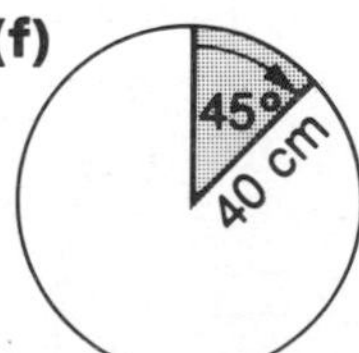

4 Find the area of card Val used to make this gift box.

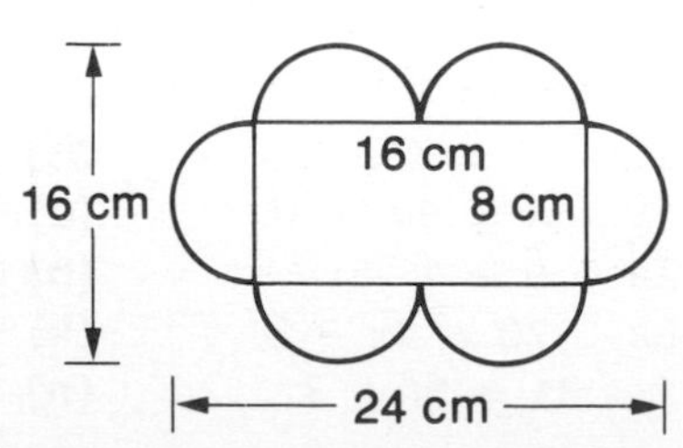

Ask your teacher what to do next.

Kay's the Chemist

Equations: $ax + b = cx + d$, negative solutions

Albert and Jenny weigh bottles of pills.
Each pill weighs one gram.
A full bottle weighs b grams.

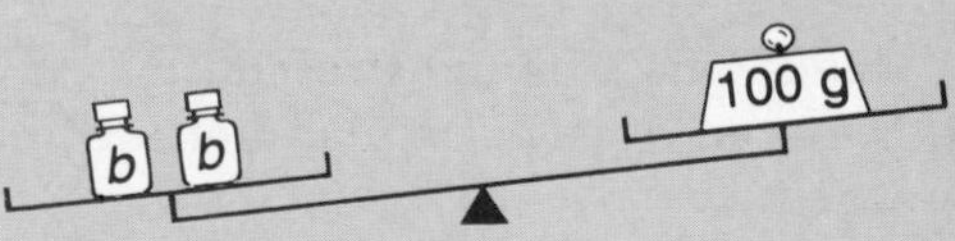

Albert balances the scales by removing 4 pills.

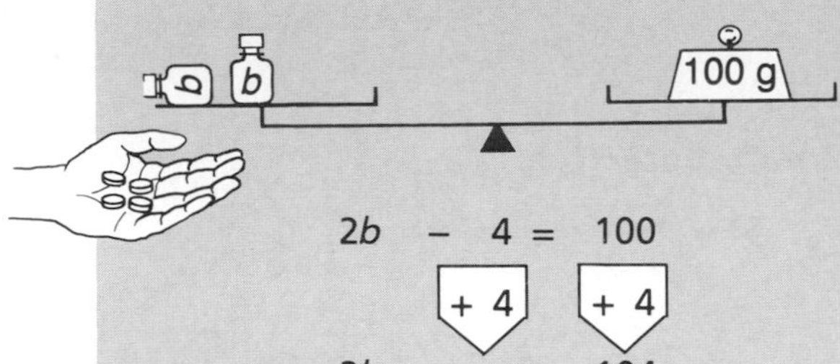

Jenny balances the scales by adding 4 grams.

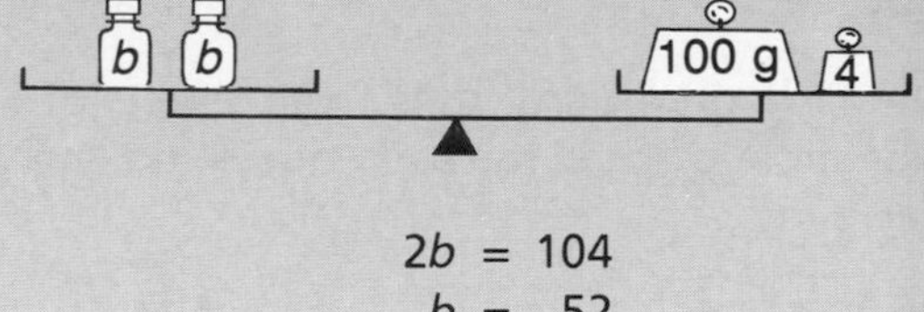

$$2b - 4 = 100$$

+ 4   + 4

$$2b = 104$$
$$b = 52$$

$$2b = 104$$
$$b = 52$$

Each full bottle weighs **52** grams.

1 Albert has started to solve these equations.
Copy and complete each solution.

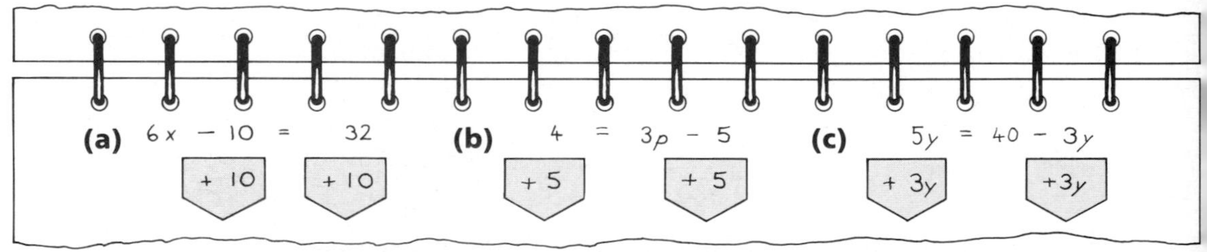

2 Solve each equation.

(a) $b - 3 = 7$ **(b)** $5t - 7 = 13$ **(c)** $8 = 3p - 1$ **(d)** $15 = 8y - 1$
(e) $4b = 10 - b$ **(f)** $x = 12 - 3x$ **(g)** $25 - 2y = 3y$ **(h)** $24 - 2p = p$

Jenny solved this equation to find the storage temperature in °C for this liquid.

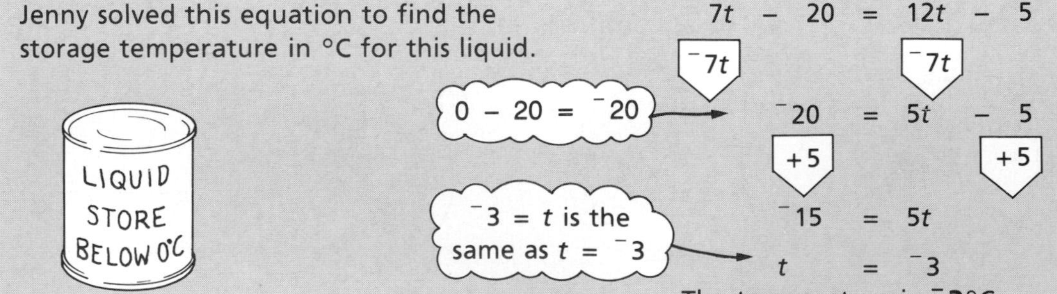

$$7t - 20 = 12t - 5$$

^-7t ^-7t

$$^-20 = 5t - 5$$

+5   +5

$$^-15 = 5t$$
$$t = {}^-3$$

The temperature is **$^-3$**°C.

3 Solve each equation. Some solutions are negative.

(a) $5w - 1 = 4w + 5$ **(b)** $9y - 8 = 2y + 20$ **(c)** $4r + 7 = 8r - 13$
(d) $5k + 4 = 44 - 3k$ **(e)** $93 - 2b = 7b + 3$ **(f)** $7 - a = 4a - 18$
(g) $2a + 9 = 1$ **(h)** $6 = 3s + 9$ **(i)** $3t - 12 = 7t$
(j) $6x - 20 = 4x - 8$ **(k)** $9y + 8 = 3y - 4$ **(l)** $p + 4 = 3p + 12$
(m) $f - 31 = 5f - 3$ **(n)** $14 - 6b = 4b + 34$ **(o)** $4 - 5x = 9x + 18$

Perimeter fences

E53
Equations: Distributive law

Kathy surrounds a rectangular field with 700 metres of electric fencing. The field is 250 metres long. How wide is the field?

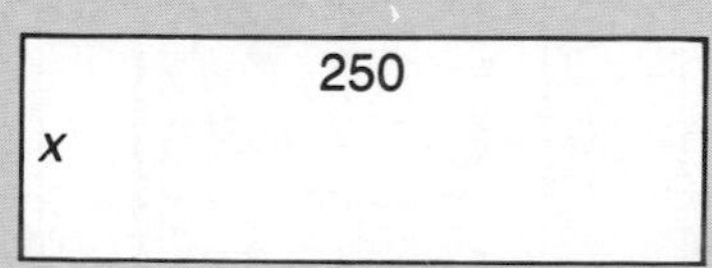

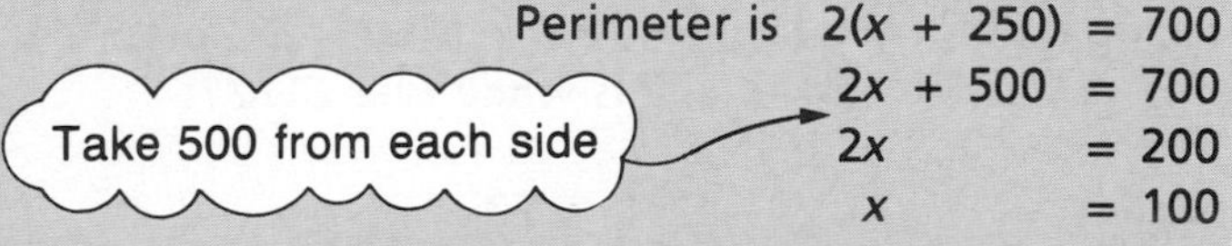

Perimeter is $2(x + 250) = 700$

$2x + 500 = 700$

$2x = 200$

$x = 100$

The field is **100** metres wide.

1 The perimeter of each of these rectangular fields is 800 metres.
For each field, form an equation and solve it to find x.

(a)

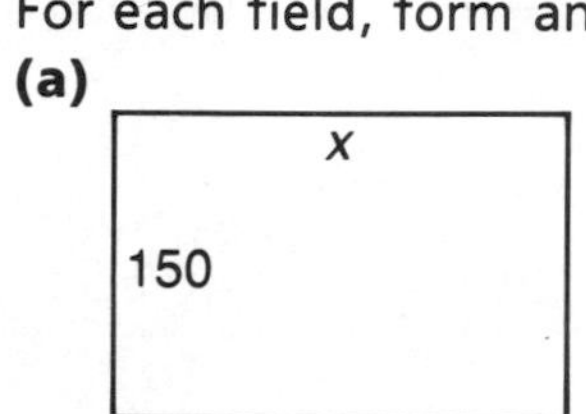

(b)

3x

70

(c)

200

2x

2 Solve these equations.

(a) $5(2x + 1) = 45$ **(b)** $4 = 2(a + 7)$ **(c)** $3(p - 5) = 6$

(d) $10 = 2(3x - 4)$ **(e)** $4(7 - y) = 8$ **(f)** $2(5 + 3r) = {}^{-}2$

(g) $6(b + 3) = 9b + 3$ **(h)** $2(3x + 3) = 3(x + 5)$ **(i)** $3(2t + 4) = 4(8 - t)$

The perimeters of these two fields are the same. Find the value of x.

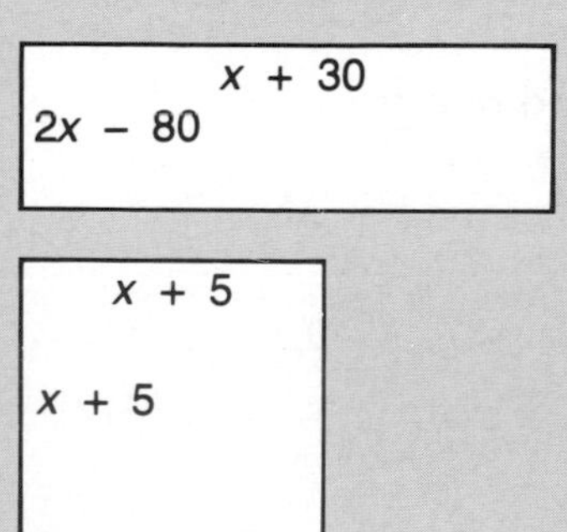

$2(x + 30) + 2(2x - 80) = 4(x + 5)$

$2x + 60 + 4x - 160 = 4x + 20$

$6x - 100 = 4x + 20$

Take 4x from each side

$2x - 100 = 20$

Add 100 to each side

$2x = 120$

$x = 60$

The square field is **65 m** long.
The rectangular field is **90 m** by **40 m**.

3 The perimeters of each pair of fields are the same. Form an equation and solve it to find the dimensions of each field.

(a)

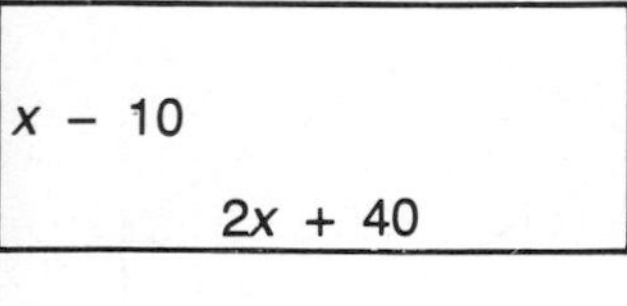

90

x

(b)

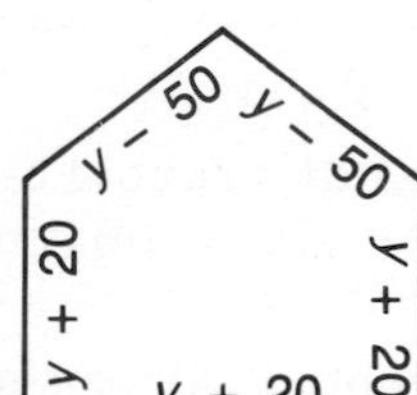

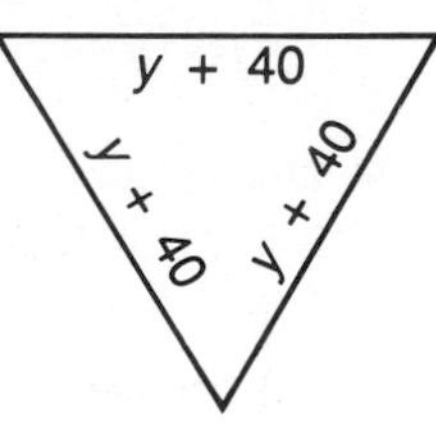

4 Solve these equations.

(a) $5(2x + 1) - 2(x + 1) = 11$ **(b)** $3(6 - d) + 4(2d + 3) = 50$

(c) $3(y - 2) + 4(3y + 1) = 2(6y + 5)$ **(d)** $5(2x - 5) - 2(8 - 2x) = x - 2$

(e) $2(2p - 7) = 1 - (3 + 2p)$ **(f)** ${}^{-}2 = 4(2c + 1) - 2(c - 3)$

Equations from formulae

Terry sells encyclopaedias. His weekly wage is calculated from the formula $W = 72 + 25n$ where W is his wage in £'s and n is the number of sets of encyclopaedias he sells that week. How many sets did he sell in a week when his wage was £172?

Formula	$W = 72 + 25n$
Substitute 172 for W	$172 = 72 + 25n$
	$100 = 25n$
	$n = 4$

Terry sold **4** sets of encyclopaedias.

1 How many sets of encyclopaedias did Terry sell in a week when he earned

(a) £247 **(b)** £372 **(c)** £497 **(d)** £697?

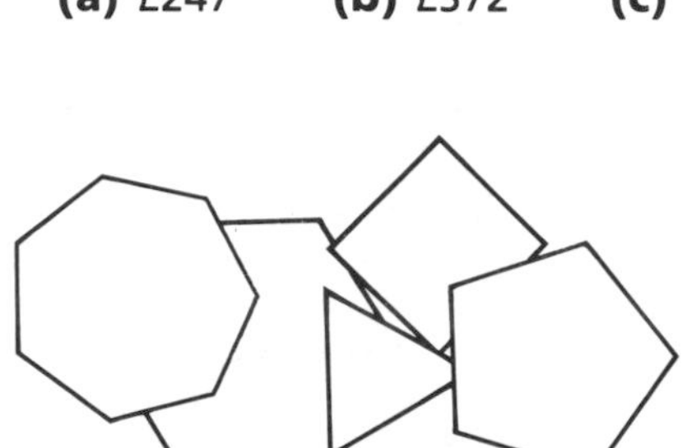

2 The sum, S (in **right angles**), of the angles in a polygon is calculated from the formula $S = 2n - 4$, where n is the number of sides. How many sides has

(a) an enneagon if its angle sum is 14 right angles

(b) a hendecagon if its angle sum is 18 right angles?

3 Paulo's Pizza Parlour sells two kinds of pizza – pastrami and quattro stagioni. Paulo's takings can be calculated from the formula $T = 2p + 3q$ where p is the number of pastrami and q is the number of quattro stagioni sold.

(a) How many quattro stagioni did he sell when the takings were £540, and 120 pastrami pizzas were sold?

(b) How many pastrami pizzas did he sell when the takings were £476, and 58 quattro stagioni were sold?

4 The perimeter of a rectangle can be calculated from the formula $P = 2(l + b)$ where l is its length and b its breadth.

(a) A rectangle has a perimeter of 50 cm and a breadth of 17 cm. What is its length?

(b) A rectangle has a perimeter of 74 cm and a length of 23 cm. What is its breadth?

5 The total surface area of a cuboid can be calculated from the formula $A = 2(lb + bh + hl)$.
Find

(a) the height of a cuboid with surface area 72 cm², length 6 cm and breadth 2 cm.

(b) the breadth of a cuboid with surface area 142 cm², length 7 cm and height 3 cm.

(c) the length of a cuboid with surface area 180 cm², height 6 cm and breadth 6 cm.

Karaoke party

E55

Equations: Simultaneous equations

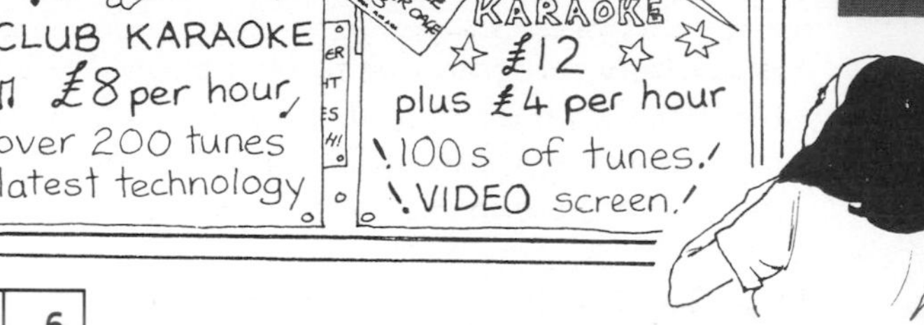

Kirsten and Rebecca want to hire a karaoke machine for their party.

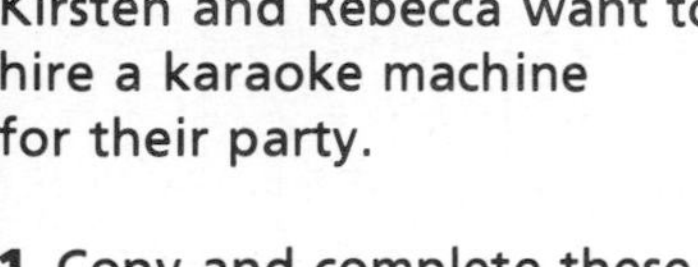

1 Copy and complete these tables.

Club Karaoke

(a)

Time in hours	1	2	3	4	5	6
Cost in £	8	16				

Laser Karaoke

(b)

Time in hours	1	2	3	4	5	6
Cost in £	16	20				

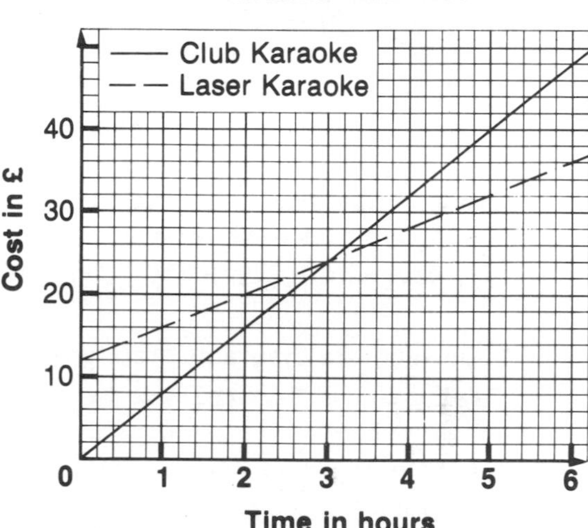

2 Kirsten drew this graph to compare the cost of hiring each machine.
Which machine is cheaper to hire for
(a) 2 hours **(b)** 5 hours?

3 **(a)** Which machine should Kirsten and Rebecca choose to hire for 3 hours? Explain.
(b) What happens to the graphs at this point?

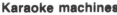

Rebecca uses a formula for the hire cost of each machine.
Club Karaoke $C = 8t$ Laser Karaoke $C = 12 + 4t$ where C is the cost in £ and t is the time in hours.

Each machine costs the same to hire for 3 hours.
We can find this • from the tables • from the graph.
We can also find this from the formulae.
When the hire costs are the same

$8t = 12 + 4t$
$4t = 12$
$t = 3$

Each machine costs £24 to hire for 3 hours.

Check by substituting $t = 3$ into

$C = 8t$ and $C = 12 + 4t$
$C = 8 \times 3$ $C = 12 + 4 \times 3$
$\mathbf{C = 24}$ $C = 12 + 12$
$\mathbf{C = 24}$

4 For each pair of adverts
- write the formulae for the hire costs
- use the formulae to find the time when the hire costs are equal
- check your answer by substituting into each formula.

(a)

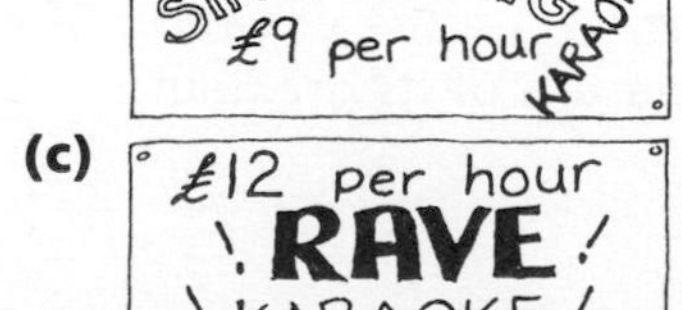

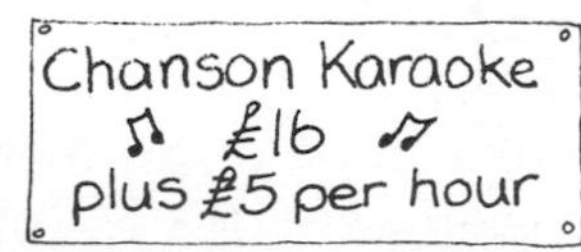

(b)

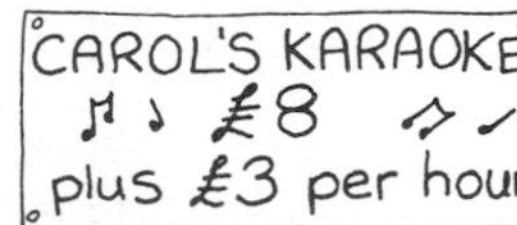

(c)

(d)

£12 per hour RAVE KARAOKE

Ask your teacher what to do next.

E56 Families of lines

Graphs of functions: Straight line, $y = mx + c$

Mike drew the graph of the equation $y = 2x + 3$.
He chose 3 values of x: 0, 1 and 3. To find the corresponding y-values Mike substituted each x-value in the equation $y = 2x + 3$.

When $x = 0$	When $x = 1$	When $x = 3$
$y = 2x + 3$	$y = 2x + 3$	$y = 2x + 3$
$y = 2 \times 0 + 3$	$y = 2 \times 1 + 3$	$y = 2 \times 3 + 3$
$y = 3$	$y = 5$	$y = 9$
Mike plots (0,3)	(1,5)	(2,9)

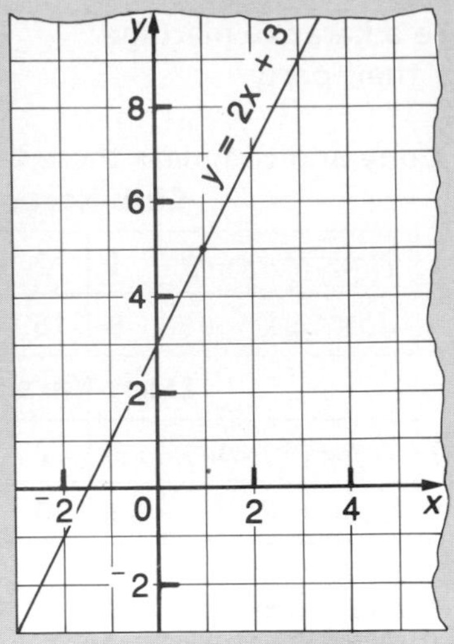

When Mike plotted the points and joined them up he found that they lay in a straight line.
He extended the line and labelled it.

1 On separate diagrams draw graphs of
(a) $y = x + 5$ **(b)** $y = 2x$ **(c)** $y = 3x - 4$ **(d)** $y = x$

2 (a) On one diagram draw this family of lines.
$y = 3x + 4$
$y = 3x$
$y = 3x - 4$

(b) What do you notice about
- the lines
- the coefficient of x in the equations?

The number in front of x is called its **coefficient**.

3 Repeat question **2** for each of these families of lines.

Family P	**Family Q**
$y = 4x + 2$	$y = x + 3$
$y = 4x$	$y = x + 1$
$y = 4x - 3$	$y = x - 1$

Lines which are parallel have the same **slope** or **gradient**. When the equation of a line is in the form $y = mx + c$ the coefficient of x is a measure of its gradient.
The line $y = \mathbf{6}x - 5$ has a gradient of **6**.

4 Write the gradient of each of the following lines.
(a) $y = 5x + 3$ **(b)** $y = 3x - 4$ **(c)** $y = 8x$
(d) $y = 4x + 7$ **(e)** $y = x - 4$ **(f)** $y = \frac{1}{2}x - 6$

5 The diagram shows another family of lines.
What do you notice about
- where the lines cross the y-axis
- the constant of each equation

The **constant** of an equation is the number on its own.

6 (a) On one diagram plot this family of lines.
Family R $y = x + 1$, $y = 2x + 1$, $y = 3x + 1$

(b) What do you notice about
- where the lines cross the y-axis
- the constant of each equation?

7 Repeat question **6** for each of these families.
Family S $y = x + 2$ $y = 2x + 2$, $y = 3x + 2$
Family T $y = x - 1$, $y = 2x - 1$, $y = 3x - 1$

When the equation of a line is in the form $y = mx + c$, the constant c, shows where the line crosses the y-axis.
The line $y = 7x + 3$ crosses the y-axis at (0,3)
The line $y = 6x - 5$ crosses the y-axis at $(0, {}^{-}5)$

8 Write the coordinates of the point where each line crosses the y-axis.
(a) $y = 4x + 7$ **(b)** $y = 6x + 5$ **(c)** $y = 4x - 7$ **(d)** $y = 2x - 9$

The graph of the equation
$y = 5x + 3$ • is a straight line • has gradient 5 • crosses the y-axis at (0,3)
$y = 7x - 4$ • is a straight line • has gradient 7 • crosses the y-axis at $(0, {}^{-}4)$

9 For each line write
- the gradient
- the coordinates of the point where it crosses the y-axis.

(a) $y = 5x + 9$ **(b)** $y = 3x + 7$ **(c)** $y = 3x - 4$ **(d)** $y = x + 1$
(e) $y = 6x - 1$ **(f)** $y = x - 9$ **(g)** $y = 7x + 8$ **(h)** $y = 6x$

Mike drew the graph of the equation $y = 7 - x$.

When $x = 0$	When $x = 2$	When $x = 4$
$y = 7 - 0$	$y = 7 - 2$	$y = 7 - 4$
$y = 7$	$y = 5$	$y = 3$
Mike plots (0,7)	(2,5)	(4,3)

When Mike joined the points he found that they lay in a straight line.
He extended the line and labelled it.

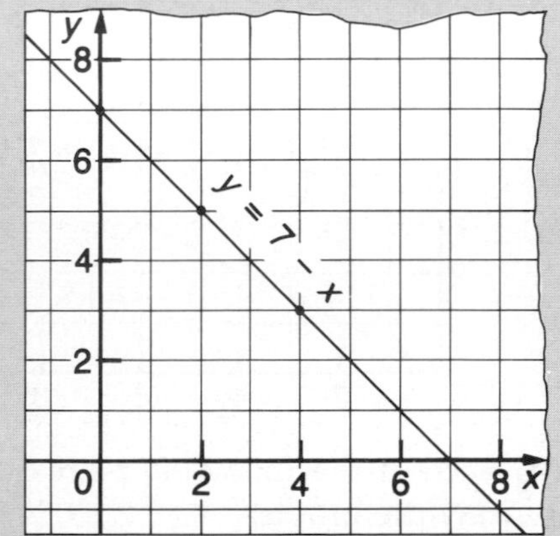

10 (a) Plot this family of lines on one diagram.
• $y = 4 - x$ • $y = 9 - x$ • $y = 6 - x$ • $y = 5 - x$ • $y = 10 - x$

(b) What do you notice about these lines?

E58 Crossed lines

Graphs of functions: Simultaneous equations

Sally drew the graphs of the equations $y = 9 - x$ and $y = x + 1$ on the same diagram.

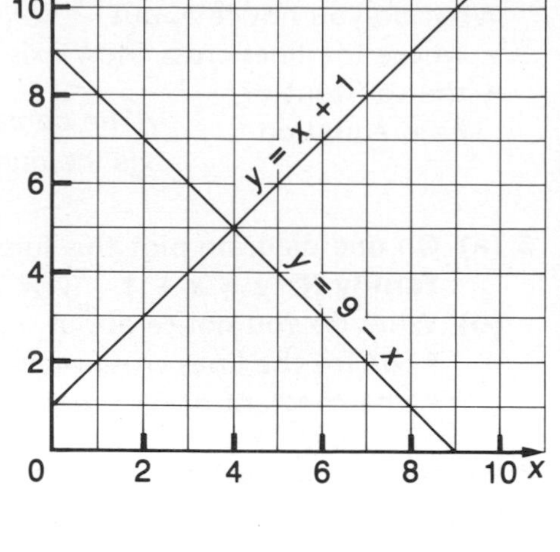

She saw that the lines intersect at **(4,5)**. The solution to this pair of equations is **$x = 4, y = 5$**

She checked by substituting **$x = 4$** in each equation.

$$y = 9 - x \qquad y = x + 1$$
$$= 9 - 4 \qquad = 4 + 1$$
$$= 5 \qquad = 5$$

1 For each of the following
- write the solution to the pair of equations
- check the solution by substitution.

(a)

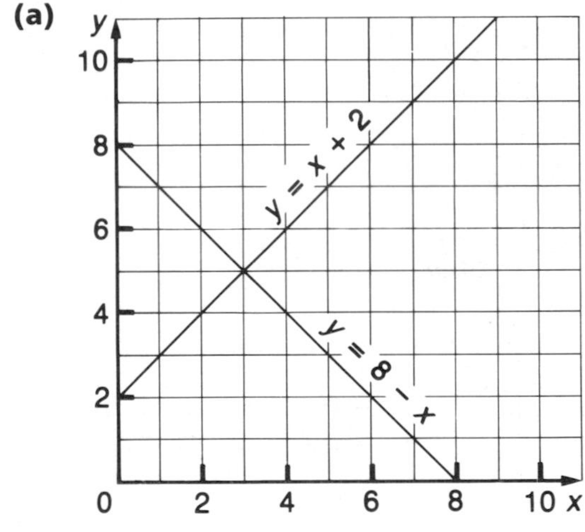

(b)

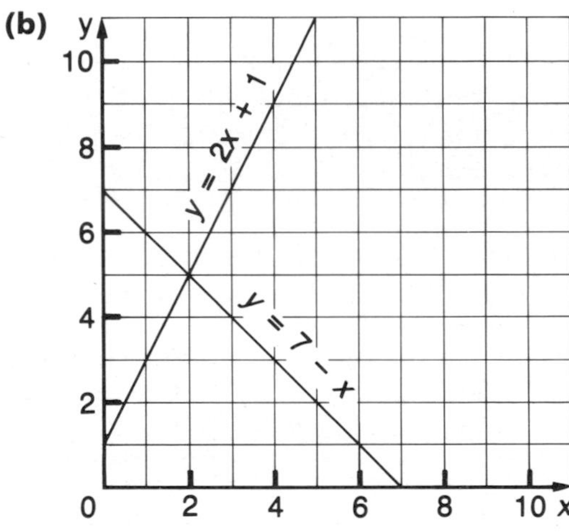

(c)

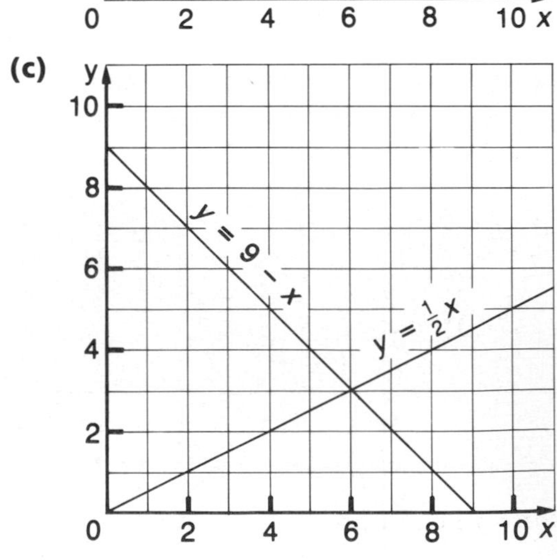

(d)

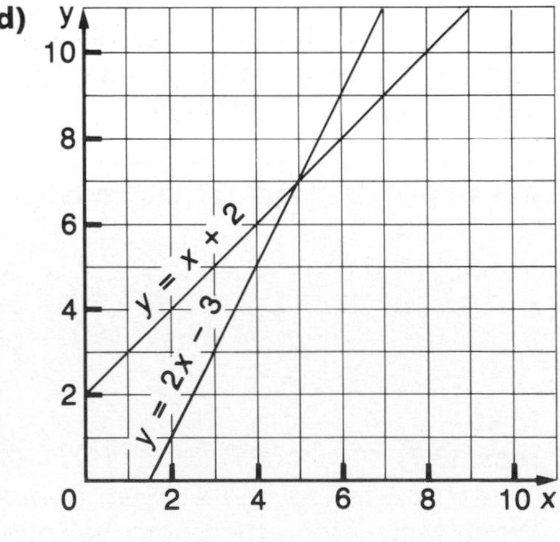

2 For each of the following pairs of equations
- draw the graphs
- write the solution
- check the solution by substitution.

(a) $y = x - 2$, $y = 10 - x$ **(b)** $y = 2x$, $y = 6 - x$ **(c)** $y = 5 - x$, $y = 3x - 3$ **(d)** $y = 2x + 1$, $y = x + 5$

Parabolic graphs

E59

Graphs of functions: The quadratic

Leena drew the graph of the equation $y = 4x - x^2$ for values of x from 0 to 4.

When $x = 0$	When $x = 1$	When $x = 2$
$y = 4 \times 0 - 0^2$	$y = 4 \times 1 - 1^2$	$y = 4 \times 2 - 2^2$
$= 0 - 0$	$= 4 - 1$	$= 8 - 4$
$= 0$	$= 3$	$= 4$
(0,0)	(1,3)	(2,4)

When $x = 3$	When $x = 4$
$y = 4 \times 3 - 3^2$	$y = 4 \times 4 - 4^2$
$= 12 - 9$	$= 16 - 16$
$= 3$	$= 0$
(3,3)	(4,0)

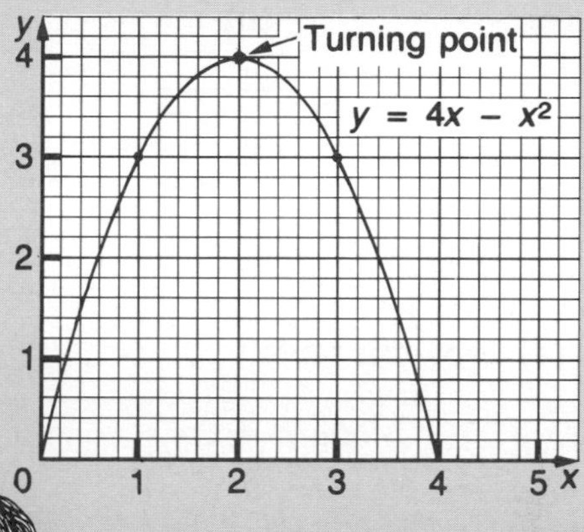

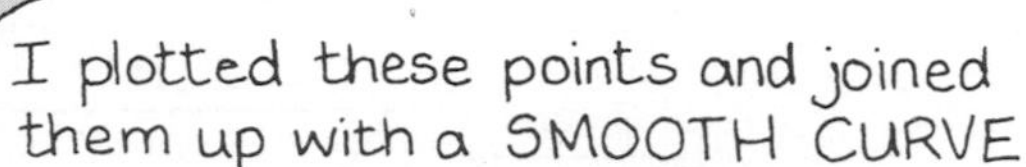

I plotted these points and joined them up with a SMOOTH CURVE.
You can see that the graph
•meets the y-axis at (0,0)
•meets the x-axis at (0,0) and (4,0)
•has a TURNING POINT at (2,4).

1 For each equation
- draw the graph
- write the coordinates of the point where the graph meets the y-axis
- write the coordinates of the points where the graph meets the x-axis
- write the coordinates of the turning point.

(a) $y = 6x - x^2$ for values of x from 0 to 6
(b) $y = x^2 - 2x$ for values of x from 0 to 4
(c) $y = 6x - x^2 - 5$ for values of x from 0 to 6
(d) $y = x^2 - 6x + 5$ for values of x from 0 to 5
(e) $y = x^2 - 4x + 3$ for values of x from 0 to 5
(f) $y = 5x - 6 - x^2$ for values of x from 0 to 6

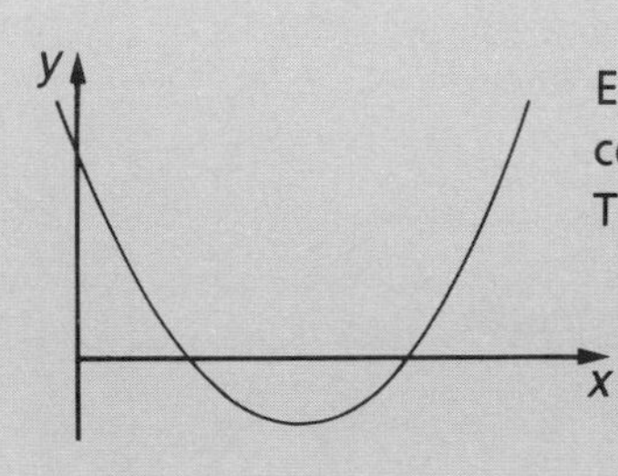

Each of the above equations contains an x^2 term.
The graph of each is a **parabola**.

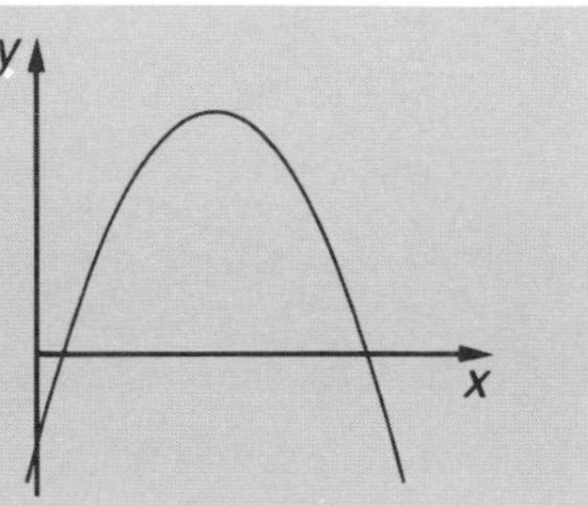

2 Without drawing, write *straight line* or *parabola* to describe the graph of each of the following equations.

(a) $y = x^2 + 4x$ **(b)** $y = 2x - 5$
(c) $y = x + 7$ **(d)** $y = 3 - x^2$
(e) $y = 2x^2 + 3x$ **(f)** $y = 6x + 1$
(g) $y = 4x - 1 + x^2$ **(h)** $y = x^2$

Ask your teacher what to do next.

E60 Triangles rule OK?

Pythagoras' Theorem: Introduction

In a right-angled triangle the longest side is called the **hypotenuse**.
The hypotenuse is the side **opposite** the right angle.
In this triangle, c is the hypotenuse.

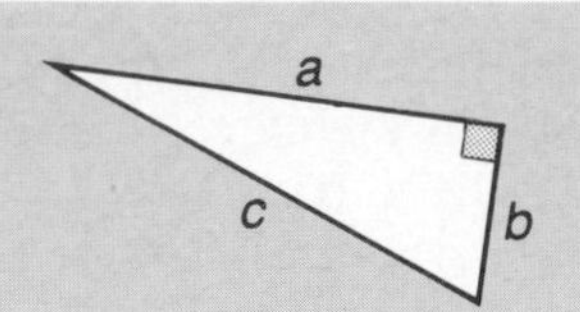

1 Name the hypotenuse in each of these triangles.

(a)

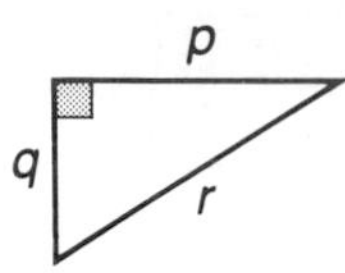

(b)

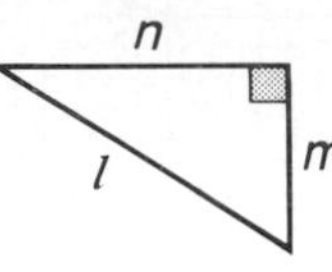

(c)

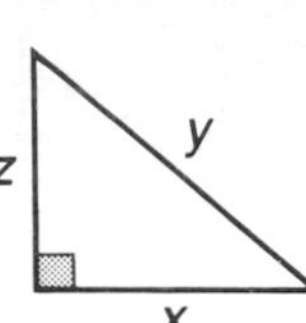

(d)

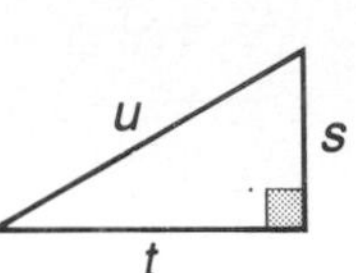

(e)

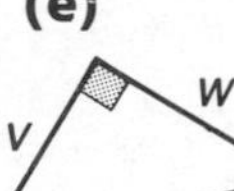

2 **(a)** Copy this table.

	length in cm				
Triangle	a	b	c	$a^2 + b^2$	c^2
P	3	4		$9 + 16 = 25$	
Q	4	6			
R					
S					
T					

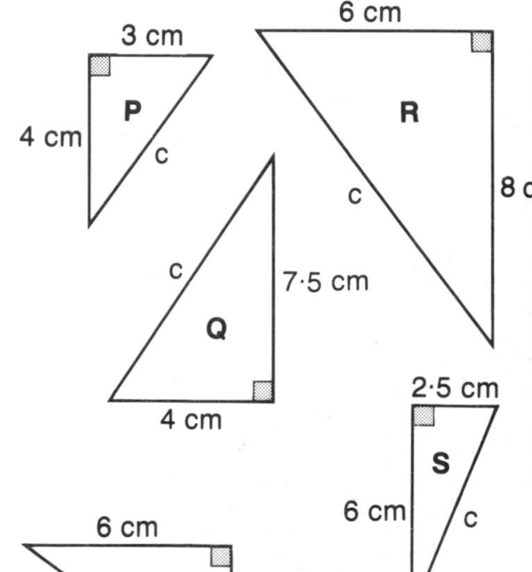

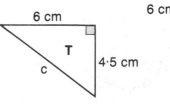

(b) For each right-angled triangle shown
- draw it accurately on $\frac{1}{2}$ cm squared paper
- measure the length of the hypotenuse, c
- complete the table.

(c) What do you notice about the last two columns of your table?

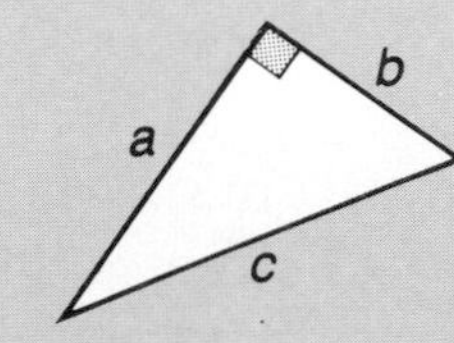

For any right-angled triangle with sides a, b and hypotenuse c

$$c^2 = a^2 + b^2$$

This is called **Pythagoras' Theorem**.

You need a set square and plain paper.

3 **(a)** Draw three right-angled triangles.
(b) For each of your triangles
- measure the length of each side
- check using Pythagoras' Theorem.

4 Find out as much as you can about Pythagoras.

Squarials

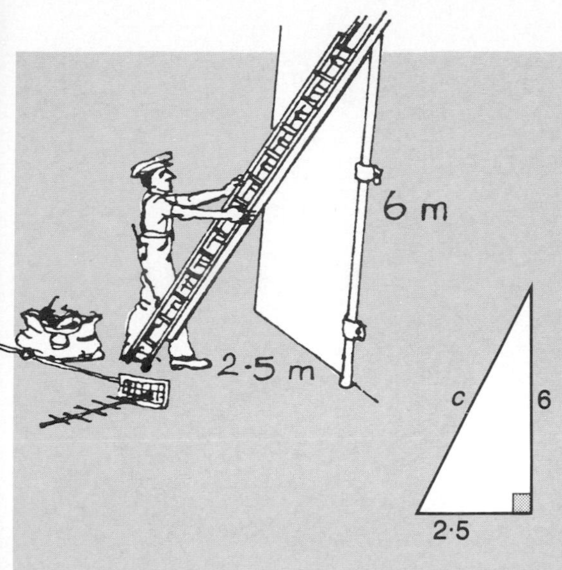

Gordon fits television aerials.
He places the ladder as shown.

You can find the length of the ladder by making a sketch and using Pythagoras' Theorem.

$$c^2 = a^2 + b^2$$
$$= 2{\cdot}5^2 + 6^2$$
$$= 6{\cdot}25 + 36$$
$$c^2 = 42{\cdot}25$$

$$c = \sqrt{42{\cdot}25}$$
$$c = 6{\cdot}5$$

The ladder is **6·5 m** long.

1 Make a sketch and use Pythagoras' Theorem to find the length of each of these ladders.

(a)
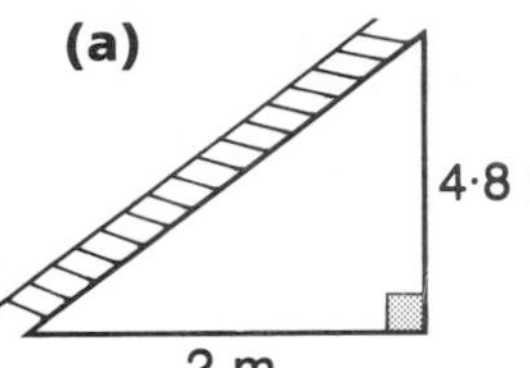

(b)
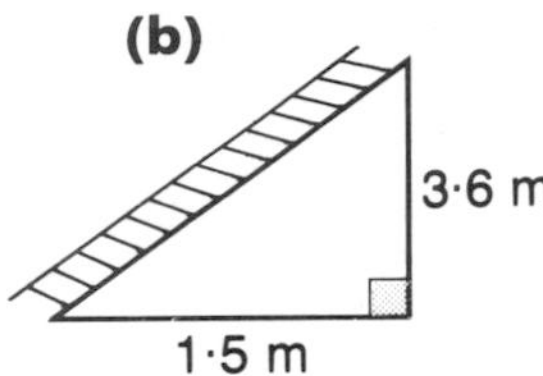

(c)
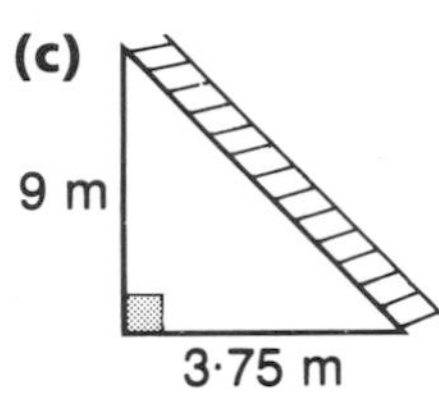

2 Find the length of the hypotenuse in each of these triangles.

(a)
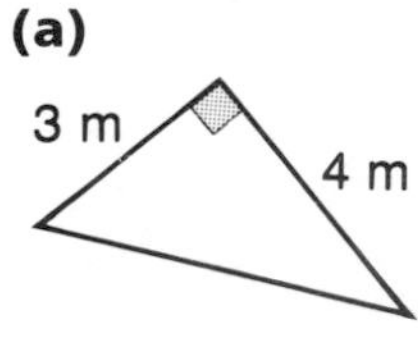

(b)
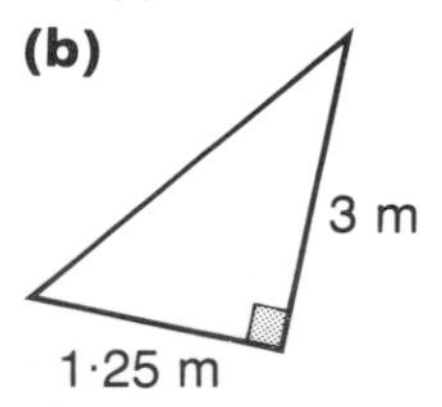

(c)
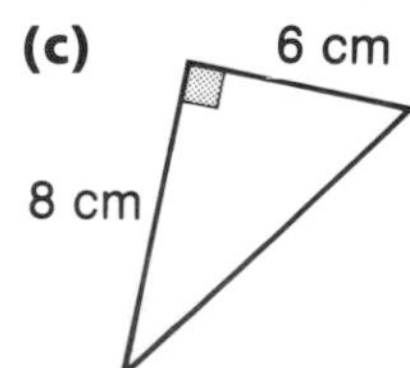

(d)
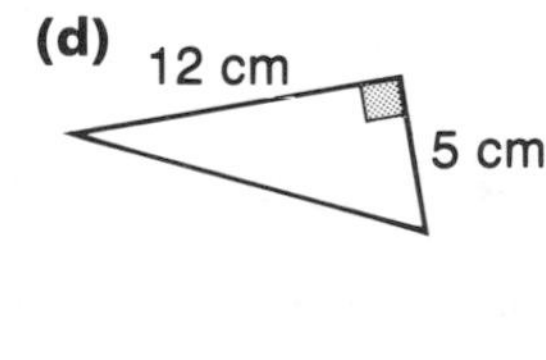

3 Gordon uses right-angled brackets to fit satellite dishes.
For each bracket, make a sketch and find the length of the longest side.

(a)
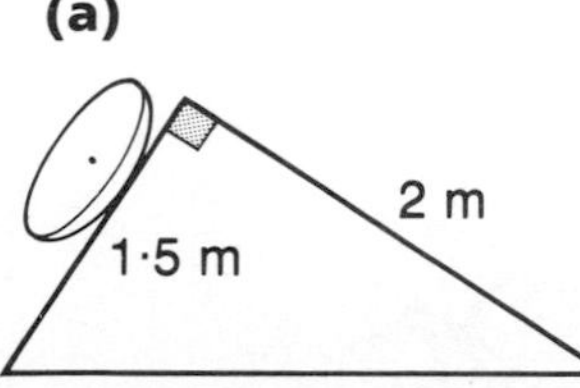

(b)
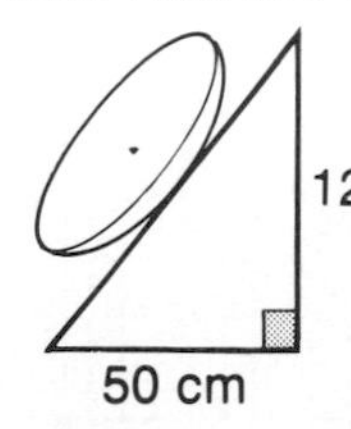

(c)
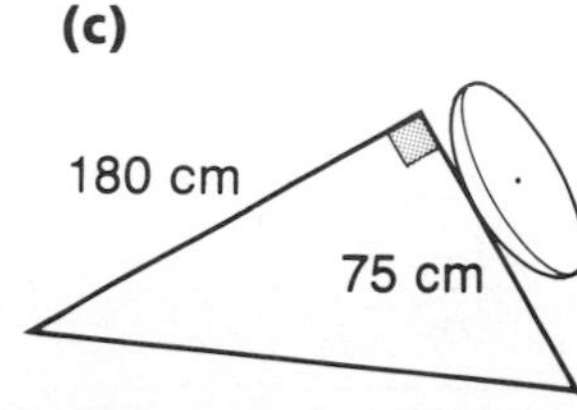

4 The size of a television screen is given by the length of its diagonal. Calculate the size of each of these screens.

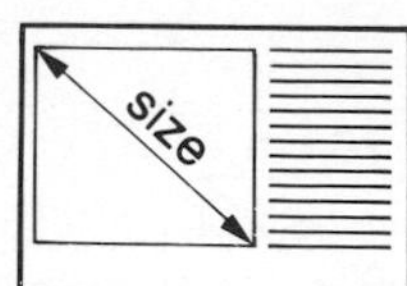

(a)
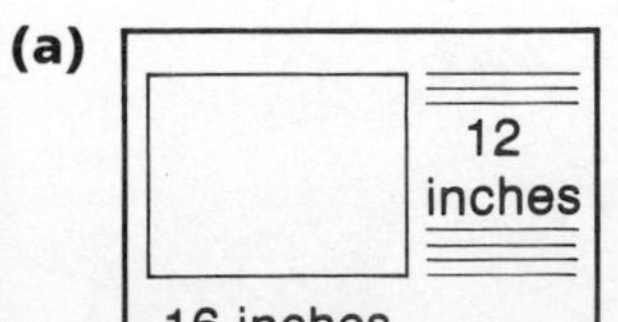

(b)
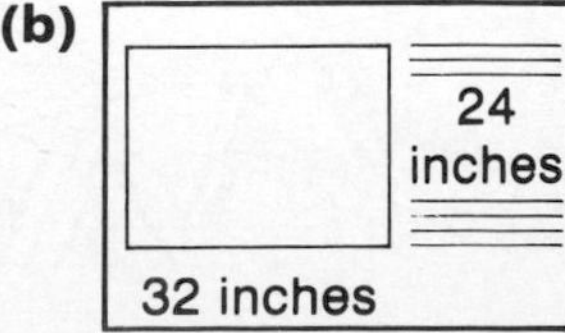

(c)
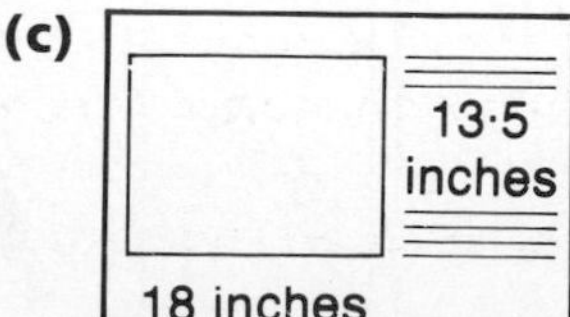

(d)
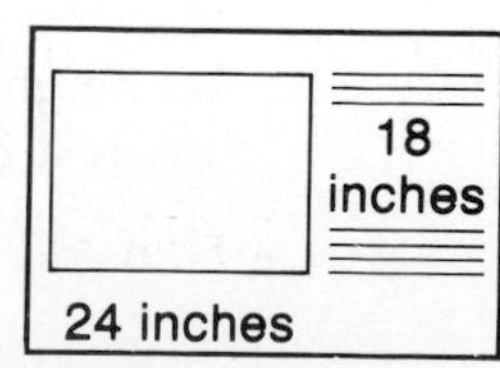

E62 Woodlea Homes

Pythagoras' Theorem: Calculating the shorter sides

Joe is a joiner with Woodlea Homes. Many of the timber frames he builds contain right-angled triangles.

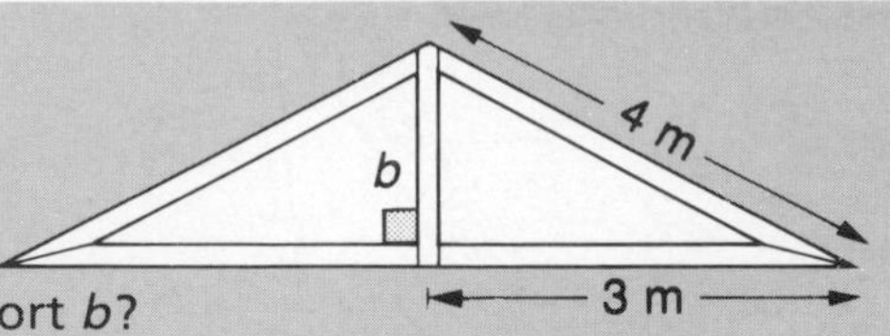

What length should Joe make the vertical support b? He makes a sketch and uses Pythagoras' Theorem.

$$4^2 = 3^2 + b^2$$
$$16 = 9 + b^2$$
$$16 - 9 = b^2$$
$$7 = b^2$$
$$b = \sqrt{7}$$
$$b = 2{\cdot}6457513$$

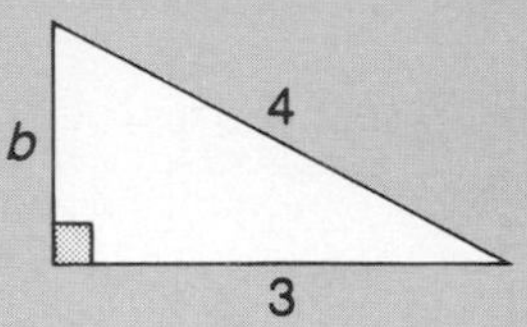

The support is **2·65 m** long, to 2 decimal places.

1 For each of these frames make a sketch and use Pythagoras' Theorem to find the length b, to 2 decimal places.

(a)

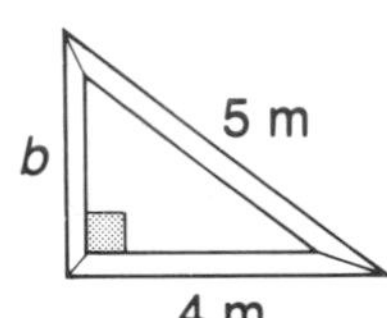

(b)

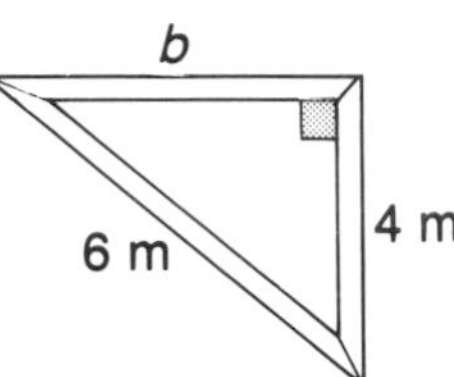

(c)

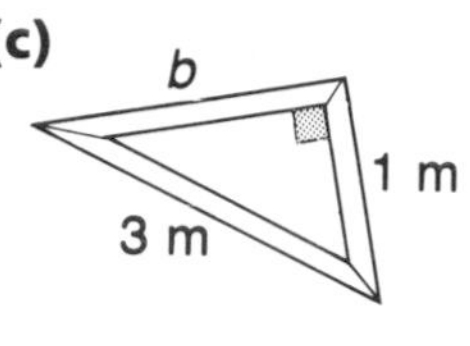

(d)

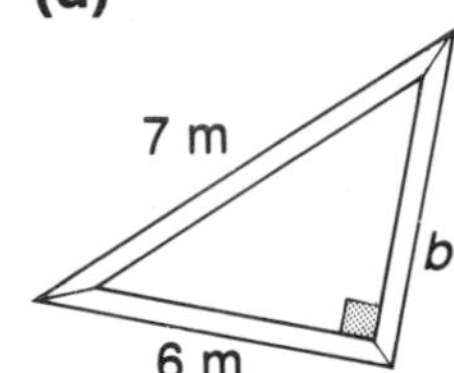

2 **(a)** What lengths should Joe make the vertical straps p and q?

(b) Find the length of support y.

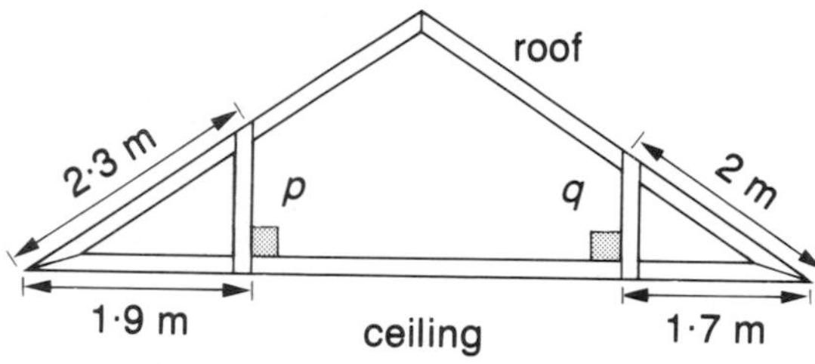

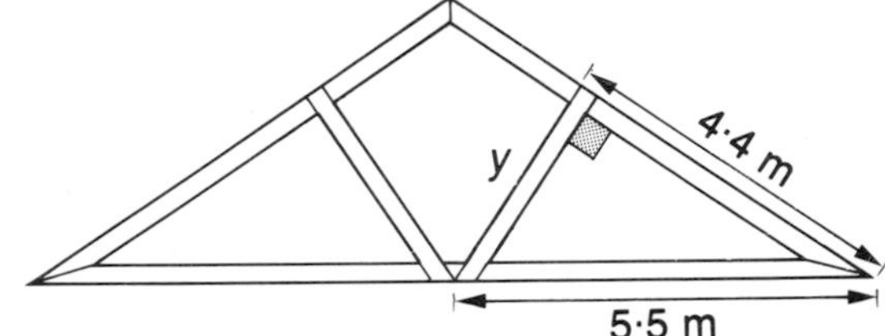

3 Find the length of d in each diagram.

(a)

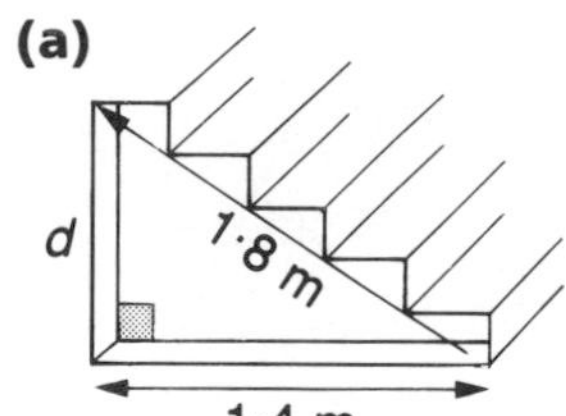

(b)

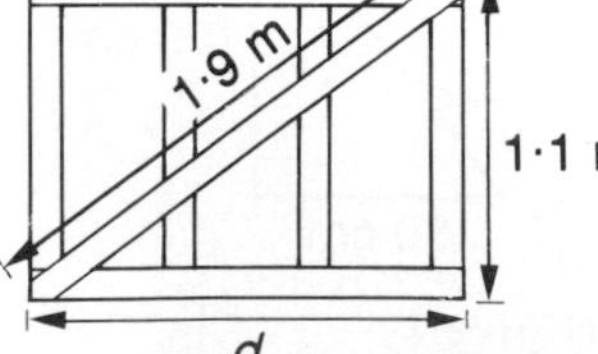

4 Joe has drawn this sketch of a door frame. Find its height to the nearest cm.

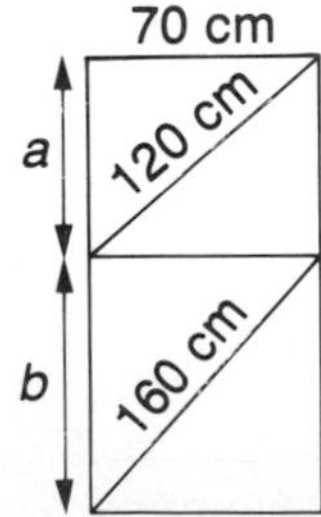

Ally the gater!

E63
Pythagoras' Theorem: Calculations

Ally makes wooden gates.
The gates are rectangular with a diagonal strut for support.

1 For each of these gates, find
- the length of wood used for the diagonal strut
- the total length of wood used for the gate.

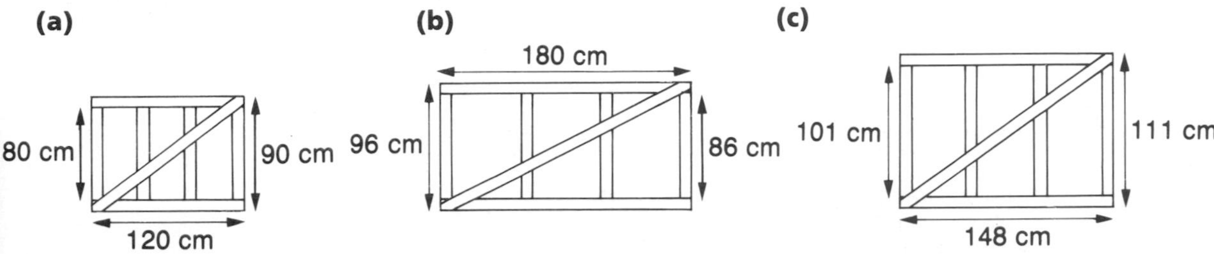

2 These pieces of wood are lying around in Ally's workshed.
Without shortening any, which pieces could he use to make a gate like those above?

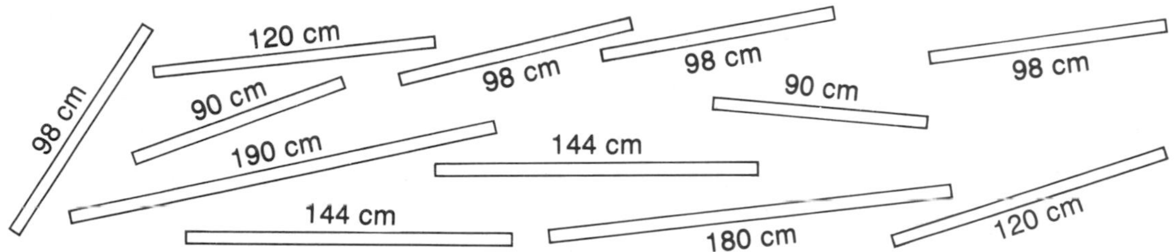

3 Here are some of Ally's sketches. Find the total length of wood used for each gate, to the nearest cm.

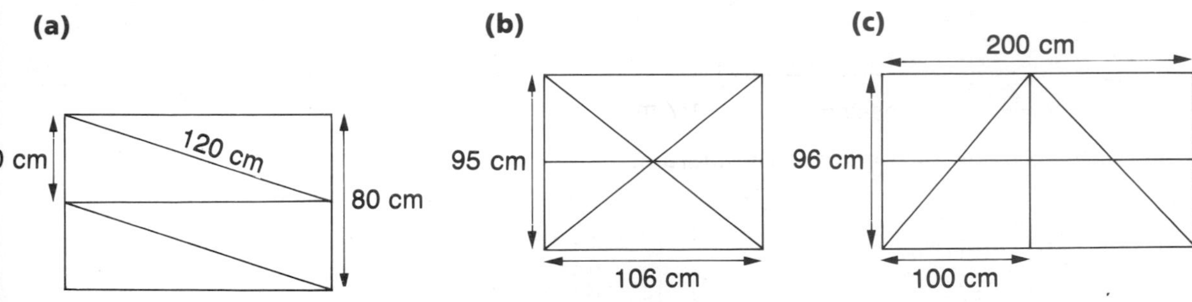

4 **(a)** Copy and complete this table to produce the squares of the whole numbers from 1 to 30.

Number	1	2	3	4	5	6
Square number	1	4	9	16	25	36

Investigation

(b) Look at the square numbers in your table.
Notice: 25 + 144 = 169
so $5^2 + 12^2 = 13^2$
5, 12 and 13 are called **Pythagorean triples**.
Use your table to find other sets of Pythagorean triples.

Ask your teacher what to do next.

Page E1 . . . from little acorns

1 (a) $60 = 6 \times 10 = 2 \times 3 \times 2 \times 5 = 2^2 \times 3 \times 5$

$60 = 5 \times 12 = 5 \times 3 \times 4 = 2^2 \times 3 \times 5$

$60 = 4 \times 15 = 2 \times 2 \times 3 \times 5 = 2^2 \times 3 \times 5$

(b) The answers are the same. **(c)** 2, 3 and 5

2 (a) 3, 5 **(b)** 2, 3 **(c)** 2, 3, 7 **(d)** 2, 3, 13
(e) 5 **(f)** 2, 3, 7 **(g)** 2, 3, 5, 7 **(h)** 2, 5, 23

3 (a) 3 **(b)** 3, 7, 11 **(c)** 2, 3 **(d)** 3, 7, 13 **(e)** 3, 5, 7
(f) 2 **(g)** 2, 3, 5 **(h)** 5, 11 **(i)** 2, 5

Page E2 Roll the dice

1 (a) 11 **(b)** 7 **(c)** 0 **(d)** 3 **(e)** 8 **(f)** 4
(g) 17 **(h)** 3 **(i)** 11 **(j)** 28 **(k)** 10 **(l)** 2

2 (a) $7 - 3 \times 2 = 1$ **(b)** $6 - 6 \div 2 = 3$ or $6 \div 6 + 2 = 3$
(c) $2 \times 3 - 6 = 0$

3 (a) 20 **(b)** 14 **(c)** 2 **(d)** 4 **(e)** 0 **(f)** 2
(g) 7 **(h)** 5 **(i)** 11 **(j)** 28 **(k)** 33 **(l)** 3

4 (a) $(10 + 8) \div 6 = 3$ **(b)** $(9 - 5) \times 7 = 28$
(c) $(3 + 17) \div 10 = 2$

5 (a) 81 **(b)** 21 **(c)** 16 **(d)** 2 **(e)** 81 **(f)** 729
(g) 36 **(h)** 2

6 (a) 7 **(b)** 3 **(c)** 39 **(d)** 2 **(e)** 18 **(f)** 6
(g) 36 **(h)** 9 **(i)** 25 **(j)** 4 **(k)** 14 **(l)** 8

Page E3 Top first

1 (a) 4 **(b)** 4 **(c)** 2 **(d)** 9 **(e)** 6·5
(f) 14 **(g)** 6 **(h)** 6·6 **(i)** 3·6 **(j)** 8
(k) 24·5 **(l)** 3·6 **(m)** 3 **(n)** 15 **(o)** 13·125
(p) 40·5 **(q)** 7·875 **(r)** 1 **(s)** 2 **(t)** 1·8

2 No. Pupil's explanation.

3 (a) 4·8 **(b)** 8·625 **(c)** 3·85 **(d)** 7·2 **(e)** 1·3 **(f)** 18

Page E4 Walter's

1 (a)

Number of soups (s)	2	3	4	5	6
Number of floor crossings (c)	3	5	7	9	11

- The increase in the number of crossings each time is 2. Number of crossings = 2 × number of soups, subtract 1. $c = 2s - 1$

(b) • 19 crossings • 39 crossings

2 (a) £10

(b)

Number of diners (d)	2	3	4	5
Total cost in £ (t)	10	17	24	31

(c) Total cost in £ = 7 × Number of diners, subtract 4
$t = 7d - 4$

(d) • £52 • £80

3 (a) $m = 3d - 2$ where m is the number of mints.
(b) • 25 mints • 43 mints • 58 mints
(c) • 10 diners • 13 diners • 18 diners

Page E5 The rules of the game

1 (a) 6 moves
(b) Pupils play game.
(c)

Size of square	2 by 2	3 by 3	4 by 4	5 by 5
Least number of moves	1	6	11	16

2 21 moves. Pupils check by playing game.

3 (a)

Term number (n)	1	2	3	4	5	6	7	8
Term	1	6	11	16	21	26	31	36

- To find the term multiply the term number by 5, subtract 4.

(b) • 46 • 96 • $5n - 4$

4 (a)

n	1	2	3	4
Term	3	5	7	9

n^{th} term $= 2n + 1$

(b)

n	1	2	3	4
Term	5	8	11	14

n^{th} term $= 3n + 2$

(c)

n	1	2	3	4
Term	2	6	10	14

n^{th} term $= 4n - 2$

5 (a) n^{th} term $= 3n - 2$ **(b)** n^{th} term $= 5n - 1$
(c) n^{th} term $= n + 5$

6 (a) 8, 11, 14, 17, 20 **(b)** 1, 3, 5, 7, 9
(c) 12, 17, 22, 27, 32 **(d)** 1, 5, 9, 13, 17
(e) 1, 8, 27, 64, 125 **(f)** $1, \frac{1}{2}, \frac{1}{3}, \frac{1}{4}, \frac{1}{5}$
(g) $\frac{1}{2}, \frac{1}{3}, \frac{1}{4}, \frac{1}{5}, \frac{1}{6}$ **(h)** $\frac{1}{2}, \frac{2}{3}, \frac{3}{4}, \frac{4}{5}, \frac{5}{6}$
(i) $\frac{1}{3}, \frac{2}{5}, \frac{3}{7}, \frac{4}{9}, \frac{5}{11}$

7 (a) n^{th} term $= n^2$ **(b)** n^{th} term $= \frac{1}{n + 2}$
(c) n^{th} term $= \frac{n}{2n - 1}$

Pages E6 and E7 Laggan Ski Club

1 Only people interested in skiing will take time to complete the questionnaire.

2 (a) To help the club set the membership fee.
(b) To help the club to buy the correct ski equipment.
(c) To enable the club to plan suitable summer activities.

3 (a) £29·50
(b) £30·00. Pupil's explanation, for example: "This is the mean rounded to the nearest £5·00."

4 T Dalgleish

5 (a) 172 cm **(b)** 41

6 A Hussain, A Smythe, R Clark, C Howard

7 A Smythe, V Thomas

8 G Rodger

9 A Sneddon, C Howard

10 A Hussain, T Dalgleish, C Howard

11 £30

12 (a) A Sneddon, C Howard, F Terry
(b) R Clark, C Thomson
(c) T Dalgleish, I Laing

13 Pupil's explanation of which techniques are biased.

Page E8 Giving it all away

1 **(a)** £20 **(b)** £2 **(c)** £1
2 **(a)** Below. Only one donation is above the mean.
(b) £1 This is the modal donation.
3 **(a)** • £18 • £10 • £10
(b) £14 400. This is 800 times the mean.
4 Mean £28·50 Median £20 Mode £50

Page E9 RelaTiVity

1 **(a)** $\frac{23}{53}$ **(b)** $\frac{26}{53}$ **(c)** $\frac{17}{53}$
2 **(a)** $\frac{20}{53}$ **(b)** $\frac{6}{53}$ **(c)** $\frac{12}{53}$ **(d)** $\frac{28}{53}$
3 **(a)** $\frac{7}{27}$ **(b)** $\frac{4}{27}$ **(c)** $\frac{2}{26}$ or $\frac{1}{13}$ **(d)** $\frac{12}{26}$ or $\frac{6}{13}$
(e) $\frac{10}{17}$ **(f)** $\frac{13}{25}$

Page E10 Road safety

1 **(a)** 1979 Bar graph A
(b) The number of accidents is decreasing. Line graph B
(c) • Bar graph A • Line graph B
2 **(a)** 1986 Pie chart D
(b) The number of injuries is decreasing. Line graph C
(c) • Line graph C • Pie chart D
(d) Pupil's reason for trend.
3 Pupil's own displays which should be
(a) Bar graph **(b)** Line graph **(c)** Pie chart.

Page E11 Rivetting stuff

1 **(a)** $\frac{1}{2}, \frac{1}{6}$ **(b)** $2\frac{7}{12}, \frac{5}{12}$ **(c)** $4\frac{5}{8}, 1\frac{1}{8}$ **(d)** $4\frac{1}{2}, \frac{7}{10}$
(e) $3\frac{1}{2}, \frac{1}{6}$
2 **(a)** $3\frac{5}{6}, 1\frac{1}{6}$ **(b)** $3\frac{11}{12}, \frac{7}{12}$ **(c)** $4\frac{11}{15}, 2\frac{1}{15}$ **(d)** $2\frac{1}{24}, \frac{17}{24}$
(e) $4\frac{5}{24}, 1\frac{11}{24}$
3 **(a)** $3\frac{8}{15}$ **(b)** $1\frac{7}{20}$ **(c)** $9\frac{9}{14}$ **(d)** $\frac{11}{12}$ **(e)** $7\frac{39}{40}$
(f) $3\frac{22}{35}$ **(g)** $8\frac{9}{10}$ **(h)** $1\frac{11}{24}$ **(i)** $5\frac{3}{20}$ **(j)** $3\frac{13}{21}$

Page E12 A sharing, caring family

1 **(a)** $\frac{1}{3}$ **(b)** $\frac{1}{5}$ **(c)** $\frac{2}{7}$ **(d)** $\frac{1}{6}$ **(e)** $\frac{3}{40}$
(f) $\frac{2}{9}$ **(g)** $\frac{3}{14}$ **(h)** $\frac{2}{7}$
2 **(a)** $\frac{1}{8}$ kg **(b)** $\frac{1}{6}$ kg **(c)** $\frac{1}{4}$ litre **(d)** $\frac{1}{15}$ kg **(e)** $\frac{1}{2}$ litre
(f) $\frac{3}{20}$ litre
3 **(a)** $\frac{1}{6}$ kg **(b)** $\frac{3}{10}$ kg
4 **(a)** $\frac{5}{8}$ litre **(b)** $\frac{21}{40}$ litre
5 **(a)** $\frac{1}{3}$ **(b)** $1\frac{1}{3}$ **(c)** $3\frac{3}{4}$ **(d)** $\frac{1}{3}$ **(e)** $3\frac{3}{5}$

Page E13 A sharing, caring family

1 **(a)** $1 \div \frac{1}{12} = 1 \times \frac{12}{1} = 12$ **(b)** $\frac{1}{3} \div \frac{1}{12} = \frac{1}{3} \times \frac{12}{1} = 4$ **(c)** $\frac{3}{4} \div \frac{1}{12} = \frac{3}{4} \times \frac{12}{1} = 9$
2 **(a)** 4 **(b)** 6 **(c)** $\frac{1}{2}$ **(d)** 6
(e) $\frac{3}{5}$ **(f)** $\frac{5}{7}$ **(g)** $2\frac{1}{2}$ **(h)** $1\frac{1}{2}$
3 **(a)** 5 scoops **(b)** 10 scoops
4 6 bowls
5 **(a)** 4 glasses **(b)** 3 tumblers
6 **(a)** 2 tumblers **(b)** 6 portions

Page E14 Wheelies

1 Practical work.
2 6 times
3 Pupil's own designs.

Page E15 Numbers in space

1 Weight of orbiter **(a)** 80 000 kg **(b)** 77 000 kg **(c)** 77 300 kg
Total weight at lift off **(a)** 2 000 000 kg **(b)** 2 100 000 kg **(c)** 2 080 000 kg
Thrust at lift off **(a)** 30 000 000 Newtons **(b)** 31 000 000 Newtons **(c)** 30 700 000 Newtons
Fuel consumption **(a)** 10 000 *l*/s **(b)** 12 000 *l*/s **(c)** 12 200 *l*/s
2 length 40 m, wing-span 20 m
3 360 km/h
4 Mars **(a)** 4 min **(b)** 4·3 min **(c)** 4·33 min
Jupiter **(a)** 30 min **(b)** 35 min **(c)** 34·9 min
Saturn **(a)** 70 min **(b)** 70 min **(c)** 69·9 min
Uranus **(a)** 3 h **(b)** 2·5 h **(c)** 2·52 h
Pluto **(a)** 5 h **(b)** 5·3 h **(c)** 5·33 h
5 **(a)** 2 years **(b)** 1·9 years **(c)** 1·88 years
6 Jupiter **(a)** 10 years **(b)** 12 years **(c)** 11·9 years
Saturn **(a)** 30 years **(b)** 29 years **(c)** 29·5 years
Pluto **(a)** 200 years **(b)** 250 years **(c)** 249 years
Uranus **(a)** 80 years **(b)** 84 years **(c)** 84·0 years

Page E16 Beetling about

1 Blister **(a)** 0·01 m **(b)** 0·015 m
Colorado **(a)** 0·03 m **(b)** 0·025 m
Golden **(a)** 0·03 m **(b)** 0·027 m
Great Water **(a)** 0·03 m **(b)** 0·031 m
Rhinoceros **(a)** 0·09 m **(b)** 0·090 m
Rove **(a)** 0·02 m **(b)** 0·024 m
Stag **(a)** 0·08 m **(b)** 0·077 m
2 0·007 m
3 A 0·003 m B 0·003 m C 0·006 m D 0·006 m
E 0·004 m F 0·004 m or 0·005 m
4 U **(a)** 0·2 m **(b)** 0·15 m **(c)** 0·153 m
V **(a)** 0·2 m **(b)** 0·17 m **(c)** 0·170 m
W **(a)** 0·1 m **(b)** 0·15 m **(c)** 0·147 m
X **(a)** 0·2 m **(b)** 0·16 m **(c)** 0·158 m
Y **(a)** 0·1 m **(b)** 0·13 m **(c)** 0·130 m
Z **(a)** 0·1 m **(b)** 0·12 m **(c)** 0·123 m
5 Answer depends on dimensions of classroom.

Page E17 Fuelling around

1 **(a)** 13·64 gallons **(b)** 15·91 gallons
(c) 29·32 gallons **(d)** 52·60 gallons

2

Fuel	*per litre*
Unleaded	49·7p
Super Unleaded	52·4p
4 star	53·2p
Diesel	49·1p

3 **(a)** Gallons 6·57, Litres 29·85 **(b)** Gallons 7·66, Litres 34·82
(c) Gallons 4·34, Litres 19·72 **(d)** This sale 28·66, Litres 58·42

4 USA The cost per litre there is 40·7p compared with 53·2 p in Great Britain.

Page E18 The product of multiplying

1 **(a)** • 120 • 12 000 • 120 000 • 12 • 1·2
(b) • It increases • It decreases

2 **(a)**

Row	*1st No.*	*2nd No.*		*Product*
1	8000	× 0·2	=	1600
2	800	× 0·2	=	160
3	80	× 0·2	=	16
4	8	× 0·2	=	1·6

(b) • It is divided by ten • It is divided by ten

(c)

Row	*1st No.*	*2nd No.*		*Product*
5	0·8	× 0·2	=	0·16
6	0·08	× 0·2	=	0·016

3 **(a)**

2 × 0·6 = 1·2	0·2 × 0·6 = 0·12
3 × 0·4 = 1·2	0·3 × 0·4 = 0·12
0·3 × 5 = 1·5	0·3 × 0·5 = 0·15
1·4 × 7 = 9·8	1·4 × 0·7 = 0·98

0·2 × 0·06 = 0·012	0·2 × 0·06 = 0·0012
0·3 × 0·04 = 0·012	0·03 × 0·04 = 0·0012
0·03 × 0·5 = 0·015	0·03 × 0·05 = 0·0015
0·14 × 0·7 = 0·098	0·14 × 0·07 = 0·0098

(b) The number of decimal places in the product is the sum of the decimal places in the two decimals.

4 **(a)** 2 **(b)** 3 **(c)** 4 **(d)** 4 **(e)** 4
(f) 3. The third decimal place is 0.

5 **(a)** • 0·24 • 0·024 **(b)** • 0·63 • 0·063 **(c)** • 0·24 • 0·024 **(d)** • 0·40 • 0·040

6 **(a)** 0·015, No, 0·015416 **(b)** 0·14, No, 0·16728
(c) 1·2, Yes, 1·15584 **(d)** 4·2 or 4·9, No, 4·70288
(e) 0·0024, No, 0·002257 **(f)** 5, Yes, 5·56412

Page E19 Marina's Aquarium

1 **(a)** 8 **(b)** 6 **(c)** 3

2 Pupils check using method shown.

3 **(a)** • $\frac{9}{90}$ • $\frac{0·9}{9}$ • $\frac{5}{50}$ • $\frac{0·09}{0·9}$
(b) It increases

4 Tank A Comet 20, 19 Veiltail 25, 25
Common Goldfish 10, 11
Tank B Koi 4, 3 Pigmy Sunfish 22, 23
Bitterling 10, 10

Pages E20 and E21 All at sea

Pupils should produce a scale drawing for each of questions 1 to 6. Answers will depend on the accuracy of their measurements.

1 **(b)** 25 m

2 150 m

3 **(a)** • 24° • 24° **(b)** They are the same.

4 500 m

5 **(a)** 12 m **(b)** 5 m

6 **(a)** 30°
(b) 26 m, No. The discrepancy is probably due to inaccurate measurements of either the angles of elevation or of the distances from the lighthouse.

7 Practical work.

Page E22 Designing Hall 2

Practical work.

Page E23 Clock-wise

1 **(a)** 1 mod 7 **(b)** 2 mod 7 **(c)** 6 mod 7 **(d)** 5 mod 7
(e) 0 mod 7 **(f)** 3 mod 7 **(g)** 5 mod 7 **(h)** 2 mod 7
(i) 0 mod 7 **(j)** 4 mod 7

2 **(a)** $y = 4$ mod 7 **(b)** $p = 4$ mod 7 **(c)** $t = 6$ mod 7
(d) $s = 3$ mod 7 **(e)** $x = 5$ mod 7 **(f)** $q = 5$ mod 7
(g) $x = 0$ mod 7 **(h)** $r = 2$ mod 7

3

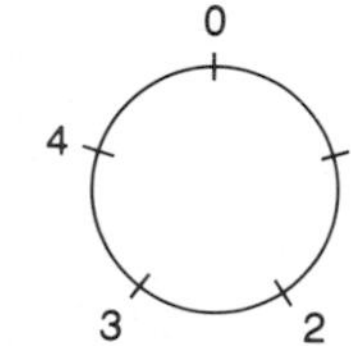

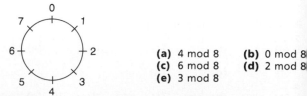

(a) 2 mod 5 **(b)** 1 mod 5
(c) 0 mod 5 **(d)** 1 mod 5
(e) 4 mod 5

4

(a) 4 mod 8 **(b)** 0 mod 8
(c) 6 mod 8 **(d)** 2 mod 8
(e) 3 mod 8

5 **(a)** mod 7 **(b)** mod 5 **(c)** mod 8 **(d)** mod 7
(e) mod 7 **(f)** mod 8 **(g)** mod 5 **(h)** mod 8

6 **(a)** 9 mod 11 **(b)** 2 mod 11 **(c)** 5 mod 11
(d) 2 mod 11 **(e)** 6 mod 11 **(f)** 10 mod 11
(g) 8 mod 11 **(h)** 9 mod 11 **(i)** 1 mod 11

7 **(a)**

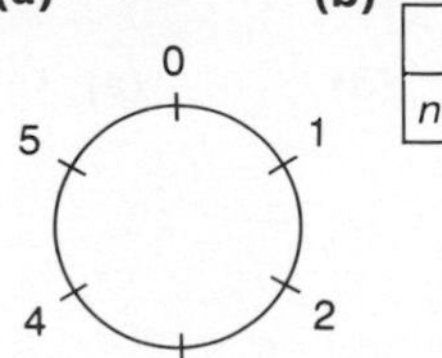

(b)

n	0	1	2	3	4	5
n + 4(mod 6)	4	5	0	1	2	3

(c)

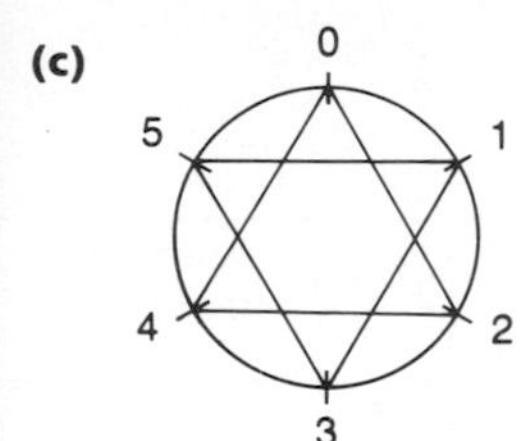

8 (a)

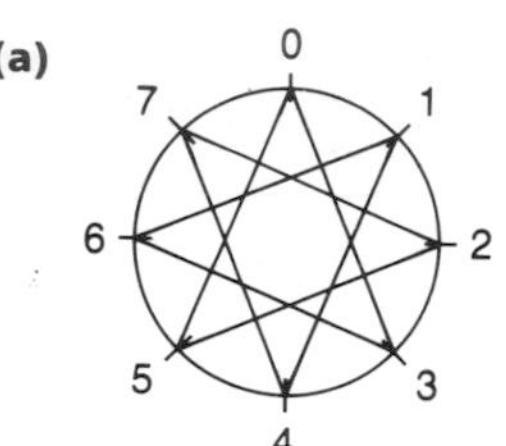

(b)

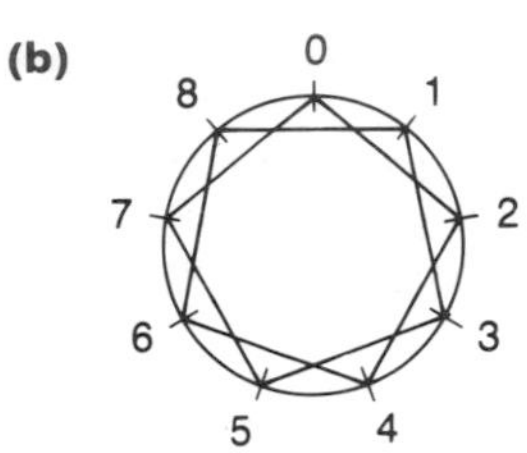

9

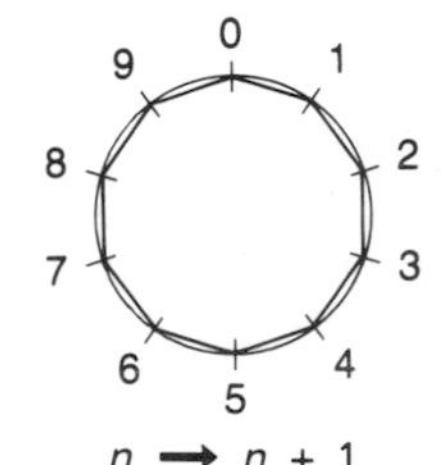

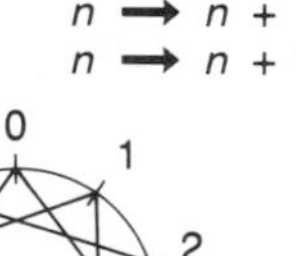

$n \rightarrow n + 1$
$n \rightarrow n + 9$

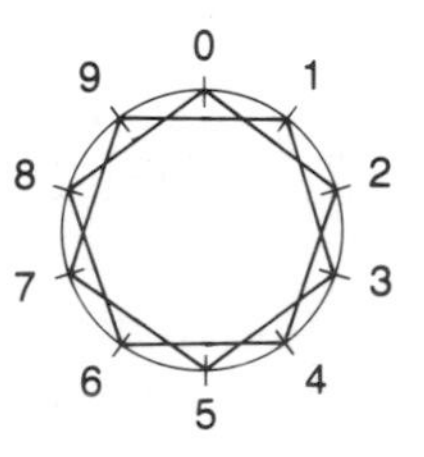

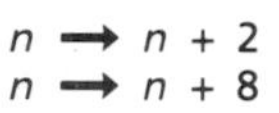

$n \rightarrow n + 2$
$n \rightarrow n + 8$

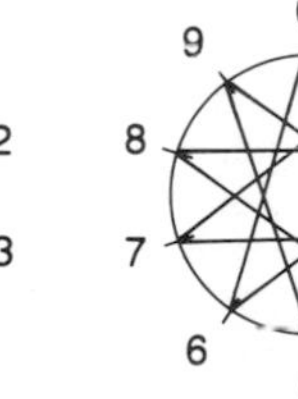

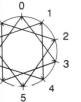

$n \rightarrow n + 3$
$n \rightarrow n + 7$

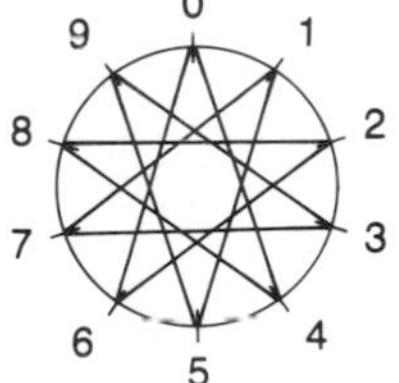

$n \rightarrow n + 4$
$n \rightarrow n + 6$

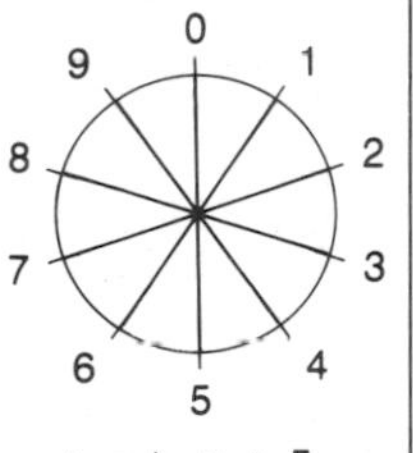

$n \rightarrow n + 5$

Pages E24 and E25 Concorde Couriers

1 (a) • 2 hours • 3 hours • $4\frac{1}{2}$ hours
(b) • The time (T) equals the distance (D) divided by the average speed (S).
• The formula is $T = \frac{D}{S}$.

2 (a) 1 hour 15 minutes **(b)** 1 hour 42 minutes
(c) 2 hours 24 minutes **(d)** 3 hours 21 minutes
3 (a) 1 hour 18 minutes **(b)** 2 hours 6 minutes
(c) 2 hours 42 minutes **(d)** 2 hours 56 minutes
4 (a) 2 hours 24 minutes **(b)** 3 hours 30 minutes
(c) 42 minutes
5 No. The inter-city delivery time is 3 hours 48 minutes so delivery could not be made before 3.02pm. However, he could 'take a chance'.
6 (a) • 108 km/h • 105 km/h • 94 km/h
(b) • The average speed (S) equals the distance (D) divided by the time (T).
• The formula is $S = \frac{D}{T}$.

7

Distance	54 km	216 km	273 km	136 km
Time	36 min	2 h 15 min	2 h 48 min	1 h 20 min
Average speed	90 km/h	96 km/h	97·5 km/h	102 km/h

8 90 km/h
9 (a) • 200 km • 300 km • 400 km
(b) • The distance (D) equals the average speed (S) multiplied by the time (T).
• The formula is $D = S \times T$.
10 (a) 384 km **(b)** 312 km **(c)** 221 km **(d)** 86 km
11 (a) 1 hour 45 minutes **(b)** 115 km/h
(c) Galway and Killarney

Page E26 Cora's coaches

1 (a) 6 minutes **(b)** 8 km
2 Other layouts are possible.

Dumglass	dep	0930
Ferrytown	arr	1000
	dep	1030
Maryport	arr	1130
	dep	1145
Dumglass	arr	1215

3 104 km
4

	Stage 1	Stage 2	Stage 3
(a)	32 km	32 km	40 km
(b)	30 min	1 hour	30 min
(c)	64 km/h	32 km/h	80 km/h

5 (a) From Maryport to Dumglass (Stage 3).
(b) From Maryport to Dumglass (Stage 3).

6 (a)

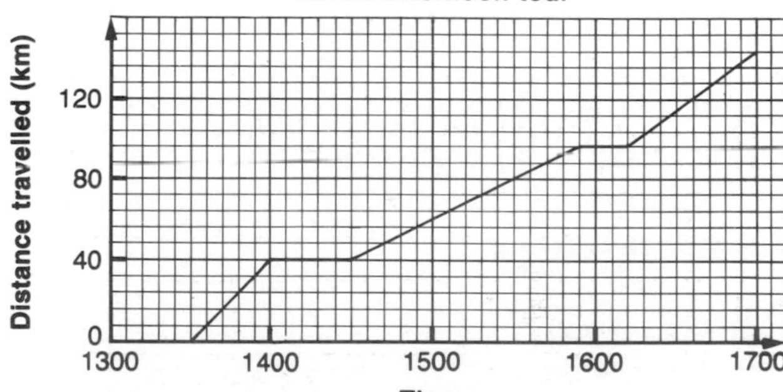

(b) • From Dumglass to Maryport (Stage 1).
• From Dumglass to Maryport (Stage 1).
(c)

Stage	*Average speed*
Stage 1	80 km/h
Stage 2	40 km/h
Stage 3	60 km/h

Page E27 Rhodes to Crete

1 • £1300 • £1140 • £1240
2 Paris £1860 Rimini £1680 Minorca £820 Crete £1440
3 (a) $c = 5p - 250$
(b) • £1750 • £2225 • £2450
4 (a) 475 fr
(b) $f = 10p - 25$
(c) • 175 fr • 325 fr • 575 fr • 1175 fr • 2475 fr
5 (a) $d = 320p - 500$ where d is the number of drachma
(b) • 9100 dr • 17 100 dr • 25 100 dr • 29 900 dr • 41 740 dr

Page E28 Formula fun

1 **(a)** 50 cm **(b)** 60 cm
(c) 88 cm **(d)** 152 cm

2 **(a)** $P = d^2$ $= 4^2$ $= 16\text{ cm}^2$
$Q = 3d^2$ $= 3 \times 4^2$ $= 3 \times 16$ $= 48\text{ cm}^2$
$R = (3d)^2$ $= (3 \times 4)^2$ $= 12^2$ $= 144\text{ cm}^2$

(b)

d	P	Q	R
5 cm	25 cm²	75 cm²	225 cm²
7 cm	49 cm²	147 cm²	441 cm²
12 cm	144 cm²	432 cm²	1296 cm²
6·2 cm	38·44 cm²	115·32 cm²	345·96 cm²

(c) $A = (3d)^2$

3 **(a)** $A = 18$ **(b)** $A = 36$ **(c)** $A = 64$ **(d)** $A = 16$
(e) $A = 54$ **(f)** $A = 144$ **(g)** $A = 20$ **(h)** $A = 15$
(i) $A = 2$ **(j)** $A = 5$ **(k)** $A = 4$ **(l)** $A = 3$
(m) $A = 2$ **(n)** $A = 3$ **(o)** $A = 90$ **(p)** $A = 410$
(q) $A = 900$ **(r)** $A = 41$ **(s)** $A = 91$ **(t)** $A = 1$

4 **(a)** 4 mg **(b)** 8 mg **(c)** 10 mg **(d)** 5 mg

Page E29 Just plug in the numbers

1 **(a)** 430°F
(b) 450°F
(c) 370°F
(d) 280°F

2 **(a)** 145 mm³
(b) 1183 cm³
(c) 128 m³
(d) 7·36 cm³
(e) 7·5 m³
(f) 16·72 mm³

3 **(a)** $M = 40$ **(b)** $R = 16$ **(c)** $w = 5{\cdot}5$
(d) $v = 50$ **(e)** $A = 423{\cdot}9$ **(f)** $V = 113{\cdot}13$
(g) $A = 1830$ **(h)** $D = 356{\cdot}25$

Page E30 The planets

1 **(a)** $1{\cdot}2 \times 10^4$ km
(b) $1{\cdot}39 \times 10^5$ km
(c) $2{\cdot}28 \times 10^3$ km

2 **(a)** $6{\cdot}5 \times 10^4$ **(b)** $3{\cdot}5 \times 10^3$ **(c)** $9{\cdot}8 \times 10^2$
(d) $7{\cdot}56 \times 10^3$ **(e)** $3{\cdot}15 \times 10^5$ **(f)** $2{\cdot}05 \times 10^4$
(g) $2{\cdot}35 \times 10^2$ **(h)** 4×10^3 **(i)** $7{\cdot}83 \times 10^4$
(j) $4{\cdot}032 \times 10^5$ **(k)** 2×10^6 **(l)** $7{\cdot}09 \times 10^6$

3 **(a)** 13 000 km
(b) 120 000 km
(c) 51 100 km
(d) 4900 km

4 **(a)** 2300 **(b)** 5 870 000 **(c)** 310 **(d)** 72 000 000
(e) 50 000 **(f)** 83 300 **(g)** 13·5 **(h)** 950 000
(i) 207 **(j)** 5 720 000 000

5

Planet	Mean distance in kilometres	
	ordinary number	standard form
Mercury	58 000 000	$5{\cdot}8 \times 10^7$
Venus	110 000 000	$1{\cdot}1 \times 10^8$
Earth	150 000 000	$1{\cdot}5 \times 10^8$
Mars	228 000 000	$2{\cdot}28 \times 10^8$
Jupiter	778 000 000	$7{\cdot}78 \times 10^8$
Saturn	1 400 000 000	$1{\cdot}4 \times 10^9$
Uranus	2 880 000 000	$2{\cdot}88 \times 10^9$
Neptune	4 500 000 000	$4{\cdot}5 \times 10^9$
Pluto	5 910 000 000	$5{\cdot}91 \times 10^9$

Page E31 Pick's Formula

1 **(a)**

Shape	Number of dots on boundary (b)	Number of dots inside boundary (i)	$\frac{1}{2}b + i$	Area (A) in square units
D	8	1	5	4
E	12	2	8	7
F	10	4	9	8
G	8	3	7	6
H	12	0	6	5

(b) Pupils' own values added to the table above.
(c) The numbers in the last column are one less than those in the previous one.
(d) $A = \frac{1}{2}b + i - 1$

2 I 14 unit² J 6 unit² K 11 unit² L 10 unit²
3 M 16 unit² N 15 unit² O 18 unit²

Pages E32 and E33 Chocolate pie

1

Nutrient	Angle	Calculation	Weight
Protein	50°	$\frac{50}{360}$ of 64 g	8·9 g
Carbohydrate	180°	$\frac{180}{360}$ of 64 g	32 g
Fat	90°	$\frac{90}{360}$ of 64 g	16 g
Others	40°	$\frac{40}{360}$ of 64 g	7·1 g
Totals	360°		64 g

2

	Carbohydrate	Fat	Others	Protein
• 18 g Ball	12·5 g	4 g	1 g	0·5 g
• 500 g box	347·2 g	111·1 g	27·8 g	13·9 g

3 **(a)** **Pluto bar**

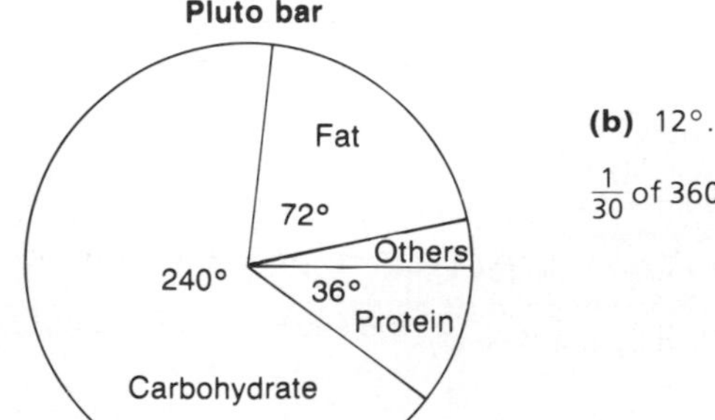

(b) 12°.

$\frac{1}{30}$ of $360° = 12°$

4 (a) Universe bar

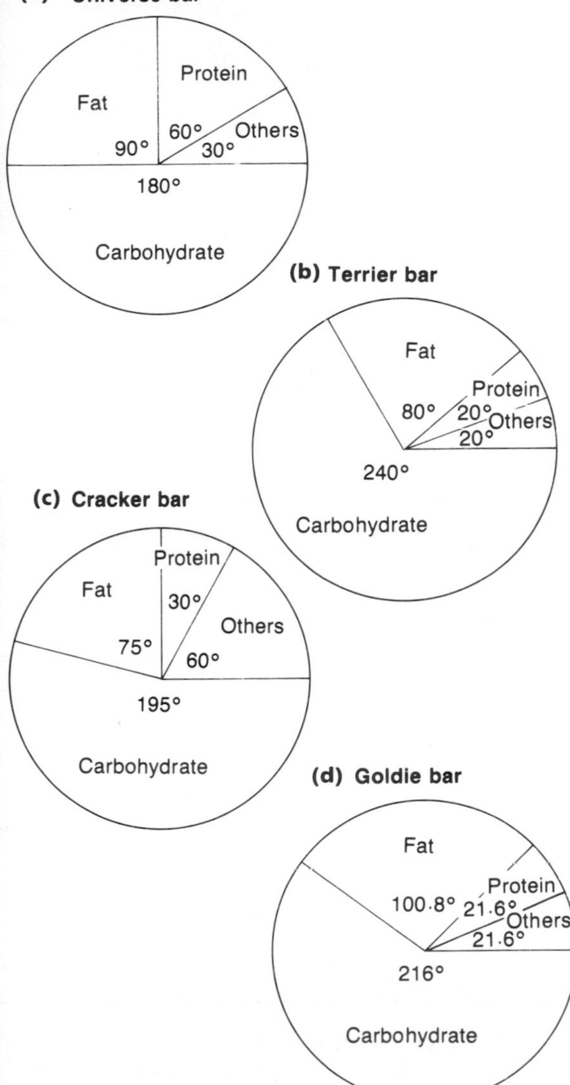

Page E34 Step by step

1 Method A • 0·6 m³ • 1·2 m³ • 1·8 m³

Method B • 0·9 m² • 1·8 m³

2 (a) 4·8 m³ **(b)** 3 m³

3 (a) 8·7 m³

(b) Yes. Total volume of rubble from the ramp and steps is 9·6 m³. This is greater than the volume of the skip but the rubble could be piled on top.

4 20 bags of cement, 39 bags of sand and 58 bags of chippings.

Page E35 What's in a can?

1–3 Practical work.

4 Yes. The numbers in the last two columns are almost the same. The differences could be due to errors in the measurements.

Page E36 Cecil's trays

1 (a) Practical work. 4 trays can be made by cutting out small squares of sides 1 cm, 2 cm, 3 cm and 4 cm.

(b) 64 cm³, 72 cm³, 48 cm³ and 16 cm³.

(c) 2 cm

2 (a) 62·5 cm³

(b) 1·5 cm with volume = 73·5 cm³.

3 A tray with maximum volume of 74·052 cm³ can be made by removing small squares of sides 1·7 cm.

Page E37 Sarah's garden

1 Practical work.

2 (a) Practical work.

(b) The same size of ellipse is drawn.

3 28 m. The distance from the circumference of the flower bed to a peg along the diameter is 6 m. Since the rope is doubled at this point, its total length is 28 m.

4 (a) The outline is an ellipse.

(b) Practical work.

Page E38 The Lunchbox Café

1 (a) $6s$ **(b)** $8s$ **(c)** $20s$ **(d)** $14s$

2 (a) $3s$ **(b)** $9s$ **(c)** $3s$ **(d)** $40s$

3 (a) $9c$ **(b)** $14c$ **(c)** $11c$
(d) $5c$ **(e)** $32c$ **(f)** $22c$

4 (a) $8s + 3c$ **(b)** $6s + 5c$ **(c)** $15s + 9c$
(d) $3p + q$ **(e)** $4p + 2q$ **(f)** $p + 2q$

5 (a) $7k + 11$ **(b)** $g + 14$ **(c)** $5t + 1$
(d) $15 + 11x$ **(e)** $3 + 13y$ **(f)** $2s + 4$
(g) $y + 2$ **(h)** $11 + 5a$ **(i)** $4 + 4d$
(j) $15x + 25$ **(k)** $50r + 37$ **(l)** $11v + 6$

Page E39 The Lunchbox Café

1 (a) $2(3s + 2c)$
$= 2 \times 3s + 2 \times 2c$
$= 6s + 4c$

(b) $3(3s + c)$
$= 3 \times 3s + 3 \times c$
$= 9s + 3c$

(c) $4(4s + 2c)$
$= 4 \times 4s + 4 \times 2c$
$= 16s + 8c$

2 (a) $10x + 20y$ **(b)** $20t + 8u$ **(c)** $6x + 18y$
(d) $21s + 56t$ **(e)** $8g + 56h$ **(f)** $15d + 30e$
(g) $6k + 36m$ **(h)** $56g + 48h$

3 (a) $15s - 5c$ **(b)** $20s - 8c$ **(c)** $21s - 28c$
(d) $8s - 16c$ **(e)** $4p - 32q$ **(f)** $60d - 100e$
(g) $12a - 44b$ **(h)** $5v - 75w$

4 (a) $35t + 45$ **(b)** $45 + 27r$ **(c)** $10s - 30$
(d) $27 - 15t$ **(e)** $24s + 16t - 24$ **(f)** $7a + 14b - 28$
(g) $8f - 6g + 14$ **(h)** $15p - 30 - 40q$

Page E40 The Jupiter rocket

1 (a) ${}^-2 + 8 = 6$ *or* $6 - {}^-2 = 8$ *or* $6 + 2 = 8$
John goes up 8 rungs.
(b) ${}^-7 + 4 = {}^-3$ *or* ${}^-3 - {}^-7 = 4$ *or* ${}^-3 + 7 = 4$
Jo goes up 4 rungs.
(c) ${}^-3 + {}^-5 = {}^-8$ *or* ${}^-8 - {}^-3 = {}^-5$ *or* ${}^-8 + 3 = {}^-5$
Lisa goes down 5 rungs.

2 (a) ${}^-4 + 7 = 3$ *or* $3 - {}^-4 = 7$ *or* $3 + 4 = 7$
Jill goes up 7 rungs.
(b) ${}^-3 + 4 = 1$ *or* $1 - {}^-3 = 4$ *or* $1 + 3 = 4$
Jill goes up 4 rungs.
(c) ${}^-3 + {}^-2 = {}^-5$ *or* ${}^-5 - {}^-3 = {}^-2$ *or* ${}^-5 + 3 = {}^-2$
Jill goes down 2 rungs.
(d) ${}^-4 + {}^-4 = {}^-8$ *or* ${}^-8 - {}^-4 = {}^-4$ *or* ${}^-8 + 4 = {}^-4$
Jill goes down 4 rungs.

3 (a) $5 - {}^-2$
$= 5 + 2$
$= 7$

(b) $3 - {}^-6$
$= 3 + 6$
$= 9$

(c) ${}^-2 - {}^-5$
$= {}^-2 + 5$
$= 3$

(d) ${}^-6 - {}^-3$
$= {}^-6 + 3$
$= {}^-3$

(e) ${}^-9 - {}^-7$
$= {}^-9 + 7$
$= {}^-2$

(f) ${}^-8 - {}^-4$
$= {}^-8 + 4$
$= {}^-4$

(g) $5 - {}^-3$
$= 5 + 3$
$= 8$

(h) ${}^-7 - {}^-1$
$= {}^-7 + 1$
$= {}^-6$

4 (a) 8 **(b)** 8 **(c)** ${}^-5$ **(d)** 5 **(e)** 0
(f) 6 **(g)** 10 **(h)** ${}^-8$ **(i)** 8 **(j)** 0

5 (a) 2 **(b)** ${}^-2$ **(c)** ${}^-3$ **(d)** 2
(e) ${}^-6$ **(f)** 1 **(g)** 6 **(h)** 9
(i) 0 **(j)** 4 **(k)** 13 **(l)** 1
(m) 8 **(n)** 5 **(o)** ${}^-6$ **(p)** 4

Page E41 Number patterns

1 (a)
$2 \times 3 = 6$
$2 \times 2 = 4$
$2 \times 1 = 2$
$2 \times 0 = 0$
$2 \times {}^-1 = {}^-2$
$2 \times {}^-2 = {}^-4$
$2 \times {}^-3 = {}^-6$

(b)
$4 \times {}^-3 = {}^-12$
$3 \times {}^-3 = {}^-9$
$2 \times {}^-3 = {}^-6$
$1 \times {}^-3 = {}^-3$
$0 \times {}^-3 = 0$
${}^-1 \times {}^-3 = 3$
${}^-2 \times {}^-3 = 6$

(c)
${}^-5 \times 2 = {}^-10$
${}^-5 \times 1 = {}^-5$
${}^-5 \times 0 = 0$
${}^-5 \times {}^-1 = 5$
${}^-5 \times {}^-2 = 10$
${}^-5 \times {}^-3 = 15$
${}^-5 \times {}^-4 = 20$

(d)
$3 \times {}^-7 = {}^-21$
$2 \times {}^-7 = {}^-14$
$1 \times {}^-7 = {}^-7$
$0 \times {}^-7 = 0$
${}^-1 \times {}^-7 = 7$
${}^-2 \times {}^-7 = 14$
${}^-3 \times {}^-7 = 21$

2 (a) ${}^-12$ **(b)** ${}^-42$ **(c)** 24 **(d)** ${}^-16$ **(e)** 45
(f) ${}^-36$ **(g)** ${}^-28$ **(h)** ${}^-35$ **(i)** 9 **(j)** 81

3 (a) ${}^-2 \times 3 \times 4$
$= {}^-6 \times 4$
$= {}^-24$

(b) $5 \times {}^-4 \times {}^-7$
$= {}^-20 \times {}^-7$
$= 140$

(c) $3 \times {}^-2 \times {}^-1$
$= {}^-6 \times {}^-1$
$= 6$

4 (a) ${}^-24$ **(b)** 10 **(c)** ${}^-30$ **(d)** 0
(e) 0 **(f)** ${}^-40$ **(g)** 120 **(h)** ${}^-125$

5 (a) ${}^-4$ **(b)** ${}^-4$ **(c)** 5 **(d)** ${}^-8$ **(e)** ${}^-6$
(f) ${}^-5$ **(g)** 7 **(h)** 21 **(i)** ${}^-7$ **(j)** 10

6 (a) $\dfrac{5 \times {}^-6}{{}^-2} = \dfrac{{}^-30}{{}^-2} = 15$

(b) $\dfrac{5 \times {}^-8}{2 \times {}^-4} = \dfrac{{}^-40}{{}^-8} = 5$

(c) $\dfrac{{}^-8 \times {}^-3}{4 \times {}^-2} = \dfrac{24}{{}^-8} = {}^-3$

(d) $\dfrac{{}^-36}{({}^-3)^2} = \dfrac{{}^-36}{9} = {}^-4$

7 (a) ${}^-8$ **(b)** 6 **(c)** ${}^-5$ **(d)** ${}^-7$
8 $({}^-1)^2 = 1$ $({}^-1)^3 = {}^-1$ $({}^-1)^4 = 1$ $({}^-1)^5 = {}^-1$
${}^-1$ to an even power is 1 and ${}^-1$ to an odd power is ${}^-1$.

Page E42 What an expression!

1 (a) $5a + 15$ **(b)** $6b + 3$ **(c)** $4c - 28$ **(d)** $10d - 6p$

2 (a) ${}^-2(3 + 4)$
$= {}^-2 \times 7$
$= {}^-14$
or ${}^-2 \times 3 + {}^-2 \times 4$
$= {}^-6 + {}^-8$
$= {}^-6 - 8$
$= {}^-14$

(b) ${}^-3(5 - 1)$
$= {}^-3 \times 4$
$= {}^-12$
or ${}^-3 \times 5 - {}^-3 \times 1$
$= {}^-15 - {}^-3$
$= {}^-15 + 3$
$= {}^-12$

3 (a) ${}^-3(a + 5)$
$= {}^-3a + {}^-15$
$= {}^-3a - 15$

(b) ${}^-2(5b + 7)$
$= {}^-10b + {}^-14$
$= {}^-10b - 14$

(c) ${}^-5(c - 2)$
$= {}^-5c - {}^-10$
$= {}^-5c + 10$

(d) ${}^-4(3f - 8)$
$= {}^-12f - {}^-32$
$= {}^-12f + 32$

4 (a) ${}^-4p - 12$ **(b)** ${}^-6q - 21$ **(c)** ${}^-15r - 35s$
(d) ${}^-7x + 21$ **(e)** ${}^-3w + 2z$ **(f)** ${}^-28 + 35j$
(g) ${}^-2t - 4u - 6$ **(h)** ${}^-12n + 28m - 20$

5 (a) $5 - (a + 2)$
$= 5 + {}^-1(a + 2)$
$= 5 - a - 2$
$= 3 - a$

(b) $7b - (2b + 1)$
$= 7b + {}^-1(2b + 1)$
$= 7b - 2b - 1$
$= 5b - 1$

(c) ${}^-2d - (7 - 3d)$
$= {}^-2d + {}^-1(7 - 3d)$
$= {}^-2d - 7 + 3d$
$= d - 7$

6 (a) $3a - 5$ **(b)** $7f + 8$ **(c)** ${}^-3c - 3$ **(d)** ${}^-2h - 7$
7 (a) $a - 1$ **(b)** $2b + 9$ **(c)** $12 - 16c$ **(d)** $15d - 64$
(e) $6 - 13e$ **(f)** $4h + 12$

Page E43 Very cross roads

1 Different layouts are possible.

(a) **(b)**

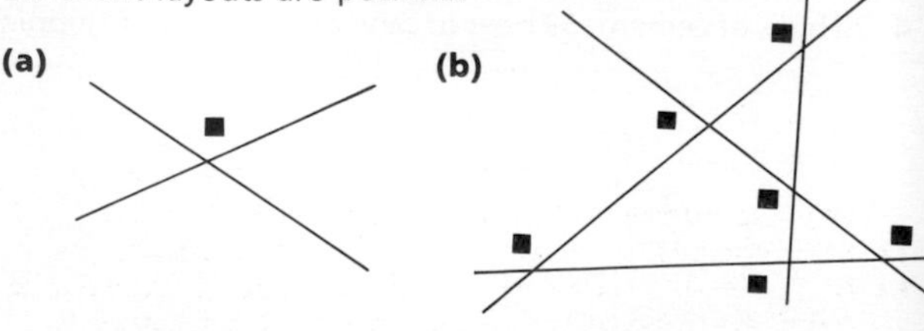

1 box 6 boxes

2, 3

Number of roads	1	2	3	4	5	6
Maximum number of control boxes	0	1	3	6	10	15

3 (b) Pupil's diagram for 5 roads.

4 28
5 (a) 3 **(b)** 3 on each road, 6 altogether
(c) 4 on each road, 10 altogether
(d) Multiply the number of roads by one less than the number of roads and then divide by 2.
6 190
7 Number of boxes = $\frac{1}{2}n\,(n - 1)$ where n is the number of roads.

Pages E44 and E45 Motorway repairs

1 (a)

Length of each section in metres	*Number of sections needed*
1	120
2	60
4	30
6	20
12	10

(b) The number of sections is halved.
2 (a) • 100 • 50 • 25
(b) The number of sections is halved.
3 (a)

Length of each stone in metres	*Number of stones needed*
0·5	400
1·0	200
2·0	100

(b) The number of stones is doubled.
4 (a) 140 **(b)** 70 **(c)** 35
5 (a) When one quantity is doubled, the other is halved.
(b) When one quantity is halved, the other is doubled.
6 $1\frac{1}{2}$ hours
7 (a) 60 minutes **(b)** 15 minutes
8 (a) 20 seconds **(b)** 80 seconds
9

Speed of the machine in mph	*Time taken in minutes*
0·5	48
1	24
2	12
4	6

10 (a)

Number of cones on each trip	*Number of trips needed*
1	48
2	24
3	16
4	12
6	8
8	6
12	4
16	3

(b) The number of trips is divided by 3.
11 (a) 18 hours **(b)** • 6 trucks • 9 trucks
12 (a) When one quantity is trebled, the other is divided by 3.
(b) When one quantity is divided by 3, the other is trebled.

Page E46 Pump action

1 (a) 10 days **(b)** 12 days **(c)** 24 days
2 15 hours
3 (a) 15 hours **(b)** 12 hours **(c)** 10 hours **(d)** $7\frac{1}{2}$ hours
4 (a) 18 hours **(b)** 9 hours **(c)** 6 hours **(d)** $4\frac{1}{2}$ hours
5 (a) 40 hours **(b)** 6 lorries **(c)** 5 lorries

Page E47 Patchworks

1 Pupils cut out shapes.
2 Other solutions may be possible.
(a)

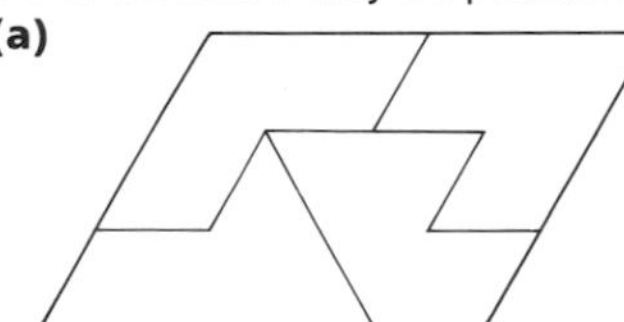

(b)

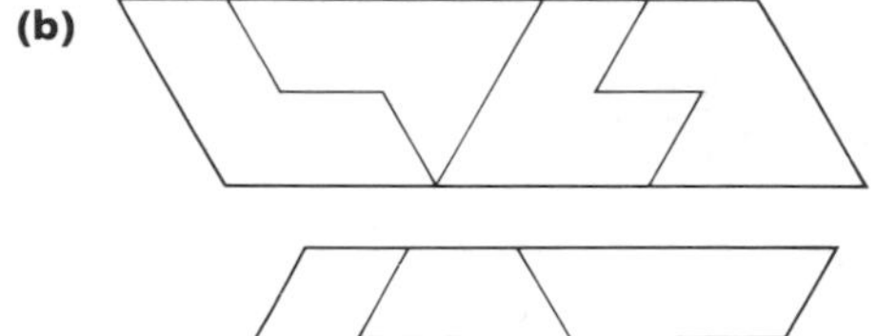

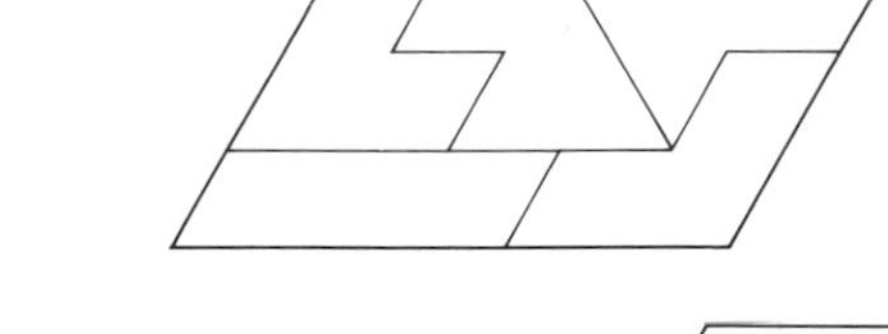

3 (a) **(b)**

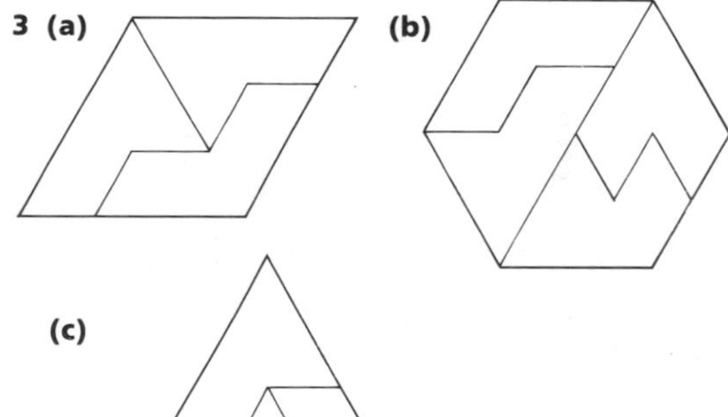

(c)

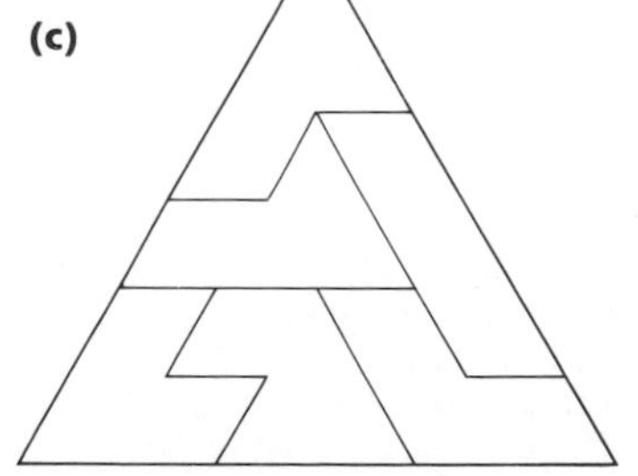

4 Pupil's own designs.

Page E48 Holby Trains

1 (a) 50 cm **(b)** 47 cm **(c)** 44 cm
2 (a) 132 cm **(b)** 75 cm **(c)** 119 cm
3

	Track 1	**Track 2**
(a)	120 cm	108 cm
(b)	4	6
(c)	94 cm	57 cm

Page E49 Holby Trains

1 (a) 442·6 cm **(b)** 369·8 cm **(c)** 172·8 cm
2 (a) 384·1 cm **(b)** 431·2 cm **(c)** 471 cm
3 (a) 89·2 cm **(b)** 105·1 cm **(c)** 81·2 cm

Page E50 Squares from circles

1 Practical Work.
(a) Pupils estimate areas of circles.
(b) Pupils complete table with estimates.
(c) The area of a circle is about $3 \times r^2$.
2 (a) 314 cm^2 **(b)** 615 cm^2 **(c)** 1256 cm^2
(d) 154 mm^2 **(e)** 50 m^2

Page E51 The Friday Fun Club

1 (a) 254 cm^2 **(b)** 452 cm^2 **(c)** 706 cm^2 or 707 cm^2
2 (a) 1413 cm^2 **(b)** 1923 cm^2
3 (a) 201 cm^2 **(b)** 393 cm^2 **(c)** 181 cm^2
(d) 471 cm^2 **(e)** 2120 cm^2 **(f)** 628 cm^2
4 279 cm^2

Page E52 Kay's the Chemist

1 (a) $6x - 10 = 32$, $6x = 42$, $x = 7$ **(b)** $4 = 3p - 5$, $9 = 3p$, $3 = p$ **(c)** $5y = 40 - 3y$, $8y = 40$, $y = 5$
2 (a) $b = 10$ **(b)** $t = 4$ **(c)** $p = 3$ **(d)** $y = 2$
(e) $b = 2$ **(f)** $x = 3$ **(g)** $y = 3$ **(h)** $p = 8$
3 (a) $w = 6$ **(b)** $y = 4$ **(c)** $r = 5$
(d) $k = 5$ **(e)** $b = 10$ **(f)** $a = 5$
(g) $a = {}^-4$ **(h)** $s = {}^-1$ **(i)** $t = {}^-3$
(j) $x = 6$ **(k)** $y = {}^-2$ **(l)** $p = {}^-4$
(m) $f = {}^-7$ **(n)** $b = {}^-2$ **(o)** $x = {}^-1$

Page E53 Perimeter fences

1 (a) $2(x + 150) = 800$, $x = 250$ **(b)** $2(3x + 70) = 800$, $x = 110$
(c) $2(2x + 200) = 800$, $x = 100$
2 (a) $x = 4$ **(b)** $a = {}^-5$ **(c)** $p = 7$
(d) $x = 3$ **(e)** $y = 5$ **(f)** $r = {}^-2$
(g) $b = 5$ **(h)** $x = 3$ **(i)** $t = 2$
3 (a) $2(x - 10) + 2(2x + 40) = 180 + 2x$, $x = 30$
First field is 20 m by 100 m.
Second field is 90 m by 30 m.
(b) $2(y - 50) + 3(y + 20) = 3(y + 40)$, $y = 80$
First field has sides of 30 m and 100 m.
Second field has sides of 120 m.
4 (a) $x = 1$ **(b)** $d = 4$ **(c)** $y = 4$
(d) $x = 3$ **(e)** $p = 2$ **(f)** $c = {}^-2$

Page E54 Equations from formulae

1 (a) 7 sets **(b)** 12 sets **(c)** 17 sets **(d)** 25 sets
2 (a) 9 sides **(b)** 11 sides
3 (a) 100 **(b)** 151
4 (a) 8 cm **(b)** 14 cm
5 (a) 3 cm **(b)** 5 cm **(c)** 4·5 cm

Page E55 Karaoke party

1 (a) Club Karaoke

Time in hours	1	2	3	4	5	6
Cost in £	8	16	24	32	40	48

(b) Laser Karaoke

Time in hours	1	2	3	4	5	6
Cost in £	16	20	24	28	32	36

2 (a) Club Karaoke **(b)** Laser Karaoke
3 (a) Either, they are the same cost.
(b) The graphs intersect.
4 Pupils check each answer by substitution.
(a) Singalong $C = 9t$ Chanson $C = 16 + 5t$
Equal when $t = 4$ hours
(b) Rave $C = 12t$ Tunes $C = 20 + 8t$
Equal when $t = 5$ hours
(c) Live $C = 2 + 6t$ Carol's $C = 8 + 3t$
Equal when $t = 2$ hours
(d) Kool $C = 30 + 5t$ Swing $C = 18 + 7t$
Equal when $t = 6$ hours

Pages E56 and E57 Families of lines

1 (a)

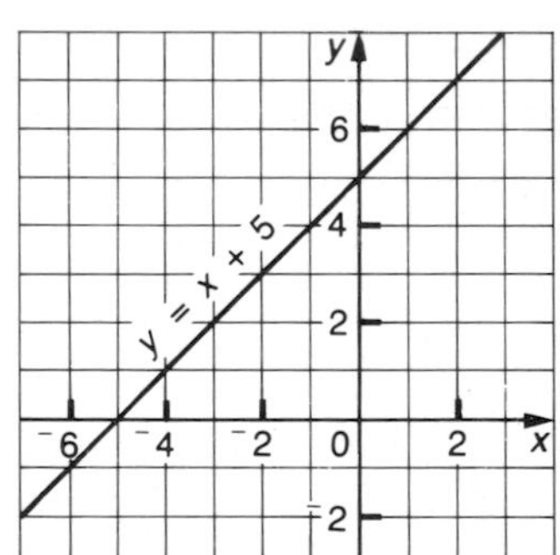

(b)

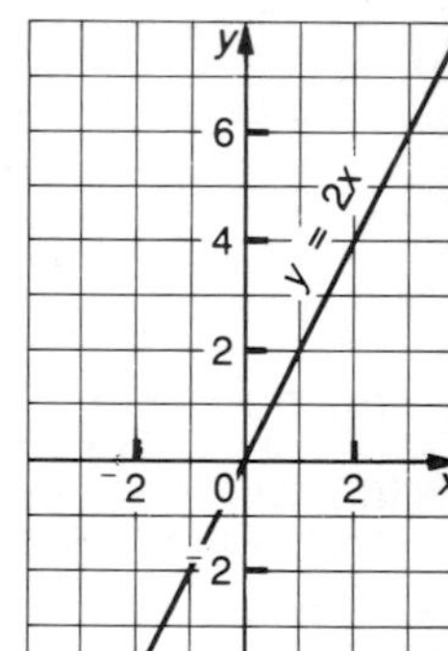

(c)

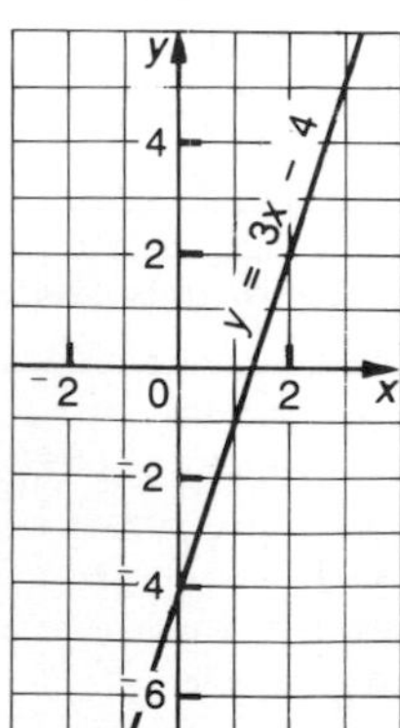

(d)

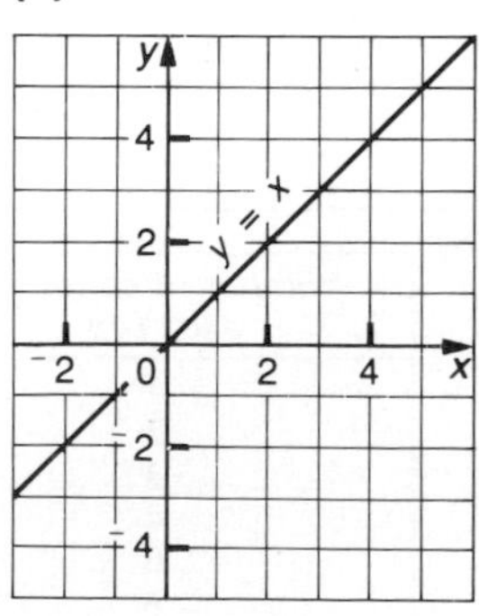

2 (a)

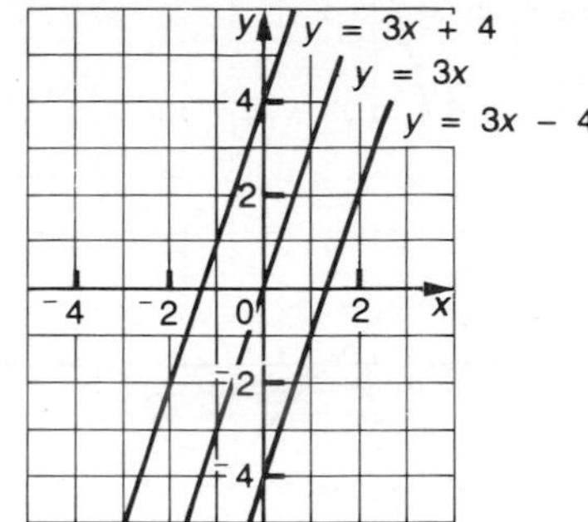

(b) • The lines are parallel.
• The coefficient of x is always 3.

3 Family P
(a)

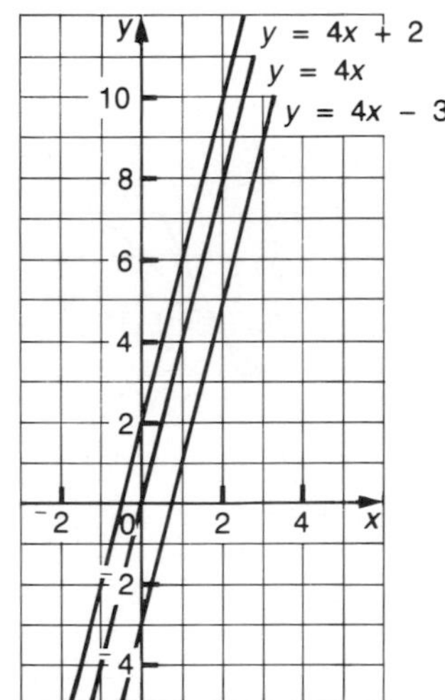

(b) • The lines are parallel.
• The coefficient of x is always 4.

Family Q
(a)

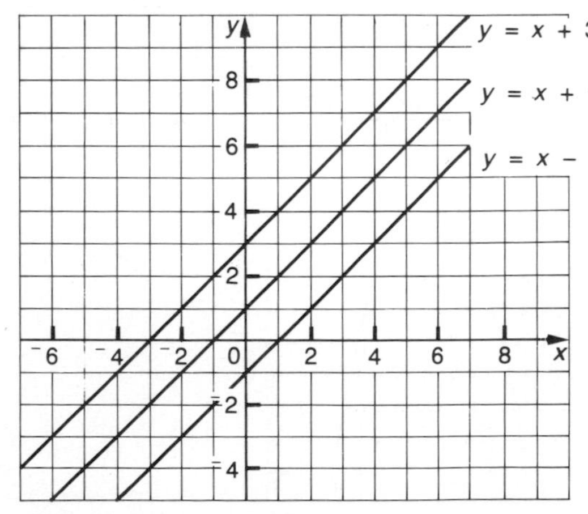

(b) • The lines are parallel.
• The coefficient of x is always 1.

4 (a) 5 **(b)** 3 **(c)** 8 **(d)** 4 **(e)** 1 **(f)** $\frac{1}{2}$

5 • The lines cross the y-axis at (0, 3).
• The constant of each equation is 3.

6 Family R
(a)

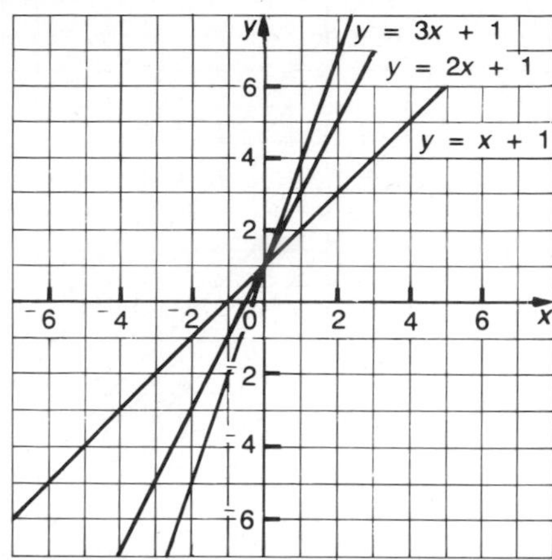

(b) • The lines cross the y-axis at (0, 1).
• The constant of each equation is 1.

7 Family S
(a)

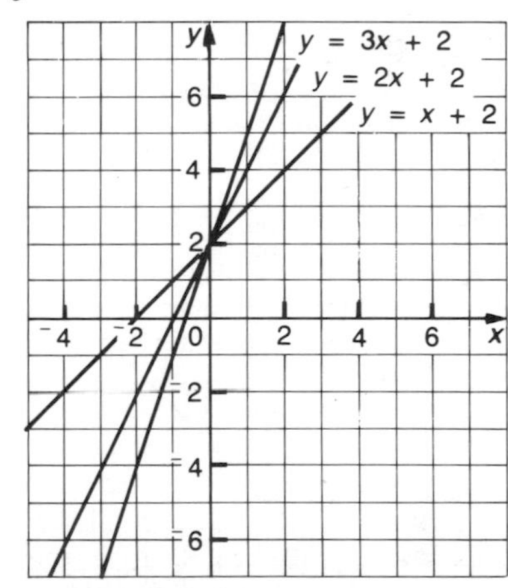

(b) • The lines cross the y-axis at (0, 2).
• The constant of each equation is 2.

Family T
(a)

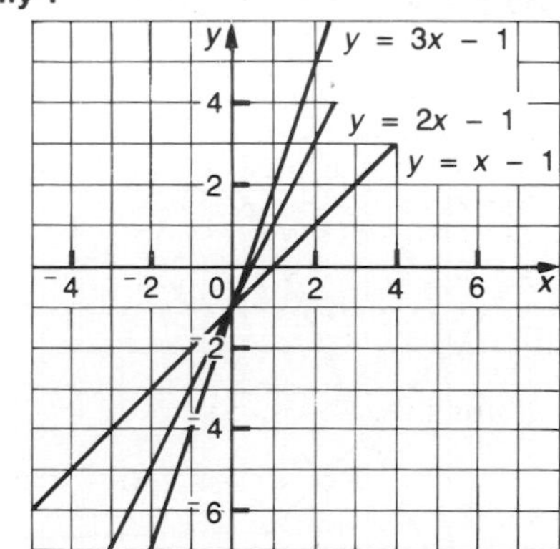

(b) • The lines cross the y-axis at (0, $^-1$).
• The constant of each equation is $^-1$.

8 (a) (0, 7) **(b)** (0, 5) **(c)** (0, $^-7$) **(d)** (0, $^-9$)

9 (a) 5, (0, 9) **(b)** 3, (0, 7) **(c)** 3, (0, $^-4$)
(d) 1, (0, 1) **(e)** 6, (0, $^-1$) **(f)** 1, (0, $^-9$)
(g) 7, (0, 8) **(h)** 6, (0, 0)

10 (a)

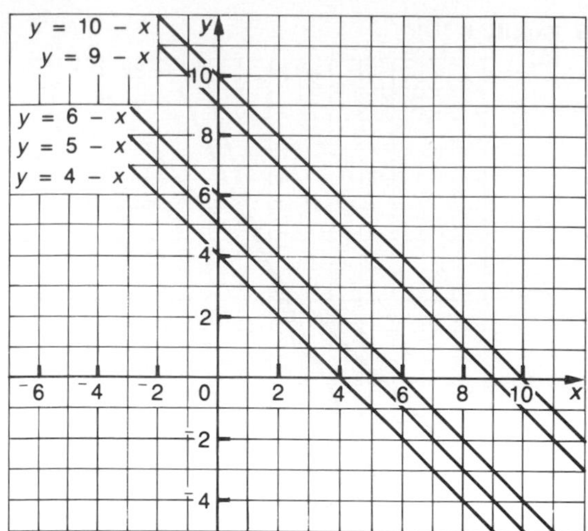

(b) The lines are parallel.

Page E58 Crossed lines

1 Pupils check each solution by substitution.
(a) $x = 3, y = 5$ **(b)** $x = 2, y = 5$
(c) $x = 6, y = 3$ **(d)** $x = 5, y = 7$

2 (a)

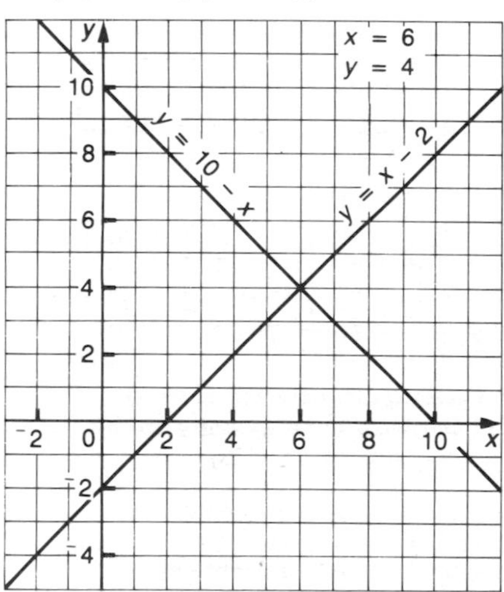

(b)

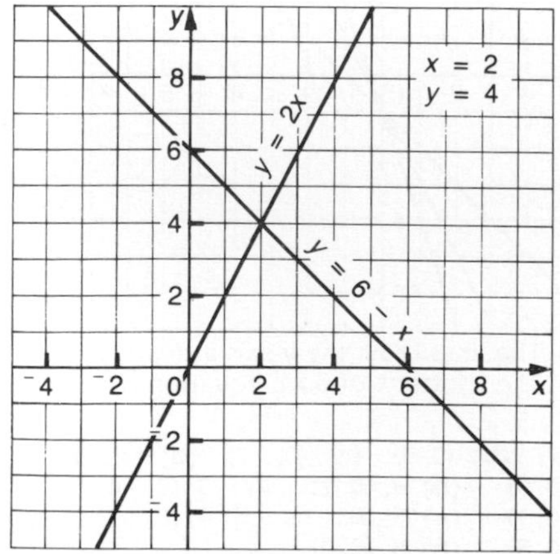

(c)

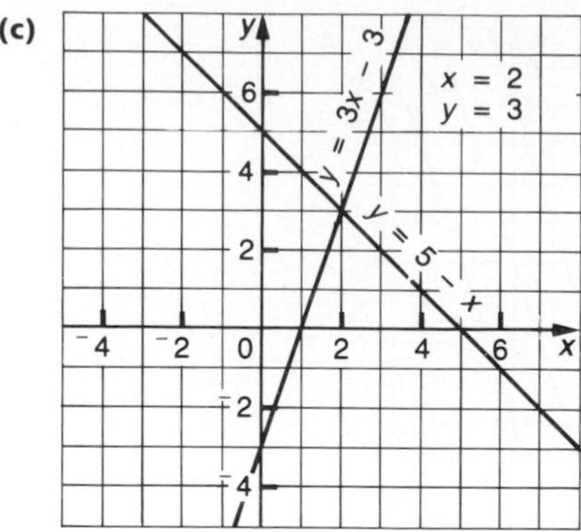

(d)

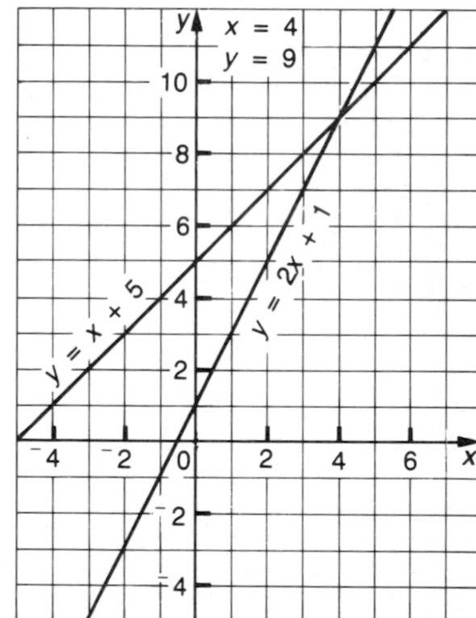

Page E59 Parabolic graphs

1 (a)

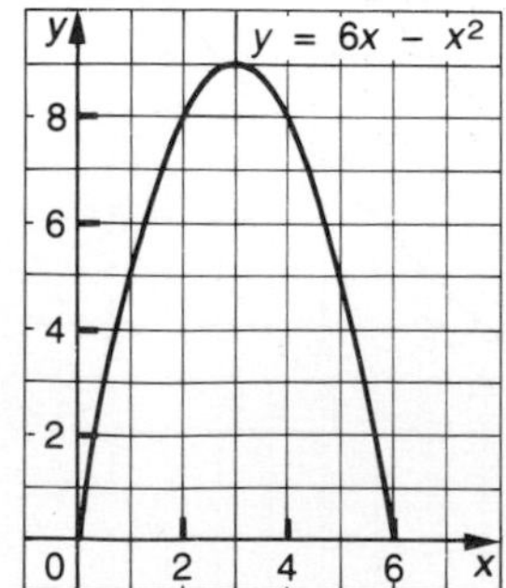

- meets y-axis at (0, 0)
- meets x-axis at (0, 0) and (6, 0)
- turning point (3, 9)

(b)

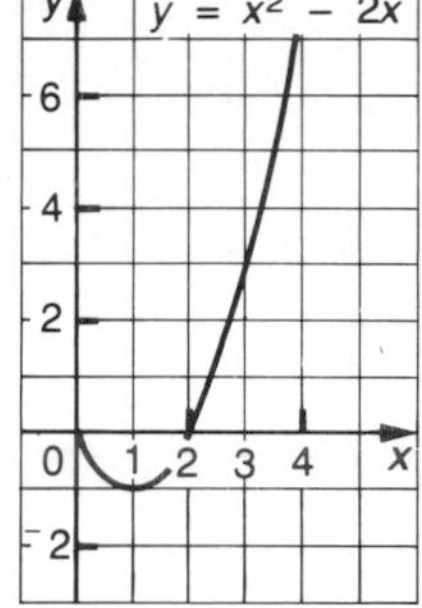

- meets y-axis at (0, 0)
- meets x-axis at (0, 0) and (2, 0)
- turning point (1, $^-1$)

(c)

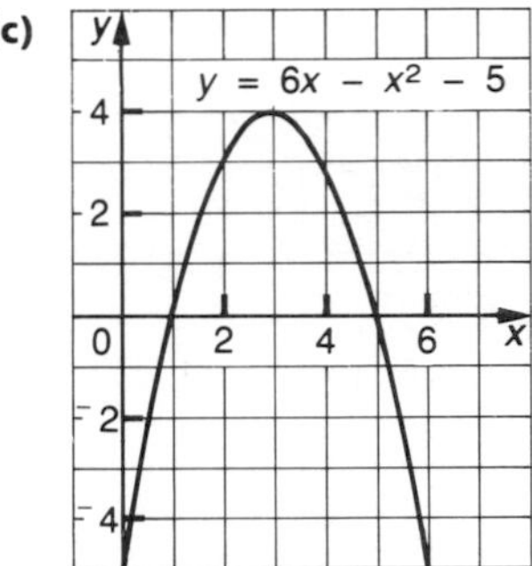

- meets y-axis at (0, $^-5$)
- meets x-axis at (1, 0) and (5, 0)
- turning point (3, 4)

(d)

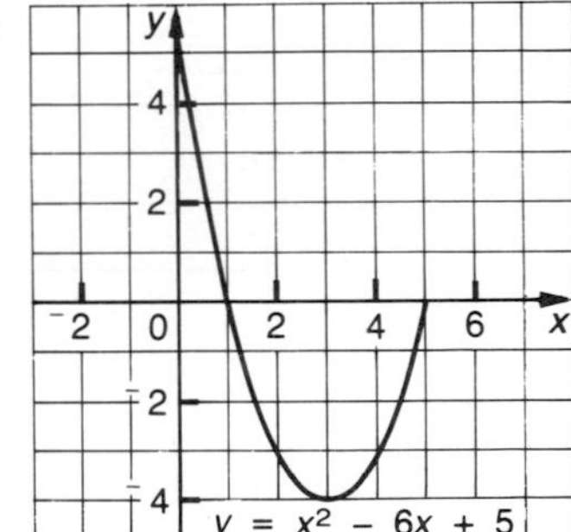

- meets y-axis at (0, 5)
- meets x-axis at (1, 0) and (5, 0)
- turning point (3, $^-4$)

(e)

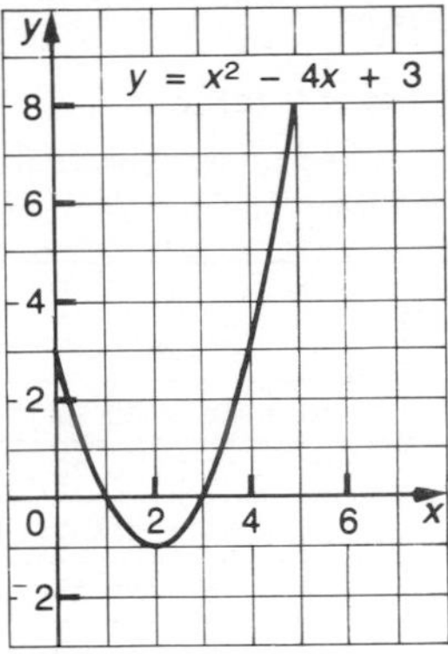

- meets y-axis at (0, 3)
- meets x-axis at (1, 0) and (3, 0)
- turning point (2, $^-1$)

(f)

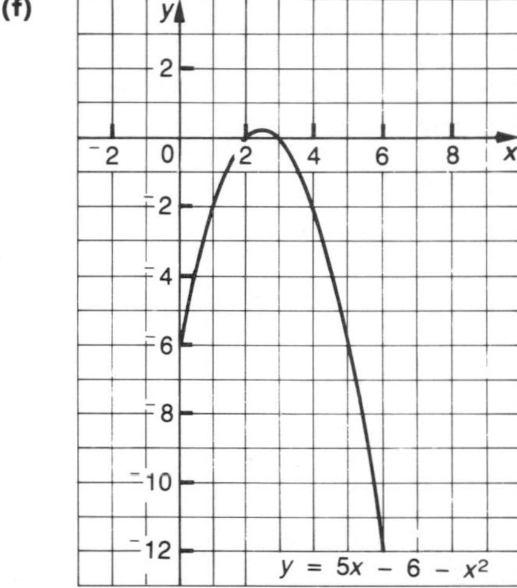

- meets y-axis at (0, $^-6$)
- meets x-axis at (2, 0) and 3, 0)
- turning point (2·5, 0·25)

2 **(a)** parabola **(b)** straight line
(c) straight line **(d)** parabola
(e) parabola **(f)** straight line
(g) parabola **(h)** parabola

Page E60 Triangles rule OK?

1 (a) *r* **(b)** *l* **(c)** *y* **(d)** *u* **(e)** *x*

2 Triangles drawn on $\frac{1}{2}$ cm squared paper. Values for *c* and hence c^2 depend on the accuracy of the measurements.

	length in cm				
Triangle	*a*	*b*	*c*	$a^2 + b^2$	c^2
P	3	4	5	9 + 16 = 25	25
Q	4	7·5	8·5	16 + 56·25 = 72·25	72·25
R	6	8	10	36 + 64 = 100	100
S	2·5	6	6·5	6·25 + 36 = 42·25	42·25
T	4·5	6	7·5	20·25 + 36 = 56·25	56·25

(c) The values are equal.

3 Practical work. Results depend on the accuracy of the measurements made.

4 The amount of detail depends on the pupil. Pythagoras was a Greek mathematician and philosopher who is believed to be the first person to prove the result known as Pythagoras' Theorem. His proof was made around 525 B.C.

Page E61 Squarials

1 (a)

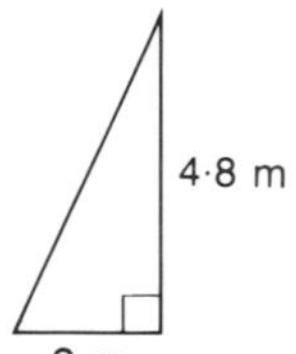

Length of ladder = 5·2 m

(b)

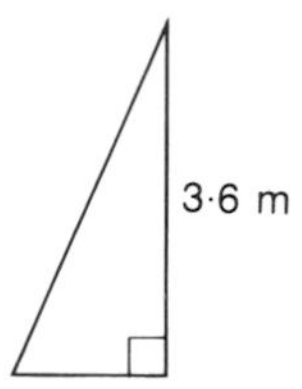

Length of ladder = 3·9 m

(c)

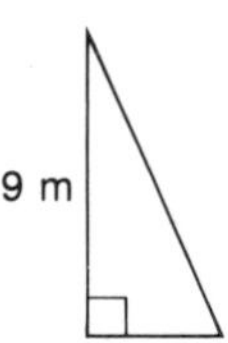

Length of ladder = 9·75 m

2 (a) 5 m **(b)** 3·25 m **(c)** 10 cm **(d)** 13 cm

3 (a)

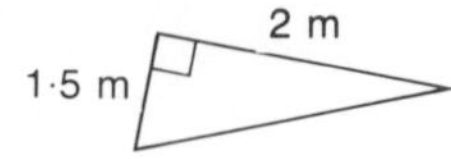

Longest side = 2·5 m

(b)

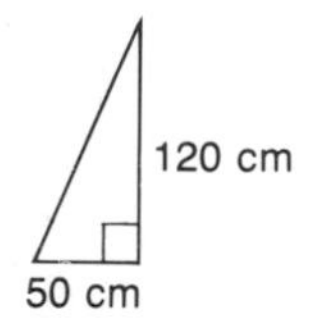

Longest side = 130 cm

(c)

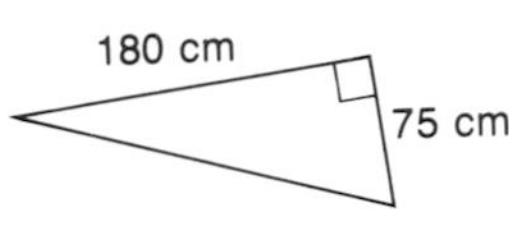

Longest side = 195 cm

4 (a) 20 inches **(b)** 40 inches
(c) 22·5 inches **(d)** 30 inches

Page E62 Woodlea Homes

1 (a)

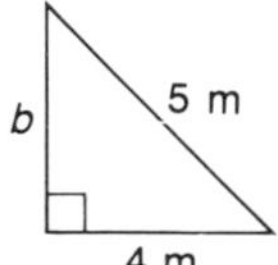

b = 3·00 m

(b)

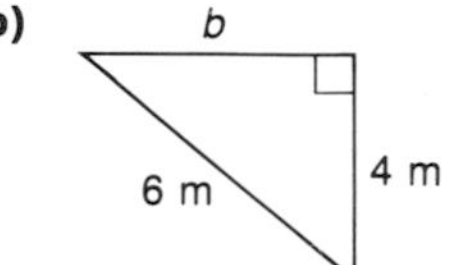

b = 4·47 m

(c)

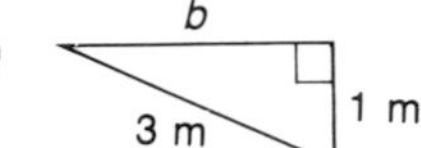

b = 2·83 m

(d)

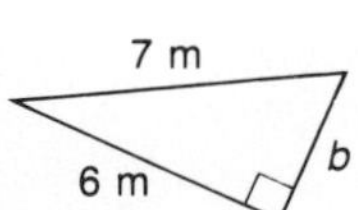

b = 3·61 m

2 (a) Strap *p* = 1·30 m, strap *q* = 1·05 m.
(b) 3·30 m

3 (a) 1·13 m **(b)** 1·55 m

4 241 cm

Page E63 Ally the gater!

1 **(a)** strut 150 cm gate 710 cm **(b)** strut 204 cm gate 908 cm **(c)** strut 185 cm gate 885 cm

2 4 pieces of 98 cm, 2 pieces of 144 cm, 1 piece of 180 cm.

3 **(a)** 739 cm **(b)** 793 cm **(c)** 1165 cm

4 **(a)**

Number	1	2	3	4	5	6	7	8	9	10
Square number	1	4	9	16	25	36	49	64	81	100

Number	11	12	13	14	15	16	17	18	19	20
Square number	121	144	169	196	225	256	289	324	361	400

Number	21	22	23	24	25	26	27	28	29	30
Square number	441	484	529	576	625	676	729	784	841	900

(b)
- 3, 4, 5
- 6, 8, 10
- 9, 12, 15
- 12, 16, 20
- 15, 20, 25
- 18, 24, 30
- 5, 12, 13
- 10, 24, 26
- 7, 24, 25
- 8, 15, 17
- 20, 21, 29

Acknowledgements
The authors and publishers would like to thank the following for permission to use photographs:

p. 1 J. Allan Cash Ltd; p. 7 Aviemore Photographic; p. 8 Save the Children; p. 27 *top* J. Allan Cash Ltd., *middle* Liba Taylor/Select, *bottom* Philip Parkhouse; p. 30 *top* SPL/Space Telescope Science Institute/NASA, *middle* SPL/US Geological Survey; p. 50 Skyscan Balloon Photography.

Heinemann Educational,
a division of Heinemann Publishers (Oxford) Ltd,
Halley Court, Jordan Hill, Oxford, OX2 8EJ

OXFORD LONDON EDINBURGH
MADRID ATHENS BOLOGNA PARIS
MELBOURNE SYDNEY AUCKLAND SINGAPORE TOKYO
IBADAN NAIROBI HARARE GABORONE
PORTSMOUTH NH (USA)

First published in 1993

93 94 95 96 10 9 8 7 6 5 4 3 2 1

ISBN 0 435 52959 5

Designed and typeset by VAP Publishing Services, Oxford

Illustrated by Fiona Plummer and Jane Bottomley

Printed in Great Britain by Thomson Litho Ltd, East Kilbride